P · O · C · K · E · T · S

SPELLING
DICTIONARY

DK PUBLISHING, INC.

A DK PUBLISHING BOOK

www.dk.com
Produced for Dorling Kindersley by
PAGE*One*, Cairn House, Elgiva Lane, Chesham,
Buckinghamshire, Great Britain

PAGE*One* team

Chris Clark, Bob Gordon, Thomas
Keenes, Neil Kelly, Helen Parker,
Charlotte Stock, Sarah Watson

DK Managing editor

Jane Yorke

Dictionary consultant
Dictionary editor   Sheila Dignen
David Morrow

First American Edition, 1998
8 10 9

Published in the United States by DK Publishing, Inc.,
95 Madison Avenue, New York, New York 10016

Published in Great Britain by
Dorling Kindersley Limited.

ISBN 0-7894-3073-8

Printed and bound in Italy by LegoPrint

USING THIS DICTIONARY

The words featured in this dictionary have been chosen because they can be difficult to spell. Since there is a limit to the total number of words that can be included, only words most likely to be used by the general reader or writer are given. Very few proper nouns appear and foreign terms are included only if they are in common usage. Thus, you will find words such as "chauffeur" and "debut," but not "habitué" or "parvenu." A few common slang words have also been given.

ALPHABETICAL ORDER

Headwords in this dictionary are all arranged in alphabetical order. Root words are not automatically followed by their derivatives, which are listed separately.

ABBREVIATIONS

In this dictionary, abbreviations have been kept to a minimum. You will, however, find the following:

eg	for example
f	feminine
m	masculine
pl	plural

ALTERNATIVE SPELLINGS

For headwords that have variant spellings, both forms are given, separated by a comma.

e.g. mediaeval, medieval
     medieval, mediaeval

     boatswain, bosun
     bosun, boatswain

In the above example, the two forms are some distance apart in the text, so an entry is given for each spelling.

When the two variants are next to each other, or fairly close together, only one entry is given at the more common spelling.

e.g. judgment, judgement

     abridgment, abridgement

     lodgment, lodgement

     adviser, advisor

MEANINGS AND DEFINITIONS

This is not a dictionary of definitions, so meanings of words are only given for clarity in the case of some words that sound the same but have completely different meanings according to the way they are spelled.

e.g. poor (lacking wealth)
     pore (of skin; to look or
          think intently)
     pour (liquid)

- For the sake of simplicity, where words with the same spelling can also have different meanings, only one entry is included.

e.g. loaf – which as a noun
          means bread, and as a
          verb means to laze around.

     rank – which as a noun
          means position, and as a
          verb means to classify.

INFLECTIONS OF VERBS

Because verbs are often formed inconsistently in English, verb inflections, such as the −ed, −ing, and −s forms, are given for verbs that could be irregular and, therefore, difficult to spell. Inflections are listed alphabetically under the headword.

- Verbs ending in −e are followed by the past and present participle to show whether or not the −e is dropped in the −ing form.

e.g. debate
    debated
    debating

- Verbs ending in a single consonant such as −t,− n, or −r are followed by −ed, −ing, and −s inflections to make clear whether they take a double or single consonant when inflected.

e.g. ban
    banned
    banning
    bans

    budget
    budgeted
    budgeting
    budgets

- Verbs ending in −y are accompanied by inflections to show whether the −y changes to −i−.

e.g. bury
    buried
    buries
    burying

    try
    tried
    tries
    trying

- Inflections of irregular verbs have their own entry with a cross-reference in brackets.

e.g. broke (*from* break)
    flung (*from* fling)

- Inflections are given for verbs that have regular inflections but look as if they might be irregular.

e.g. echo
    echoed
    echoes
    echoing

PLURALS

Plurals are not listed where they are formed regularly by simply adding –s to the root word (see p. 8). However, irregular noun plurals are always listed immediately after the headword and are followed by *pl*. This is true even where verb inflections are also listed under the same headword.

e.g. man
    men *pl*
    manned
    manning
    mans

    fancy
    fancies *pl*
    fancied
    fancies
    fancying

- Plurals of words ending in –y are always given to distinguish whether or not the –y becomes –ies

e.g. baby
    babies *pl*

    toy
    toys *pl*

- Plurals are always given of words that end in –um, –us, or –a because these words often look as if they might have an irregular plural.

e.g. auditorium
    auditoria *pl*

    circus
    circuses *pl*

- Plurals of words ending in –o are always given since there are no strict rules on whether these take –oes or –os.

e.g. piccolo
    piccolos *pl*

    potato
    potatoes *pl*

    gizmo
    gizmos *pl*

COMMON SPELLING RULES

English spelling is notoriously inconsistent, and spellings can often seem illogical. Here are a few basic rules, with examples and exceptions, that will help make spelling easier.

VERB INFLECTIONS

- To form the past tense of a regular verb, add –ed to the root. To form the present continuous, simply add –ing. Many of these inflections are also used as adjectives.

e.g. hunt+ed   hunted
      laugh+ing   laughing

ADVERBS

- Adverbs are formed regularly by adding –ly to the root of the adjective.

e.g. free+ly   freely
      foolish+ly   foolishly

- Adjectives ending in –ic add –ally to form the adverb.

e.g. basic+ally   basically
      historic+ally historically
      cynic+ally   cynically

Exception: publicly

- When –ly is added to an adjective that ends in a consonant followed by –le, the –le is usually dropped.

e.g. gentle+ly   gently
      subtle+ly   subtly

PLURALS

- Regular plurals are formed by simply adding an s.

e.g. heart   hearts
      book   books

- The plurals of nouns that end in a consonant+y are formed by substituting –ies for –y.

e.g. ambiguity   ambiguities
      category   categories
      penny   pennies

- Nouns ending in a vowel + y form plurals regularly by adding an s.

e.g. array   arrays
     key   keys
     chimney   chimneys

- If a word ends in –sh, –ch, –s, or –x, the plural is formed by adding –es.

e.g. wish   wishes
     finch   finches
     boss   bosses
     fox   foxes

DOUBLING CONSONANTS IN COMPOUND WORDS

- When an ending that begins with a vowel is added to a word that ends in a single vowel plus a consonant, the consonant is doubled.

e.g. dot+ed   dotted
     admit+ance   admittance
     excel+ent   excellent

- When an ending that begins with –e, –i, or –y is added to a word that ends in –c, a –k– is inserted between the two to keep the hard sound.

e.g. frolic+ing   frolicking
     panic+y   panicky

LOSING A CONSONANT IN COMPOUND WORDS

- Compound words made up of smaller words ending in –ll often drop an –l–.

e.g. all+mighty   almighty
     un+till   until
     well+fare   welfare

Exceptions: farewell, fulfill

I BEFORE E EXCEPT AFTER C

- The rule –i– before –e– except after –c– can generally be relied upon where the sound is "ee."

e.g. believe, friend, receive

Exceptions: either, weird, seize, caffeine; proper names such as Keith and Sheila

- Where words are not pronounced "ee," –ei– is always correct.

e.g. deign
     freight
     weight
     veil

Y TO I

- When an ending is added to a word that ends in a consonant+y, the –y changes to –i. If the ending begins with –i, the –y– is retained.

e.g. pretty+est prettiest
   pity+ful pitiful
   pity+ing pitying

THE SILENT E

- Verbs that end in a silent –e generally drop the –e when an ending that begins with a vowel is added, such as –ed, –ing, –er, or –able.

e.g. line+ed lined
   chase+ing chasing
   argue+able arguable

- The silent –e is retained before a consonant.

e.g. value+less valueless
   pave+ment pavement

Exception: argument, truly

- In words that end in –ce or –ge, the silent –e is usually retained to keep the soft sound of the consonant.

e.g. change+able changeable
   courage+ous courageous

ALTERNATIVE SPELLINGS

Some words are accepted with various spellings, both of which are correct. You will often find that one spelling is more common than the other. However, the most important thing when writing is to be consistent. Decide which spelling to use and stick to it.

abridgement	abridgment
briar	brier
disc	disk
dispatch	despatch
encyclopedia	encyclopaedia
hello	hallo (or hullo)
inquire	enquire
judgment	judgement
loth	loath
medieval	mediaeval
rateable	ratable
spelled	spelt

WORDS THAT NEVER USE –IZE

The words listed below never use –ize. Many of these end in –cise, –mise, –prise, and –vise. As a rule, if the part of the word preceding the ending is not recognizable as an English word, the ending is unlikely to be –ize.

e.g. advertise

advise

apprise

arise

braise

chastise

circumcise

comprise

compromise

concise

demise

despise

devise

disfranchise

disguise

emprise

enfranchise

enterprise

excise

exercise

expertise

franchise

guise

improvise

incise

merchandise

misadvise

precise

premise

reprise

revise

supervise

surmise

surprise

televise

treatise

COMMONLY CONFUSED WORDS

In English, there are many words that sound the same, but have completely different spellings and meanings. Here are some of the most commonly confused words.

accede (to agree to)
exceed (to go beyond)

accept (to take)
except (to exclude)

access (right of way)
excess (too much)

adapter (someone who adapts)
adaptor (piece of equipment that adapts)

addition (something added)
edition (number of copies of a book, newspaper, etc.)

adverse (unfavorable)
averse (disinclined)

advice (recommendation)
advise (to recommend)

affect (to influence)
effect (to accomplish, result)

aid (help)
aide (assistant)

allay (to make less)
alley (a narrow street)
ally (friendly country or person)

all ready (completely ready)
already (previously, so soon)

allude (to mention in passing)
elude (to escape or avoid)

allusion (a brief mention)
illusion (a false impression)

altar (platform in a church)
alter (to change)

arc (a curved line)
ark (a type of boat)

artist (a person who is skilled in fine arts)
artiste (a theater performer)

ascent (climb, rise)
assent (agreement, permission)

aural (by ear)
oral (by mouth)

bail (money given to release a prisoner)
bale out (to remove water from a boat)

base (basis, foundation)
bass (low part in music, fish)

bazaar (marketplace, fair)
bizarre (strange)

birth (being born)
berth (a mooring place)

bloc (a group of nations)
block (a solid mass)

born (given birth)
borne (carried, produced)

bough (a tree branch)
bow (form of greeting)

boy (a male child)
buoy (a floating object)

brake (to slow and stop)
break (to fracture, damage)

breach (to break)
breech (rear part of a gun)

bridal (belonging to the bride)
bridle (a horse's harness)

broach (to bring up a subject)
brooch (a piece of jewelry)

cannon (gun)
canon (law)

canvas (cloth)
canvass (to solicit opinions, votes, etc.)

choose (to select)
chose (past tense of to choose)

chord (musical tones)
cord (thin rope)

cite (to quote)
sight (power of seeing)
site (place)

coarse (rude, rough)
course (series, route)

complement (something that completes or balances)
compliment (praise)

dairy (milk farm)
diary (daily record book)

desert (arid region, to leave or abandon)
dessert (final course of a meal)

dual (of two, double)
duel (fight)

flair (aptitude, style)
flare (to burn, burst out)

foreword (introduction to a written work)
forward (onward, ahead)

idle (inactive)
idol (image of a god)

immigrant (person coming into a country)
emigrant (person leaving a country)

its (belonging to it)
it's (it is)

lead (a metal, to guide)
led (past tense of lead)

lightening (becoming lighter in weight or color)
lightning (as in thunder)

miner (one who mines)
minor (underage person)

moral (relating to good behavior)
morale (level of spirits)

naval (of the navy)
navel (umbilicus)

palate (the roof of the mouth, taste)
palette (an artist's paintboard)
pallet (crude bed, platform)

passed (past tense of pass)
past (former time)

pastel (artist's crayons)
pastille (type of sweet)

pedal (foot lever)
peddle (to sell)

personal (belonging to someone, intimate)
personnel (staff)

plane (airplane, level)
plain (ordinary, open land)

precede (to go before)
proceed (to continue)

prey (animal killed for food)
pray (to say a prayer)

principal (chief, head person)
principle (rule)

rapped (knocked)
rapt (fascinated)
wrapped (covered)

raze (to destroy totally)
raise (to lift up, increase)

reign (of a monarch)
rein (part of a horse's harness)

review (a report)
revue (amusing theater show)

rhyme (short poem)
rime (frost)

skeptic (unbeliever)
septic (infected)

stationary (fixed)
stationery (paper supplies)

stile (steps over a wall)
style (manner of doing things)

their (belonging to them)
there (at that place)
they're (they are)

to (toward)
too (also, excessive)
two (number)

waive (to give up)
wave (to salute, on ocean)

weather (state of atmosphere)
whether (if)

who's (who is)
whose (of whom)

you're (you are)
your (belonging to you)

SPELLING
DICTIONARY

aback
abacus
  abacuses *pl*
abandon
  abandoned
  abandoning
  abandons
abandonment
abase
abasement
abash
abate
  abated
  abating
abatement
abattoir
abbess (nun)
abbey (building)

abbeys *pl*
abbot
abbreviate
  abbreviated
  abbreviating
abbreviation
abdicate
  abdicated
  abdicating
abdication
abdomen
abdominal
abduct
  abducted
  abducting
abduction
abductor
aberrant

aberration
abet
  abets
  abetted
  abetting
abetter, abettor
abeyance
abhor
  abhorred
  abhorring
  abhors
abhorrence
abhorrent
abidance
abide
  abided
  abiding
ability
  abilities *pl*
abject (miserable)
abjection
abjectly
abjure
  abjured
  abjuring
abjuration
ablative
ablaze
able
able-bodied
ablution

ably	above	absentminded
abnegate	aboveboard	absinth (plant)
abnegated	abracadabra	absinthe (drink)
abnegating	abrade	absolute
abnegation	abraded	absolutely
abnormal	abrading	absolve
abnormality	abrasion	absolved
abnormalities *pl*	abrasive	absolving
abnormally	abreast	absolution
abnormity	abridge	absorb
abnormities *pl*	abridging	absorbency
aboard	abridged	absorbent
abode	abridgment,	absorption
abolish	abridgement	absorptive
abolition	abroad	abstain
abolitionary	abrogate	abstained
abominable	abrogated	abstaining
abominably	abrogating	abstainer
abominate	abrogation	abstention
abominated	abrupt	abstemious
abominating	abscess	abstemiously
abomination	abscesses *pl*	abstinence
aboriginal	abscissa	abstinent
aborigine	abscissas, abscissae	abstract
abort	*pl*	abstraction
abortion	abscond	abstruse
abortionist	absent	abstrusely
abortive	absence	abstruseness
abound	absentee	absurd
about	absenteeism	absurdity
about-face	absently	absurdities *pl*

absurdly
abundance
abundant
abundantly
abuse
  abused
  abusing
abusive
abusively
abut
  abuts
  abutted
  abutting
abutment
abysmal
abysmally
abyss (deep hole)
  abysses pl
acacia
  acacias pl
academy
  academies pl
academia
academic
academically
academician
accede (to agree)
  acceded
  acceding
accelerate
  accelerated

  accelerating
acceleration
accelerator
accent
accentuate
  accentuated
  accentuating
accentuation
accept
acceptability
acceptable
acceptance
access
accessary (crime)
  accessaries pl
accessibility
accessible
accessibly
accession
accessory (extra)
  accessories pl
accident
accidental
accidentally
acclaim
acclamation
acclimatize
  acclimatized
  acclimatizing
acclimatization
accolade

accommodate
  accommodated
  accommodating
accommodation
accompany
  accompanied
  accompanies
  accompanying
accompaniment
accompanist
accomplice
accomplish
accomplishment
accord
accordance
accordion
accordionist
accost
account
accountability
accountable
accountancy
accountant
accouterments
accredit
  accredited
  accrediting
accreditation
accretion
accrual
accrue

accrued
accruing
accumulate
  accumulated
  accumulating
accumulation
accumulator
accuracy
accurate
accurately
accursed
accusation
accusative
accusatory
accuse
  accused
  accusing
accuser
accustom
  accustomed
  accustoming
ace
acerbate
  acerbated
  acerbating
acerbic
acerbity
acetate
acetic (acid)
acetylene
ache

ached
aching
achievable
achieve
  achieved
  achieving
achievement
achromatic
acid
acidic
acidify
  acidified
  acidifies
  acidifying
acidity
acidosis
acknowledge
  acknowledged
  acknowledging
acknowledgement,
  acknowledgment
acme
acne
acolyte
aconite
acorn
acoustic
acoustical
acoustically
acoustics
acquaint

acquaintance
acquaintanceship
acquiesce
  acquiesced
  acquiescing
acquiescence
acquiescent
acquire
  acquired
  acquiring
acquisition
acquisitive
acquit
  acquits
  acquitted
  acquitting
acquittal
acre
acreage
acrid
acridity
acrimonious
acrimoniously
acrimony
acrobat
acrobatic
acrobatically
acronym
acrophobia
acropolis
across

acrostic
acrylic
act
action
actionable
activate
  activated
  activating
activation
active
actively
activism
activist
activity
  activities *pl*
actor
actress
actual
actuality
  actualities *pl*
actually
actuary
  actuaries *pl*
actuarial
actuate
  actuated
  actuating
actuation
acuity
acumen
acupuncture

acupuncturist
acute
acutely
acuteness
adage
adagio
  adagios *pl*
adamant
adapt
adaptability
adaptable
adaptation
adapter, adaptor
adaption
adaptive
add
addendum
  addenda *pl*
adder
addict
addiction
addictive
addition (sum)
additive
addle
  addled
  addling
address
addressee
adduce
adduced

adducing
adenoid
adenoidal
adept
adequate
adequacy
adequately
adhere
  adhered
  adhering
adherence
adherent
adhesion
adhesive
ad hoc
adieu
  adieus, adieux *pl*
ad infinitum
adipose
adiposity
adjacency
adjacent
adjacently
adjectival
adjectivally
adjective
adjoin
adjourn
adjournment
adjudicate
  adjudicated

adjudicating
adjudication
adjudicator
adjunct
adjust
adjustable
adjuster
adjustment
adjutant
adjuvant
ad-lib
  ad-libbed
  ad-libbing
  ad-libs
adman
  admen *pl*
administer
administrate
  administrated
  administrating
administration
administrative
administrator
admirable
admirably
admiral
admiralty
admiration
admire
  admired
  admiring

admirer
admissibility
admissible
admissibly
admission
admit
  admits
  admitted
  admitting
admittance
admixture
admonish
admonition
admonitory
ad nauseam
ado
adolescence
adolescent
adopt
adopter
adoption
adoptive
adorable
adorably
adoration
adore
  adored
  adoring
adorer
adorn
adornment

adrenaline
adrift
adroit
adsorb
adsorbent
adsorption
adulate
  adulated
  adulating
adulation
adult
adulterant
adulterate
  adulterated
  adulterating
adulteration
adultery
adulterer
adulteress
adulterous
adulterously
advance
  advanced
  advancing
advancement
advantage
advantageous
advantageously
advent (arrival)
Advent (time before
  Christmas)

adventitious
adventitiously
adventure
adventurer
adventurous
adventurously
adverb
adverbial
adversary
  adversaries *pl*
adverse
adversely
adversity
advert
advertise
  advertised
  advertising
advertisement
advertiser
advice (suggestion)
advisability
advisable
advise (to give
  advice)
  advised
  advising
advisedly
adviser, advisor
advisory
advocacy
advocate

advocated
advocating
advocation
aegis
  aegises *pl*
aeon
aerate
  aerated
  aerating
aeration
aerator
aerial
aerially
aerobatics
aerobic
aerobics
aerodynamics
aeronaut
aeronautical
aeronautics
aerosol
aerospace
afar
affability
affable
affably
affair
affect (to influence)
affectation
affection
affectionate

affectionately
affidavit
affiliate
  affiliated
  affiliating
affiliation
affinity
  affinities *pl*
affirm
affirmation
affirmative
affirmatively
affix
afflict
affliction
affluence
affluent
afford
afforest
  afforested
  afforesting
afforestation
affray
  affrays *pl*
affront
aficionado
afield
afloat
aforesaid
afraid
afresh

Afrikaans
after
aftermath
afternoon
afterthought
afterwards
again
against
agape
agate
age
  aged
  aging, ageing
ageless
agelessness
agency
  agencies *pl*
agenda
agent
agglomerate
agglomeration
aggrandize
  aggrandized
  aggrandizing
aggrandizement
aggravate
  aggravated
  aggravating
aggravation
aggregate
  aggregated

aggregating
aggregation
aggression
aggressive
aggressively
aggressiveness
aggressor
aggrieve
  aggrieved
  aggrieving
aghast
agile
agilely
agility
aging (*from* age)
agitate
  agitated
  agitating
agitation
agitator
aglow
agnostic
agnosticism
ago
agog
agony
  agonies *pl*
agonize
  agonized
  agonizing
agoraphobia

agrarian
agree
agreeable
agreeably
agreement
agriculture
agricultural
agriculturist,
  agriculturalist
aground
ague
ahead
ahoy
aid
aide (helper)
aide-de-camp
  aides-de-camp *pl*
AIDS
ail (to be ill)
ailing
aileron
ailment
aim
aimless
aimlessly
aimlessness
air
airborne
air-conditioned
aircraft
airdrome

airfield

air force

airily

airiness

airing

airless

airlessness

airlift

airline

airliner

air lock

airmail

airman

  airmen *pl*

airplane

airport

air raid

airspace

airtight

airworthiness

airworthy

airy

aisle

ajar

akimbo

akin

alabaster

à la carte

alacrity

à la mode

alarm

alarmist

alas

albatross

albeit

albino

  albinos *pl*

albinism

album

albumen (white of

  egg)

albumin (protein)

alchemy

alchemist

alcohol

alcoholic

alcoholism

alcove

alderman

  aldermen *pl*

ale (beer)

alert

alertly

alertness

alfresco

alga

  algae *pl*

algebra

algebraic

algebraical

algebraically

alias

aliases *pl*

alibi

  alibis *pl*

alien

alienable

alienate

  alienated

  alienating

alienation

alienator

alight

align

alignment

alike

aliment (food)

alimentary (food)

alimony

alive

alkali

  alkalis, alkalies *pl*

alkaline

alkalinity

all (every)

allay (to reduce,

  lessen)

allegation

allege

  alleged

  alleging

allegedly

allegiance

allegory (story)
  allegories *pl*
allegorical
allegorically
allegretto
  allegrettos *pl*
allegro
  allegros *pl*
alleluia, halleluiah,
  hallelujah
allergic
allergy
  allergies *pl*
alleviate
  alleviated
  alleviating
alleviation
alley
  alleys *pl*
alliance
alligator
alliteration
allocate
  allocated
  allocating
allocation
allocution (a speech)
allot
  allots
  allotted
  allotting

allotment
allow
allowable
allowance
alloy
  alloys *pl*
all right
allude (to mention)
  alluded
  alluding
allure
allurement
alluring
allusion (mention)
allusive (mentioning)
alluvial
ally
  allies *pl*
  allied
  allying
alliance
alma mater
almanac
almighty
almond
almoner
almost
alms (charity)
aloe
aloft
alone

along
aloof
aloofly
aloofness
aloud (speak)
alp
alpine
alpaca
alphabet
alphabetical
alphabetically
already
also
also-ran
altar (in church)
alter (to change)
alterable
alteration
altercate
  altercated
  altercating
altercation
alternate
  alternated
  alternating
alternation
alternative
alternatively
alternator
although
altimeter

altitude
alto
  altos pl
altogether
altruism
altruist
altruistic
altruistically
alum
aluminum
always
Alzheimer's
am (from be)
amalgam
amalgamate
  amalgamated
  amalgamating
amalgamation
amanuensis
  amanuenses pl
amass
amateur
amateurish
amateurishly
amateurishness
amateurism
amaze
  amazed
  amazing
amazement
ambassador

ambassadorial
amber
ambidextrous
ambience
ambient
ambiguity
  ambiguities pl
ambiguous
ambiguously
ambit
ambition
ambitiously
ambivalence
ambivalent
amble
  ambled
  ambling
ambulance
ambulant
ambush
ameliorate
  ameliorated
  ameliorating
amelioration
amen
amenable
amenably
amend
amendment
amenity
  amenities pl

American
Americana
Americanism
Americanization
Americanize
  Americanized
  Americanizing
amethyst
amiable
amiability
amiably
amicable
amicability
amicably
amid
amidships
amidst
amiss
amity
ammeter
ammonia
ammunition
amnesia
amnesty
  amnesties pl
amniocentesis
  amniocenteses pl
amniotic
amoeba
  amoebas,
    amoebae pl

amoebic
amok, amuck
among
 amongst
amoral
amorally
amorous
amorously
amorousness
amorphous
amortization
amortize
 amortized
 amortizing
amount
amour
amp
amperage
ampere
ampersand
amphetamine
amphibian
amphibious
amphitheater
ample (enough)
amplitude
amplifier
amplify
 amplified
 amplifies
 amplifying

amplification
amplifier
amply
ampoule (bottle)
amputate
 amputated
 amputating
amputation
amputee
amuck, amok
amulet
amuse
 amused
 amusing
amusement
anachronism
anachronistic
anaerobic
anagram
anal
analgesia
analgesic
analogous
analog (computer)
analogical
analogue (similar)
analogy
 analogies pl
analyze
 analyzed
 analyzing

analysis
 analyses pl
analyst
analytic
analytical
analytically
anarchic
anarchical
anarchism
anarchist
anarchy
anathema
 anathemas pl
anatomic
anatomical
anatomically
anatomist
anatomize
 anatomized
 anatomizing
anatomy
 anatomies pl
ancestor
ancestral
ancestry
 ancestries pl
anchor
 anchored
 anchoring
anchorage
anchovy

anchovies *pl*
ancient
ancillary
 ancillaries *pl*
anecdotal
anecdote
anemia
anemic
anemometer
anemone
aneroid
anesthesia
anesthetic
anesthetist
anesthetize
 anesthetized
 anesthetizing
aneurysm
anew
angel (spiritual)
angelic
angelical
angelically
anger
angina
angle (fishing; maths)
angler
Anglican
Anglicanism
anglicization
anglicize

anglicized
anglicizing
Anglophile
Anglophobe
Anglophobia
angostura
angry
 angrier
 angriest
anguish
angular
angularity
anhydrous
aniline
animal
animalcule
animate
 animated
 animating
animatedly
animation
animosity
 animosities *pl*
animus
aniseed
ankle
anklet
annal (story of one
 year)
annalist
anneal (to toughen, *eg*

metal)
annex (building)
annex (join)
 annexed
 annexes
 annexing
annexation
annihilate
 annihilated
 annihilating
annihilation
anniversary
 anniversaries *pl*
annotate
 annotated
 annotating
annotation
annotator
announce
 announced
 announcing
announcement
announcer
annoy
 annoyed
 annoying
annoyance
annual (yearly)
annually
annuity
 annuities *pl*

annuitant
annul (cancel)
  annulled
  annulling
  annuls
annular (ring-like)
annularity
annulment
annunciate
  annunciated
  annunciating
annunciation
anode
anodyne
anoint
anomalous
anomalously
anomaly
  anomalies *pl*
anon. (anonymous)
anon (soon)
anonymity
anonymous
anonymously
anorak
another
answer
  answered
  answering
answerable
antacid

antagonize
  antagonized
  antagonizing
antagonism
antagonist
Antarctic
antecedence
antecedent
antechamber
antedate
  antedated
  antedating
antediluvian
antelope
antenatal
antenna (of insect)
  antennae *pl*
antenna (radio)
  antennas *pl*
anterior
anteriority
anteroom
anthem
anther
anthology
  anthologies *pl*
anthologist
anthracite
anthrax
anthropoid
anthropology

anthropological
anthropologist
anthropomorphic
anthropomorphism
antiaircraft
antibiotic
antibody
  antibodies *pl*
antic
antichrist
anticipate
  anticipating
  anticipated
anticipation
anticipative
anticipatory
anticlimactic
anticlimax
anticlockwise
anticyclone
anticyclonic
antidepressant
antidote
antifreeze
antigen
antihistamine
antilogarithm
antimacassar
antimony
antipathy
  antipathies *pl*

antipathetic

antipodean

antipodes

antiquarian

antiquary

  antiquaries *pl*

antiquated

antique

antiquity

  antiquities *pl*

antirrhinum

  antirrhinums *pl*

anti-Semite

anti-Semitic

anti-Semitism

antiseptic

antiseptically

antisepsis

antisocial

antisocially

antithesis

  antitheses *pl*

antitoxic

antitoxin

antler

antonym

anus

anvil

anxiety

  anxieties *pl*

anxious

anxiously

any

anybody

anyhow

anyone

anything

anyway

anywhere

aorta

  aortas *pl*

apace

apart

apartheid

apartment

apathetic

apathetically

apathy

ape

aperient

aperitif

aperture

apex

  apexes, apices *pl*

aphasia

aphid

aphorism

aphoristic

aphrodisiac

apiary

  apiaries *pl*

apiarist

apiculture

apiece

aplomb

apocalypse

apocalyptic

apocrypha

apocryphal

apogee

apologia

  apologias *pl*

apologetic

apologetically

apologize

  apologized

  apologizing

apology

  apologies *pl*

apophthegm

apoplectic

apoplectically

apoplexy

apostasy

  apostasies *pl*

apostate

apostatize

  apostatized

  apostatizing

a posteriori

apostle

apostolate

apostolic

apostrophe
apostrophize
  apostrophized
  apostrophizing
apothecary
  apothecaries *pl*
apotheosis
  apotheoses *pl*
appall
  appalled
  appalling
  appalls
apparatus
  apparatuses *pl*
apparel
apparent
apparently
apparition
appeal
  appealed
  appealing
appear
  appeared
  appearing
appearance
appease
  appeased
  appeasing
appeasement
appeaser
appellant

appellation
append
appendage
appendicitis
appendix (addition to
  a book)
  appendices *pl*
appendix (in
  anatomy)
  appendixes *pl*
appertain
appetite
appetizer
appetizing
applaud
applause
apple
applecart
appliqué
apply
  applied
  applies
  applying
appliance
applicable
applicant
application
appoint
appointment
apportion
apposite (apt)

appraisal
appraise
  appraised
  appraising
appraisement
appreciable
appreciably
appreciate
  appreciated
  appreciating
appreciation
appreciative
apprehend
apprehension
apprehensive
apprentice
apprenticeship
apprise
  apprised
  apprising
apprize
  apprized
  apprizing
approach
approachable
approbation
appropriate
  appropriated
  appropriating
appropriately
appropriateness

appropriation
appropriator
approve
　approved
　approving
approval
approximate
　approximated
　approximating
approximately
approximation
appurtenance
apricot
a priori
apron
apropos
apt
aptitude
aptly
aptness
aquarium
　aquaria, aquariums *pl*
aquatic
aquatint
aqueduct
aqueous
aquiline
arabesque
Arabian
Arabic
arable

arbiter
arbitrage
arbitrarily
arbitrariness
arbitrary
arbitrate
　arbitrated
　arbitrating
arbitration
arbitrator
arbor
arc (curve)
arcade
arch
archaeological
archaeologically
archaeologist
archaeology
archaic
archaism
archaistic
archangel
archbishop
archbishopric
archdeacon
archdeaconry
archdiocese
archduke
archducal
archduchess
archduchy

　archduchies *pl*
archenemy
　archenemies *pl*
archer
archery
archetypal
archetype
archiepiscopal
archiepiscopate
archipelago
　archipelagos,
　　archipelagoes *pl*
architect
architectural
architecturally
architecture
architrave
archive
archivist
archly
archness
arctic
ardent
ardently
ardor
arduous
arduously
are (*from* be)
aren't
area (space)
arena

arenas *pl*

argosy

argot

arguable

arguably

argue

argued

arguing

argument

argumentative

aria (song)

arias *pl*

arid

aridity

aright

arise

arisen

arises

arising

arose

aristocracy

aristocracies

aristocrat

aristocratically

arithmetic

arithmetical

arithmetically

arithmetician

ark

arm

arms (weapons)

armada

armadas *pl*

Armageddon

armament

armature

armchair

armful

armistice

armlet

armor

armorer

armory

armories *pl*

armorial

arms

army

armies *pl*

aroma

aromas *pl*

aromatherapy

aromatic

arose (*from* arise)

around

arousal

arouse

aroused

arousing

arpeggio

arpeggios *pl*

arraign

arraignment

arrange

arrangement

arrant (utter, thorough)

array

arrears

arrest

arrive

arrived

arriving

arrival

arrogance

arrogant

arrogantly

arrogate

arrogated

arrogating

arrogation

arrow

arrowroot

arsenal

arsenic

arsenical

arsenious

arson

arsonist

art

arterial

artery

arteries *pl*

artesian

artful
artfully
artfulness
arthritic
arthritis
artichoke
article
articulate
  articulated
  articulating
articulately
articulation
artifact
artifice
artificer
artificial
artificiality
artificially
artillery
artilleryman
  artillerymen *pl*
artisan
artist (*eg* painter)
artiste (performer)
artistic
artistically
artistry
artless
artlessly
artlessness
arty

Aryan
asbestos
asbestosis
ascend (to go up)
ascendancy,
  ascendency
ascendant
ascension
ascent (going up)
ascertain
ascertainable
ascertainment
ascetic (hermit)
ascetically
asceticism
ascribable
ascribe
  ascribed
  ascribing
ascribing
ascription
asepsis
aseptic
asexual
asexually
ash
ashamed
ashen
ashore (on the beach)
ashtray
ashy

Asia
Asiatic
aside
asinine
asininity
ask
askance
askew
asleep
asp
asparagus
aspect
aspen
asperity
  asperities *pl*
aspersion
asphalt
asphyxia
asphyxiant
asphyxiate
  asphyxiated
  asphyxiating
asphyxiation
aspic
aspidistra
  aspidistras *pl*
aspirant
aspirate
  aspirated
  aspirating
aspiration

aspire
  aspired
  aspiring
aspirin
ass
assail
assailant
assassin
assassinate
  assassinated
  assassinating
assassination
assault
assaulter
assay (to test)
  assays *pl*
assayer
assemblage
assemble
  assembled
  assembling
assembly
  assemblies *pl*
assent (agreement)
assert
assertion
assertive
assess (measure)
assessable
assessment
assessor

asset
assiduity
assiduous
assiduously
assign
assignable
assignation
assignee
assignment
assimilate
  assimilated
  assimilating
assimilation
assist
assistance
assistant
assizes
associate
  associated
  associating
association
assonance
assonant
assort
assorted
assortment
assuage
  assuaged
  assuaging
assuagement
assume

  assumed
  assuming
assumption
assurance
assure (to guarantee)
  assured
  assuring
assuredly
assurer
aster (plant)
asterisk
asteroid
astern
asthma
asthmatic
astir (moving about)
astigmatism
astigmatic
astonish
astonishment
astound
astral
astrakhan
astray
astride
astringency
astringent
astrologer
astrology
astronaut
astronautics

astronomy
astronomer
astronomic
astronomical
astronomically
astroturf
astute
astutely
astuteness
asunder
asylum
  asylums *pl*
asymmetric
asymmetrical
asymmetrically
asymmetry
ate (*from* eat)
atheism
atheist
athlete
athletic
athletics
atlas
atmosphere
atmospheric
atoll
atom
atomic
atomically
atomization
atomize

atomized
atomizing
atomizer
atone
  atoned
  atoning
atonement
atrocious
atrociously
atrocity
  atrocities *pl*
atrophy
  atrophied
  atrophies
  atrophying
attach
attachable
attaché
attaché case
attachment
attack
attacker
attain
attainable
attainment
attempt
attend
attendance
attendant
attention
attentive

attentively
attenuate
  attenuated
  attenuating
attenuation
attenuator
attest
attestation
attestor, attestator
attic
attire
  attired
  attiring
attitude
attorney
  attorneys *pl*
attract
attraction
attractive
attractiveness
attributable
attribute
  attributed
  attributing
attribution
attributive
attributively
attrition
attune
  attuned
  attuning

atypical
atypically
auburn
auction
auctioneer
audacious
audaciously
audacity
audibility
audible
audibly
audience
audiometer
audiometric
audiometry
audiovisual
audit
  audited
  auditing
auditor
audition
auditorium
  auditoriums,
  auditoria pl
auger (tool)
augment
augmentation
au gratin
augur (to predict)
augury
  auguries pl

August (month)
august (noble)
auk
aunt (relation)
au pair
aura
  auras pl
aural (by ear)
aurally
auspices
auspicious
auspiciously
austere
austerely
austerity
  austerities pl
autarchy (absolute
  power)
  autarchies pl
autarky (self-
  sufficiency)
authentic
authentically
authenticate
  authenticated
  authenticating
authentication
authenticity
author
authorship
authority

authorities pl
authoritarian
authoritative
authoritatively
authorization
authorize
  authorized
  authorizing
autism
autistic
autobiographic
autobiographical
autobiographically
autobiography
  autobiographies pl
autocracy
  autocracies pl
autocrat
autocratic
autocratically
autogenous
autogiro, autogyro
  autogiros, autogyros
  pl
autograph
automatic
automatically
automation
automatism
automaton
  automatons,

automata *pl*
automobile
automotive
autonomous
autonomy
autopilot
autopsy
  autopsies *pl*
autostrada
  autostrade *pl*
autosuggestion
autumn
autumnal
auxiliary
  auxiliaries *pl*
avail
availability
available
avalanche
avant-garde
avarice
avaricious
avenge
  avenged
  avenging
avenger
avenue
aver
  averred
  averring
  avers

average
averse
aversion
avert
avertible, avertable
aviary
  aviaries *pl*
aviation
aviator
avid
avidity
avidly
avocado
  avocados *pl*
avocation
avoid (evade)
avoidable
avoidably
avoidance
avuncular
await
awake
  awakes
  awaking
  awoke
  awoken
award
aware
awareness
away
awe (fear)

awesome
awful
awfully
awfulness
awhile
awkward
awkwardly
awkwardness
awl
awning
awry
ax
  axed
  axing
axial
axially
axiom
axiomatic
axiomatically
axis
  axes *pl*
axle
ay, aye
ayah
ayatollah
azalea
  azaleas *pl*
azimuth
azimuthal
azure

babble (to chatter)
  babbled
  babbling
babbler
babe
Babel (tower of)
baboon
baby
  babies *pl*
babyish
baby-sit
  baby-sat
  baby-sits
  baby-sitting
baby-sitter
baccarat
bacchanalia
bachelor

bachelorhood
bacillary
bacillus
  bacilli *pl*
back
backache
backbite
backbiter
backbiting
backbone
backbreaking
backdate
  backdated
  backdating
backer
backfire
  backfired
  backfiring

backgammon
background
backpack
backstairs
backup
backward
backwardness
backwater
bacon
bacterial
bacteriological
bacteriologist
bacteriology
bacterium
  bacteria *pl*
bad (not good)
bade (*from* bid)
badge
badger
badly
badminton
bad-tempered
baffle
  baffled
  baffling
bag
  bagged
  bagging
  bags
bagatelle
baggage

baggy
  baggier
  baggiest
bagpipe
baguette
bail (to scoop water)
  bailed
  bailing
bailiff
  bailiffs *pl*
bait (fishing)
  baited
  baiting
baize
bake
  baked
  baking
baker
bakery
  bakeries *pl*
baksheesh,
  backsheesh
balaclava
  balaclavas *pl*
balalaika
  balalaikas *pl*
balance
  balanced
  balancing
balcony
  balconies *pl*

bald (hairless)
balderdash
baldheaded
baldness
bale (to bundle)
  baled
  baling
baleful
balefully
balk
ball (round shape)
ballad
ballast
ballbearing
ballerina
  ballerinas *pl*
ballet
ballistic
balloon
  ballooned
  ballooning
ballot
  balloted
  balloting
ballpoint
ballyhoo
balm
balmy (weather)
  balmier
  balmiest
baloney

balsam
baluster
balustrade
bamboo
bamboozle
  bamboozled
  bamboozling
ban (to prohibit)
  banned
  banning
  bans
banal
banality
  banalities *pl*
banally
banana
  bananas *pl*
band (strip; group)
bandage
  bandaged
  bandaging
bandit
banditry
bandoleer, bandolier
bandsman
  bandsmen *pl*
bandy
  bandied
  bandies
  bandying
bandy-legged

bane

baneful

banefully

bang

  banged

  banging

bangle

banish

banishment

banister, bannister

banjo

  banjos *pl*

bank

banker

banknote

bankrupt

bankruptcy

  bankruptcies *pl*

banner

banns (for marriage)

banquet

  banqueted

  banqueting

banshee

bantam

banter

  bantered

  bantering

baptism

baptize

  baptized

  baptizing

bar

  barred

  barring

  bars

barb

barbarian

barbaric

barbarism

barbarous

barbarously

barbecue

  barbecued

  barbecuing

barbed wire

barber

barbitone

barbiturate

barbituric

bard (poet)

bare (uncovered)

  bared

  baring

bareback

barefaced

barefoot

bareheaded

barelegged

barely

bareness

bargain

barge

  barged

  barging

baritone

barium

bark

bark, barque (ship)

barley

barmaid

barman

  barmen *pl*

barmy (silly)

  barmier

  barmiest

barn

barnacle

barnyard

barometer

barometric

baron (nobleman)

baroness

baronet

baronial

barony

  baronies *pl*

baroque

barque, bark (ship)

barrack

barrage

barrel

  barrels

barreled | basis | bather
barreling | bases *pl* | bathos
barren (sterile) | bask | batik
barrenness | basket | baton (conductor's)
barricade | basketball | batsman
  barricaded | bas-relief | batsmen *pl*
  barricading | bas-reliefs *pl* | battalion
barrier | bass (fish; music) | batten (to close)
barrister | bass, bast (fiber) | batter
barrow | basset | battery
bartender | bassoon | batteries *pl*
barter | bastard | battle
  bartered | bastardy | battled
  bartering | baste | battling
barterer | basted | battleax
basalt | basting | battledress
base (to found) | bastion | battlement
  based | bat | battleship
  basing | bats | batty
baseball | batted | battier
baseless | batting | battiest
basely | batch | bauble
basement | bate (to hold) | bauxite
baseness | bated | bawdy
bashful | bating | bawdier
bashfully | bated breath | bawdiest
bashfulness | bath | bawl (to shout)
basic | bathe (to go | bawled
basically | swimming) | bawling
basil | bathed | bay
basin | bathing | bayed

baying
bays
bay leaf
bayonet
bazaar (market)
bazooka
  bazookas *pl*
be (to exist)
  am
  are
  been
  being
  is
  was
beach (shore)
  beaches *pl*
beachcomber
beachhead
beacon
bead
  beaded
  beading
beadle
beady
beagle
beak
beaker
beam
  beamed
  beaming
bean (vegetable)

beansprout
beanstalk
bear (animal; to carry)
  bearing
  bears
  bore
  borne
bearable
beard
bearer
bearing (of a
  machine)
beast
beastliness
beastly
  beastlier
  beastliest
beat (to hit)
  beaten
  beating
  beats
beater
beatific
beatnik
beau (suitor)
  beaux *pl*
beauty
  beauties *pl*
beauteous
beautician
beautiful

beautifully
beautify
  beautified
  beautifies
  beautifying
beaver
becalm
because
beckon (to signal)
  beckoned
  beckoning
become
  became
  becomes
  becoming
bed
  bedded
  bedding
  beds
bedaub
bedclothes
bedevil
  bedevils
  bedeviled
  bedeviling
bedlam
Bedouin
bedraggle
  bedraggled
  bedraggling
bedridden

bedrock
bee (insect)
beech (tree)
  beeches pl
beef
  beefed
  beefing
beefeater
beefsteak
beefy
  beefier
  beefiest
beehive
beeline
been (from be)
beer (ale)
beery
beeswax
beet (vegetable)
beetle (insect)
beetroot
befall
  befallen
  befalling
  befalls
  befell
befit
  befits
  befitted
  befitting
before

beforehand
befoul
befriend
beg
  begged
  begging
  begs
beget
  begets
  begetting
  begot
  begotten
begetter
beggar
beggarliness
beggarly
beggary
begin
  began
  beginning
  begins
  begun
beginner
begone
begonia
  begonias pl
begrudge
  begrudged
  begrudging
beguile
  beguiled

  beguiling
beguilement
beguiler
behalf
behave
  behaved
  behaving
behavior
behead
  beheaded
  beheading
behind
behindhand
behold
  beheld
  beholding
  beholds
beholden
beholder
behoove
  behooved
  behooving
beige
being (from be)
belabor
  belabored
  belaboring
belated
belay
  belayed
  belaying

belays

belch

beleaguer

belfry

belfries *pl*

belie

belied

belies

belying

belief

believable

believe

believed

believing

believer

belittle

belittled

belittling

belittler

bell (for ringing)

belladonna

belladonnas *pl*

belle (pretty girl)

belles lettres

bellicose

bellicosity

belligerence

belligerent

bellow

bellows

belly

bellies *pl*

bellyful

belong

beloved

below (under)

belt

bemoan

bemoaned

bemoaning

bemuse

bemused

bemusing

bench

bencher

bend

bending

bends

bent

beneath

benediction

benefaction

benefactor

benefactress

benefice

beneficence

beneficent

beneficial

beneficially

beneficiary

beneficiaries *pl*

benefit

benefited

benefiting

benefiter

benevolence

benevolent

benevolently

benighted

benign

benignancy

benignant

benison

bent

benumb

benzene (coal tar)

benzine (gas)

bequeath

bequest

berate

berated

berating

bereaved

bereavement

bereft

beret (cap)

berry (fruit)

berries *pl*

berserk

berserker

berth (nautical)

beryl

beseech

beset
  besets
  besetting
beside
besides
besiege
  besieged
  besieging
besom
besotted
besought (*from*
  beseech)
bespeak
  bespeaking
  bespeaks
  bespoke
  bespoken
best
bestial
bestialism
bestiality
  bestialities *pl*
bestially
bestir
  bestirred
  bestirring
  bestirs
bestow
bestowal
bestride
  bestrides

bestriding
bestrode
bet
  bets
  betted
  betting
better
bête noire
  bêtes noires *pl*
betel nut
betide
betoken
betray
  betrayed
  betraying
betrayal
betroth
betrothal
betrothed
better
  bettered
  bettering
betterment
between
betwixt
bevel
  bevels
  beveled
  beveling
beverage
bevy

bevies *pl*
bewail
beware
bewilder
bewilderment
bewitch
beyond
biannual (twice a
  year)
biannually
bias
  biased, biassed
  biases
  biasing, biassing
bible (general)
Bible (Christian or
  Jewish scriptures)
biblical
bibliography
  bibliographies *pl*
bibliographer
bibliographic
bibliographical
bibliographically
bibliophile
bibulous
bicarbonate
bicentenary
  bicentenaries *pl*
bicentennial
biceps

bicker
bicycle
bicyclist
bid
  bade
  bidden
  bidding
  bids
bide
  bided
  biding
bidet
biennial (every two
  years)
biennially
bier (coffin stand)
bifocal
bifurcate
  bifurcated
  bifurcating
bifurcation
big
  bigger
  biggest
bigamist
bigamous
bigamously
bigamy
bigot, bight (bay)
bigoted
bigotry

bigwig
bijou
  bijoux *pl*
bike
bikini
bilateral
bilaterally
bilberry
  bilberries *pl*
bile
bilge
biliary
bilingual
bilingualism
bilinguist
bilious
biliousness
bilk
bill
billet
billet doux
  billets doux *pl*
billiards
billion
billionaire
billow (of a wave)
billowy
bimonthly
bin
  binned
  binning

bins
binary
binaural
bind
  binding
  binds
  bound
binder
bindery
  binderies *pl*
binge
  binged
  binging
bingo
binnacle
binocular
binomial
biochemical
biochemist
biochemistry
biodegradable
biodegrade
  biodegraded
  biodegrading
biodiversity
biography
  biographies *pl*
biographer
biographical
biographically
biological

biologically
biologist
biology
bionics
biopsy
  biopsies *pl*
biorhythms
bipartisan
bipartite
biped
biplane
bipolar
birch
bird
birdie
bird's-eye
birth (born)
birthday
birthplace
birthrate
birthright
biscuit
bisect
bisection
bisector
bisexual
bisexually
bishop
bishopric
bismuth
bison

bistro
bit
bitch
  bitches *pl*
bite (with teeth)
  bit
  biter
  bites
  biting
  bitten
bitter
bitterly
bittern (bird)
bitterness
bitumen
bituminous
bivalve
bivouac
  bivouacs
  bivouacked
  bivouacking
bizarre (unusual)
bizarrely
bizarreness
blab
  blabbed
  blabbing
  blabs
black
blackberry
  blackberries *pl*

blackbird
blackboard
blacken
blackguard
blackguardly
blackmail
blackmailer
black market
black marketeer
blackness
blackout (loss of
  consciousness)
black out (to lose
  consciousness)
blacksmith
bladder
blade
blame
  blamed
  blaming
blameless
blamelessly
blanch
blancmange
bland
blandish
blandishment
blandly
blank
blanket
blare

blared
blaring
blarney
blasé
blaspheme
blasphemer
blasphemous
blasphemy
  blasphemies *pl*
blast
blast-off
blatancy
blatant
blatantly
blaze
  blazed
  blazing
blazer
blazon
bleach
bleak
bleakly
bleakness
blear
blearily
bleariness
bleary
bleary-eyed
bleat
  bleated
  bleating

bleed
  bled
  bleeding
  bleeds
blemish
  blemishes *pl*
blench
blend
blender
bless
  blessed (sacred)
  blesses
  blessing
  blest
blew (*from* blow)
blight
blighter
blind
blind alley
  blind alleys *pl*
blindfold
blindly
blink
blinkered
bliss
blissful
blissfully
blissfulness
blister
  blistered
  blistering

blithe
blithely
blitheness
blithering
blizzard
bloat
  bloated
  bloating
bloater
blob
  blobbed
  blobbing
  blobs
bloc (group)
block (to stop; solid
  piece)
blockade
blockage
blockbuster
blockhead
bloke
blond (male)
blonde (female)
blood
bloodcurdling
bloodhound
blood pressure
bloodshed
bloodshot
bloodthirsty
blood vessel

bloody
  bloodied
  bloodies
  bloodying
  bloodier
  bloodiest
bloom
  bloomed
  blooming
bloomer
blossom
  blossomed
  blossoming
blot
  blots
  blotted
  blotting
blotch
  blotches *pl*
blotchy
  blotchier
  blotchiest
blotter
blouse
blow
  blew
  blown
  blows
blower
blowzy (red-faced)
blub

blubbed
  blubbing
  blubs
blubber (of whale)
blubbery
bludgeon
blue (color)
bluebell
blueberry
  blueberries *pl*
blue-chip
blue-collar
blue-eyed
blueness
bluff
bluffness
blunder
blunderbuss
blunderer
blunt
bluntly
bluntness
blur
  blurred
  blurring
  blurs
blurb
blurriness
blurry
blurt
blush

bluster
blustery
boa
  boas *pl*
boa constrictor
boar (male pig)
board (wooden plank)
boarder (lodger)
boast
boaster
boastful
boastfully
boastfulness
boat
boatswain, bosun
bob
  bobbed
  bobbing
  bobs
bobbin
bobby
  bobbies *pl*
bobsled, bobsleigh
bode
  boded
  boding
bodice
bodied
bodiless
bodily
bodkin

body
  bodies *pl*
bodyguard
bogey (golf; goblin;
    nasal mucus)
  bogeys *pl*
boggle
  boggled
  boggling
bogie (wheeled
    undercarriage)
  bogies *pl*
bogus
boil
  boiled
  boiling
boiler
boisterous
boisterously
bold (brave)
bolder
boldly
bole (tree trunk)
bollard
bologna
Bolshevik
Bolshevism
Bolshevist
bolster
  bolstered
  bolstering

bolt
bomb
bombard
bombardier
bombardment
bombast
bombastic
bombastically
bomber
bombshell
bona fide (in good
  faith)
bona fides (good
  faith)
bonanza
  bonanzas *pl*
bond
bondage
bone
  boned
  boning
boneless
bonfire
bonhomie
bonnet
bonny
  bonnier
  bonniest
bony
  bonier
  boniest

bonsai
bonus
  bonuses *pl*
bon voyage
boo
  boos *pl*
  booed
  booing
  boos
booby
  boobies *pl*
book
  booked
  booking
bookable
bookie
bookkeeper
bookkeeping
booklet
boom
  boomed
  booming
boomerang
boor (lout)
boorish
boost
booster
boot
  booted
  booting
bootee (baby's shoe)

booth
bootleg
  bootlegs
    bootlegged
    bootlegging
  bootlegger
bootless
booty (plunder)
booze
  boozed
  boozing
boozer
boozy
boracic
borax
border (edge)
bore
  bored
  boring
boredom
born (of a baby)
borne (*from* bear)
borough (town)
borrow (*eg* money)
borrower
bosh
bosom
boss
bossily
bossiness
bossy

bossier
bossiest
bosun, boatswain
botanical
botanist
botany
botch
both
bother
bothersome
bottle
  bottled
  bottling
bottleneck
bottom
  bottomed
  bottoming
bottomless
bottommost
botulism
boudoir
bough (branch)
bought (*from* buy)
boulder
boulevard
bounce
  bounced
  bouncing
bound
boundary
  boundaries *pl*

bounder
boundless
bounteous
bountiful
bounty
  bounties *pl*
bouquet
bourbon
bourgeois
bourgeoisie
bout
boutique
bovine
bow (to bend)
bowdlerize
  bowdlerized
  bowdlerizing
bowel (intestine)
bower
bowlegged
bowlegs
bowl (dish)
bowler
bowling
bowtie
box
boxer
boy (male child)
  boys *pl*
boycott
boyfriend

boyhood
boyish
boyishly
boyishness
bra (brassiere)
  bras *pl*
brace
  braced
  bracing
bracelet
bracken
bracket
brackish
brad
brag
  bragged
  bragging
  brags
braggart
braid
  braided
  braiding
Braille
brain
brainless
brainwashed
brainwashing
brainwave
brainy
  brainier
  brainiest

braise (to cook)
  braised
  braising
brake (to slow down)
  braked
  braking
bramble
bran
branch
brand
brand-new
brandy
  brandies *pl*
brash
brass
brasserie (restaurant)
brassiere (bra)
brat
bravado
brave
  braved
  braving
bravely
bravery
bravo (cry of
  approval)
  bravos *pl*
bravo (ruffian)
  bravoes *pl*
bravura
brawl

brawn
brawny
bray
  brayed
  braying
  brays
braze (to solder)
  brazed
  brazing
brazen
brazenness
brazier (burner)
breach (break)
  breached
  breaches
  breaching
bread (food)
breadth (width)
break (to split)
  breaking
  breaks
  broke
  broken
breakable
breakage
breakfast
breakthrough
bream (fish)
breast
breast-feed
  breast-fed

breast-feeding
breast-feeds
breath (air)
breathalyze
breathalyzed
breathalyzing
breathalyzer
breathe (to take
  breaths)
breathed
breathing
breather
breathless
breathtaking
breech (of gun)
breeches (trousers)
breechloader
breech-loading
breed
  bred
  breeding
  breeds
breeze
  breezed
  breezing
breezily
breezy
  breezier
  breeziest
brethren
brevity

brew (to make beer)
brewer
brewery
  breweries pl
briar, brier
bribe
  bribed
  bribing
bribable
bribery
bric-a-brac
brick
brickbat
bricklayer
bricklaying
bridal (of bride)
bride
bridegroom
bridesmaid
bridge
  bridged
  bridging
bridgehead
bridle (of horse)
  bridled
  bridling
bridlepath
Brie
brief
  briefed
  briefing

briefs
briefcase
briefly
brier, briar
brigade
brigadier
brigand
bright
brighten
  brightened
  brightening
brightly
brilliance
brilliant
brilliantly
brim (to fill)
  brimmed
  brimming
  brims
brimful
brimstone
brine
bring
  bringing
  brings
  brought
brink
briny
briquette
brisk
brisket

briskly
bristle
  bristled
  bristling
bristly
Britain (country)
British
Brittany
brittle
brittleness
broach (to open)
broad
broadcast
broadcaster
broaden
broadly
broadminded
broadside
brocade
broccoli
brochure
brogue
broil
  broiled
  broiling
broiler
broke (*from* break)
broken (*from* break)
brokenhearted
broker
brokerage

bromide
bronchial
bronchitic
bronchitis
bronco
  broncos *pl*
bronze
bronzed
brooch (jewelry)
  brooches *pl*
brood (to worry)
  brooded
  brooding
broody
brook
brooklet
broom
broth
brothel
brother
brotherhood
brother-in-law
  brothers-in-law *pl*
brotherliness
brotherly
brougham (carriage)
brought (*from* bring)
brow (eyebrow; edge)
browbeat
  browbeaten
  browbeating

brown
brownie
browse
  browsed
  browsing
bruise
  bruised
  bruising
bruiser
bruising
brunette
brunt
brush
brusque
brusquely
brusqueness
Brussels (city)
Brussels sprouts
brutal
brutality
  brutalities *pl*
brutalization
brutalize
  brutalized
  brutalizing
brutally
brute
bubble
  bubbled
  bubbling
bubbly

buccaneer
buck
bucket
bucketful
  bucketfuls *pl*
buckle
  buckled
  buckling
buck passer
buck passing
buckram
buck-toothed
bucolic
bud
  budded
  budding
  buds
Buddha
Buddhism
Buddhist
buddleia
  buddleias *pl*
budge
  budged
  budging
budgerigar
budget
  budgeted
  budgeting
budgetary
buff

buffalo
  buffaloes *pl*
buffer
buffet
  buffeted
  buffeting
buffoon
buffoonery
  buffooneries *pl*
bug
  bugged
  bugging
  bugs
bugbear
buggy
  buggies *pl*
bugle
bugler
build
  building
  builds
  built
builder
building
bulb
bulbous
bulge
  bulged
  bulging
bulimia
bulk

bulkhead
bulky
  bulkier
  bulkiest
bull
bulldoze
  bulldozed
  bulldozing
bulldozer
bullet
bulletproof
bulletin
bullfighter
bullfinch
  bullfinches *pl*
bullion
bullish
bullock
bull's-eye
bully
  bullies *pl*
  bullied
  bullies
  bullying
bullyrag
bulrush
bulwark
bum
  bummed
  bumming
  bums

bumblebee
bump
bumper
bumpily
bumpiness
bumpy
  bumpier
  bumpiest
bumpkin
bumptious
bumptiously
bumptiousness
bun
bunch
  bunches *pl*
bundle
  bundled
  bundling
bung
bungalow
bungle
  bungled
  bungling
bungler
bunion
bunk
bunker (in golf)
bunkum
bunny
  bunnies *pl*
Bunsen burner

bunting
buoy (float)
  buoys *pl*
buoyancy
buoyant
buoyantly
burble
  burbled
  burbling
burden
  burdened
  burdening
burdensome
bureau
  bureaux, bureaus *pl*
bureaucracy
  bureaucracies *pl*
bureaucrat
bureaucratic
bureaucratically
burgeon
burgeoning
burglar
burglary
  burglaries *pl*
burgle
  burgled
  burgling
burgomaster
burgundy
  burgundies *pl*

burial
burlesque
burliness
burly
  burlier
  burliest
burn
  burned
  burning
  burns
  burnt
burner
burnish
  burnished
  burnisher
burr, bur (of a plant)
burr (sound)
burrow
bursar
bursary
  bursaries *pl*
burial
burst
bury
  buried
  buries
  burying
bus
  buses *pl*
bush
  bushes *pl*

bushel
bushy
  bushier
  bushiest
business
  businesses *pl*
businesslike
businessman
  businessmen *pl*
businesswoman
  businesswomen *pl*
busk
busker
bust
bustle
  bustled
  bustling
busy
  busied
  busies
  busying
  busier
  busiest
busybody
  busybodies *pl*
busyness (being busy)
but (contrary)
butcher
butcherer
butler
butt (to adjoin;

  container)
butted
butting
butts
butter
  buttered
  buttering
buttercup
butterfingered
butterfly
  butterflies *pl*
buttery
  butteries *pl*
buttock
button
  buttoned
  buttoning
buttress
buxom
buxomness
buy (to purchase)
  bought
  buying
  buys
buyer
buzz
buzzard
buzzer
by (close to)
by and by
by-election

bygone
bylaw
byline, byline
bypass
bypath
byplay
by-product
byroad
bystander
byte (computer)
byword

cab
cabaret
cabbage
cabby
  cabbies *pl*
cabin
cabinet
cable
  cabled
  cabling
cablegram
cache (hide)
cackle
  cackled
  cackling
cacophonous
cacophony
  cacophonies *pl*

cactus
  cacti, cactuses *pl*
cad
cadaver
cadaverous
caddie, caddy (golf)
  caddied
  caddies
  caddying
caddis
caddish
caddishly
caddisworm
caddy (tea)
  caddies *pl*
cadence
cadenza
  cadenzas *pl*

cadet
cadet corps
cadge
  cadged
  cadging
cadmium
Caesar
café
  cafés *pl*
cafeteria
  cafeterias *pl*
caffeine
cage
caged
cagey
  cagier
  cagiest
  cagily
  caginess
cagoule
cairn
caisson
cajole
  cajoled
  cajoling
cajolery
cake
  caked
  caking
calabash
calamine

calamity
  calamities *pl*
calamitous
calcification
calcify
  calcified
  calcifies
  calcifying
calcium
calculable
calculate
  calculated
  calculating
calculation
calculator
calculus
calendar (of dates)
calender (machine)
calends, kalends
calf
  calves *pl*
caliber
calibrate
  calibrated
  calibrating
calibration
calico
  calicoes, calicos *pl*
caliper
caliph
caliphate

calisthenic
calisthenics
call (to shout out)
caller
calligrapher
calligraphic
calligraphist
calligraphy
callosity
callous (unfeeling)
callously
callousness
callow
callus (hard skin)
  calluses *pl*
calm
calmly
calmness
calomel
calorie
  calories *pl*
calorific
calorimeter
calorimetric
calorimetry
calumniate
  calumniated
  calumniating
calumniator
calumnious
calumny

calumnies *pl*
calve (give birth
  to a calf)
  calved
  calving
calypso
calyx
  calyxes, calyces *pl*
cam
camaraderie
camber
cambered
cambric
camcorder
came (*from* come)
camel
camel-hair
Camembert
cameo
  cameos *pl*
camera
  cameras *pl*
camisole
camomile
camouflage
  camouflaged
  camouflaging
camp
campaign
camphor
camphorated

campsite
campus
  campuses *pl*
can (to put in tins)
  canned
  canning
  cans
can (to be able to)
  could
canal
canalization
canalize
  canalized
  canalizing
canary (bird)
  canaries *pl*
can-can
cancel
  cancels
  canceled
  canceling
cancellation
cancer
cancerous
candelabra,
  candelabrum
candelabra,
  candelabras,
  candelabrums *pl*
candid (open)
candidacy

candidacies *pl*
candidate
candidly
candle
candlelight
candlestick
candor
candy
  candies *pl*
  candied
  candies
  candying
cane
  caned
  caning
canine
canister
canker
cannabis
cannery
  canneries *pl*
cannibal
cannibalism
cannibalization
cannibalize
  cannibalized
  cannibalizing
cannily
canniness
cannon (gun)
cannonade

cannot
canny
  cannier
  canniest
canoe
  canoes *pl*
canoeing
canoeist
canon (law)
canonical
canonization
canonize
  canonized
  canonizing
canonry
canopied
canopy
  canopies *pl*
can't (cannot)
cant (hypocrisy)
cantabile
cantaloupe, cantaloup
cantankerous
cantankerously
cantata
  cantatas *pl*
canteen
canter
  cantered
  cantering
cantilever

canto
  cantos *pl*
canton
cantonal
cantonment
cantor
canvas (cloth)
  canvases *pl*
canvass (for votes)
  canvassed
  canvasses
  canvassing
canvasser
canyon
cap
  capped
  capping
  caps
capability
  capabilities *pl*
capable
capably
capacious
capacitance
capacitive
capacitor
capacity
  capacities *pl*
cape
caper (to jump)
capillary

  capillaries *pl*
capital (city, letter)
capitalism
capitalist
capitalistic
capitalization
capitalize
  capitalized
  capitalizing
capitally
capitation
Capitol (building)
capitulate
  capitulated
  capitulating
capitulation
capon
cappuccino
caprice
capricious
capriciously
capsizable
capsize
  capsized
  capsizing
capstan
capsular
capsule
captain
captaincy
  captaincies *pl*

caption
  captioned
  captioning
captious
captiously
captiousness
captivate (to delight)
  captivated
  captivating
captivation
captive
captivity
capture
  captured
  capturing
captor
car
carabiniere
  carabinieri *pl*
carafe
caramel
carat (weight)
caravan
caraway
  caraways *pl*
carbide
carbine
carbohydrate
carbolic
carbon
carbon dioxide

carbonaceous
carbonate
carbonic
carbonization
carbonize
  carbonized
  carbonizing
carboy
  carboys *pl*
carbuncle
carburetor
carcass, carcase
  carcasses, carcases *pl*
carcinogenic
carcinoma
  carcinomas *pl*
card
cardboard
card-carrying
cardiac
cardigan
cardinal (of Church)
cardiogram
cardiograph
cardiographer
cardiographic
cardiography
care
  cared
  caring
careen

careened
careening
career
  careered
  careering
careerist
carefree
careful
carefully
careless
carelessly
carelessness
caress
caretaker
careworn
cargo
  cargoes *pl*
caricature
  caricatured
  caricaturing
caricaturist
caries (decay)
carillon
carjack
carjacking
carminative
carmine
carnage
carnal
carnally
carnation

carnival
carnivorous
carol
  carols
  caroled
  caroling
caroler
carotid
carouse
  caroused
  carousing
carousel (merry-go-
  round)
carousing
carp
carpenter
carpentry
carpet
  carpeted
  carpeting
carriage
carrion
carrot (vegetable)
carrier
carry (to bear)
  carried
  carries
  carrying
cart
cartage
carte blanche

cartel
carter
cartilage
cartilaginous
cartographer
cartographic
cartography
carton (cardboard)
cartoon (drawing)
cartoonist
cartridge
carve (to cut up)
  carved
  carving
caryatid
cascade
  cascaded
  cascading
cascara
case
  cased
  casing
casein
casement
cash (money)
cashew
cashier
cashmere
casino
  casinos pl
cask

casket
casserole
cassette
cassock
cast (throw)
castanets
castaway
  castaways pl
caste (social class)
casteless
castellated
cast-off
castigate
  castigated
  castigating
castigation
castle
castor, caster
castor oil
castrate
  castrated
  castrating
castration
castrato (singer)
  castrati pl
casual
casually
casualness
casualty
  casualties pl
casuist

casuistry
cat
catabolism
cataclysm (upheaval)
cataclysmal
cataclysmic
cataclysmically
catacomb
catalepsy
cataleptic
cataloged
  cataloging
cataloger
catalyst
catalytic
catalyze
  catalyzed
  catalyzing
catalyzer
catamaran
catapult
cataract
catarrh
catarrhal
catastrophe
catastrophic
catastrophically
catcall
catch
  catches
  catching

caught
catchment
catechism
catechize
  catechized
  catechizing
categoric
categorical
categorically
categorize
  categorized
  categorizing
category
  categories *pl*
cat's eye
cater
caterer
caterpillar
caterwaul
catgut
catharsis
cathartic
cathedral
catheter
cathode
cathodic
catholic
catholicism
catholicity
catkin
catnap

cattily
cattish
catty
  cattier
  cattiest
catsup
cattle
caucus
  caucuses *pl*
caught (*from* catch)
caul (of a baby)
cauldron
cauliflower
caulk (to make
  watertight)
causal
causation
causative
cause
  caused
  causing
causeway
  causeways *pl*
caustic
caustically
cauterization
cauterize
  cauterized
  cauterizing
cautery
  cauteries *pl*

caution
cautionary
cautious
cautiously
cavalcade
cavalier
cavalry
  cavalries *pl*
cave
  caved
  caving
caveat
cavern
cavernous
caviar, caviare
cavil
  cavils
  caviled
  caviling
cavity
  cavities *pl*
cavort
caw (bird sound)
cayenne
CD
CD ROM
cease
ceasefire
ceaseless
ceaselessly
cedar

cede (yield)
  ceded
  ceding
cedilla
  cedillas *pl*
ceiling (of a room)
celandine
celebrant
celebrate
  celebrated
  celebrating
celebration
celebrator
celebrity
  celebrities *pl*
celeriac
celerity
celery (vegetable)
celestial
celestially
celibacy
celibate
cell (*eg* prison)
cellar (basement)
cellarage
cellist
cello
  cellos *pl*
cellophane
cellular
cellulite

celluloid
cellulose
Celsius
Celt
Celtic
cement
cemetery
  cemeteries *pl*
cenotaph
censer (for incense)
censor (official)
censorious
censorship
censure (blame)
  censured
  censuring
census
  censuses *pl*
cent (money)
centaur
centenary
  centenaries *pl*
centenarian
centennial
centigrade
centigram
centiliter
centime
centimeter
centipede
central

centralization
centralize
  centralized
  centralizing
centrally
center
  centered
  centering
centerpiece
centrifugal
centrifugally
centrifuge
centripetal
centrist
centuple
centurion
century
  centuries *pl*
cephalic
cephalitis
ceramic
cereal (grain)
cerebellum
  cerebellums,
  cerebella *pl*
cerebral
cerebral palsy
cerebration
cerebrospinal
cerebrum
  cerebra *pl*

ceremonial
ceremonially
ceremonious
ceremoniously
ceremony
  ceremonies *pl*
cerise
certain
certainly
certainty
  certainties *pl*
certifiable
certificate
  certificated
  certificating
certification
certify
  certified
  certifies
  certifying
certitude
cervical
cervix
cesarean section
cessation
cession (yielding)
cesspit
cesspool
chafe (rub)
  chafed
  chafing

chaff (straw)
chaffinch
  chaffinches *pl*
chagrin
chain
chair
  chaired
  chairing
chairman
  chairmen *pl*
chairwoman
  chairwomen *pl*
chaise longue
  chaises longues *pl*
chalcedony
  chalcedonies *pl*
chalet
chalice
chalk
chalky
challenge
  challenged
  challenging
challenger
chamber
chamberlain
chambermaid
chameleon
chamfer (groove)
chamois
champ, chomp

champagne
champion
championships
chance
  chanced
  chancing
chancel
chancellery
  chancelleries *pl*
chancellor
chancery
  chanceries *pl*
chancy
  chancier
  chanciest
chandelier
chandler
change
  changed
  changing
changeable
changeling
channel
  channels
  channeled
  channeling
chant
chantry
  chantries *pl*
chaos
chaotic

chaotically
chap
  chapped
  chapping
  chaps
chapel
chaperon
  chaperoned
  chaperoning
chaperonage
chaplain
chaplaincy
chaplet
chapter
char
charred
  charring
  chars
character
characteristic
characteristically
characterization
characterize
  characterized
  characterizing
charade
charcoal
charge
  charged
  charging
chargeable

chargé d'affaires
  chargés d'affaires pl
chariot
charioteer
charisma
charismatic
charity
  charities pl
charitable
charitably
charlatan
charlotte
charlotte russe
charm
charmer
chart
charter
charterer
charily
chariness
chary
chase (to pursue)
  chased
  chasing
chaser
chasm
chassis
  chassis pl
chaste (pure)
chastely
chasten

chastise
  chastised
  chastising
chastisement
chastity
chat
  chats
  chatted
  chatting
château
  châteaus, châteaux
chatelaine
chatter
chatterbox
chatty
  chattier
  chattiest
chattel
chauffeur
  chauffeurs pl
chauvinism
chauvinist
chauvinistic
cheap (low priced)
cheaper
cheaply
cheapness
cheat
  cheated
  cheating
check (control; stop)

checkered
checkmate
cheek
cheekily
cheekiness
cheeky
  cheekier
  cheekiest
cheep (chick's chirp)
cheer
cheerily
cheerless
cheery
  cheerier
  cheeriest
cheerful
cheerfully
cheerfulness
cheese
cheetah (animal)
chef
chemical
chemically
chemise
chemist
chemistry
cherish
cheroot
cherry
  cherries pl
cherub

cherubic
cherubically
chess
chessboard
chest
chestnut
chevalier
chevron
chevroned
chew (to eat)
  chewed
  chewing
  chews
chewy
  chewier
  chewiest
Chianti
chic (elegant)
chicanery
chichi
chick (young bird)
chicken
chickenpox
chickweed
chicory
chide
  chid
  chidden
  chided
  chiding
chief

chiefs pl
chieftain
chiffon
chilblain
child
  children pl
childbirth
childhood
childish
chill
chilled
chilli, chili (spice)
  chillies, chilies pl
chilly
  chillier
  chilliest
chime
  chimed
  chiming
chimney
  chimneys pl
chimpanzee
chin
China
china (porcelain)
Chinese
chink
chinos
chintz
  chintzes pl
chip

chipped
chipping
chips
chipmunk
chiropodist
chiropody
chiropractic
chiropractor
chirp
chisel (tool)
chisel (to cheat)
  chisels
  chiseled
  chiseling
chiseler
chit
chit-chat
chivalrous
chivalrously
chivalry
chive
chlorate
chloride
chlorinate
  chlorinated
  chlorinating
chlorination
chlorine
chlorodyne
chlorofluorocarbon
chloroform

chlorophyll
chock
chock-a-block
chock-full
chocoholic
chocolate
choice
choicely
choiceness
choicest
choir
choke
  choked
  choking
choker
choler (anger)
cholera
choleric
cholesterol
chomp, champ
choose (select)
  chooses
  choosing
  chose
  chosen
choosy
chop
  chopped
  chopping
  chops
chopper

choppy
  choppier
  choppiest
chopstick
chop-suey
choral (of a choir)
choral (hymn)
chorally
chord (music)
chore
choreographer
choreographic
choreography
chorister
chortle
  chortled
  chortling
chorus
  choruses *pl*
chose (*from* choose)
chosen (*from* choose)
chow (dog)
chow mein
Christ
christen
Christendom
christening
Christian
Christianity
Christmas
Christmassy

chromate
chromatic
chromatin
chrome
chromic
chromium
chromosome
chromosphere
chronically
chronicle
  chronicled
  chronicling
chronological
chronologically
chronology
  chronologies *pl*
chronometer
chrysalis
  chrysalises *pl*
chrysanthemum
  chrysanthemums *pl*
chub
chubby
  chubbier
  chubbiest
chuck
chuckle
chuckling
chuffed
chug
  chugged

  chugging
  chugs
chum
chummy
chump
chunk
chunky
  chunkier
  chunkiest
church (general)
  churches *pl*
Church (Christian)
churchgoer
churchwarden
churlish
churn
chute (sloping
  passage)
chutney
  chutneys *pl*
cicada
  cicadas, cicadae *pl*
cicatrize
  cicatrized
  cicatrizing
cider
cigar
cigarette
cinder
Cinderella
cinema

cinemas *pl*
cinematic
cinematograph
cinematography
cineraria
  cinerarias *pl*
cinerarium
  cinerariums *pl*
cinerary
cinerary urn
cinnamon
cipher
circa
circle
  circled
  circling
circuit
circuitous
circuitry
  circuitries *pl*
circular
circularize
  circularized
  circularizing
circulate
  circulated
  circulating
circulation
circumcise
  circumcised
  circumcising

circumcision
circumference
circumflex
circumlocution
circumnavigate
  circumnavigated
  circumnavigating
circumnavigation
circumscribe
  circumscribed
  circumscribing
circumscription
circumspect
circumspection
circumstance
circumstantial
circumstantially
circumvent
  circumvented
  circumventing
circumvention
circus
  circuses *pl*
cirrhosis
cirrus
  cirri *pl*
cist
cistern
citadel
citation
cite (quote)

cited
citing
citizen
citizenship
citrate
citric
citron
citrus
city
  cities *pl*
civet
civic
civic center
civil
civilian
civility
  civilities *pl*
civilization
civilize
  civilized
  civilizing
civilly
civvies
clad
cladding
claim
claimable
claimant
clairvoyance
clairvoyant
clam (shellfish)

clamant
clamber
clamminess
clammy
clamor
clamorous
clamp
clan
clandestine
clandestinely
clang
clangor (noise)
clannish
clap
  clapped
  clapping
  claps
claptrap
claret
clarification
clarify
  clarified
  clarifies
  clarifying
clarinet
clarinetist, clarinettist
clarion
clarity
clash
clasp
class

classic

classical

classically

classicism

classicist

classics

classifiable

classification

classify

  classified

  classifies

  classifying

classless

classroom

classy

  classier

  classiest

clatter

  clattered

  clattering

clause

claustral

claustrophobia

claustrophobic

clavichord

clavicle

clavicular

claw

clay

clean

  cleaned

  cleaning

cleanable

cleaner

cleanliness

cleanly

cleanse

  cleansed

  cleansing

clear

clearance

clear-cut

clearly

cleave

  cleaved

  cleaving

  cleft

  clove

  cloven

clef

  clefs *pl*

clematis

clemency

clement

clench

clergy

cleric

clerical

clerk

clever

cleverly

clew (thread)

cliché

click

client

clientele

cliff

climactic

  (culminating)

climate

climatic (of climate)

climatically

climatology

climax

  climaxes *pl*

climb (to ascend)

climbable

climber

clime (region)

clinch

cling

  clinging

  clings

  clung

clinic

clinical

clinically

clink

clinker

clip

  clipped

  clipping

  clips

clipboard
clipper
clique
cliquey
cliquish
clitoris
  clitorides *pl*
cloak
cloakroom
clobber
cloche
clock
clockwise
clockwork
clod
clodhopper
clog
  clogged
  clogging
  clogs
cloister
cloistered
cloistral
clone
  cloned
  cloning
close
  closed
  closing
closet
  closeted

  closeting
closure
clot
  clots
  clotted
  clotting
cloth (material)
clothe (to dress)
  clothed
  clothing
clothes (garments)
clothier
cloud
  clouded
  clouding
cloudy
  cloudier
  cloudiest
clout
clove (spice)
cloven
clover
cloverleaf
clown
cloy
club
  clubbed
  clubbing
  clubs
cluck
clue

clueless
clump
clumsily
clumsiness
clumsy
  clumsier
  clumsiest
clung (*from* cling)
cluster
  clustered
  clustering
clutch
clutter
  cluttered
  cluttering
coach
  coaches *pl*
coachman
coagulate
  coagulated
  coagulating
coagulation
coal
coalesce
  coalesced
  coalescing
coalescence
coalescent
coalition
coarse (rough)
coarsely

coarsen
  coarsened
  coarsening
coarseness
coast
coastal
coaster
coastguard
coat (garment;
    to cover)
  coated
  coating
coax
coaxial
cob
cobalt
cobble
  cobbled
  cobbling
cobbler
cobra
  cobras *pl*
cobweb
cocaine
coccygeal
coccyx
cochineal
cochlea
  cochleae *pl*
cock
cockade

cockatoo
  cockatoos *pl*
cockerel
cockeyed
cockily
cockle
cockney
  cockneys *pl*
cockpit
cockroach
  cockroaches *pl*
cocksure
cocktail
cocky
  cockier
  cockiest
coco (tree)
cocoa (drink)
coconut
cocoon
cocotte
cod
coda
  codas *pl*
coddle
  coddled
  coddling
code
  coded
  coding
codeine

codger
codicil
codification
codify
  codified
  codifies
  codifying
codling
coeducation
coeducational
coefficient
coerce
  coerced
  coercing
coercion
coexist
coexistence
coffee
coffer
coffin
cog
cogency
cogent
cogently
cogitate
  cogitated
  cogitating
cogitation
cognac
cognate
cognizance

cognizant
cognition
cognitive
cognomen
cog-wheel
cohabit
  cohabited
  cohabiting
cohabitation
cohere
  cohered
  cohering
coherence
coherent
coherently
coherer
cohesion
cohesive
cohort
coiffeur (hairdresser)
  coiffeurs *pl*
coiffeuse
  coiffeuses *pl*
coiffure (hair style)
coil
  coiled
  coiling
coin
coinage
coincide
  coincided

  coinciding
coincidence
coincident
coincidental
coincidentally
coiner
coir (fiber)
coition
coitus
coke
colander
cold
cold-blooded
coldly
cold-shoulder
cole (cabbage)
coleslaw
colic
colicky
colitis
collaborate
  collaborated
  collaborating
collaboration
collaborator
collage (patchwork
  picture)
collapse
  collapsed
  collapsing
collapsible

collar (around neck)
  collared
  collaring
collate
  collated
  collating
collateral
collation
collator
colleague
collect
collectible,
  collectable
collection
collective
collectively
collectivism
collectivist
collector
colleen
college
collegial
collegian
collegiate
collide
  collided
  colliding
collie
collier
colliery
  collieries *pl*

collision
collocate
  collocated
  collocating
collocation
colloid
colloidal
colloquial
colloquialism
colloquially
colloquy
  colloquies *pl*
collude
  colluded
  colluding
colitis
collusion
collusive
cologne
colon (bowel,
  punctuation)
colonel (military)
colonial
colonialism
colonizer
colonist
colonization
colonize
  colonized
  colonizing
colonnade

colony
  colonies *pl*
color
  colored
  coloring
coloration
coloratura
  coloraturas *pl*
colorful
colorfully
colorless
colossal
colossally
colosseum
colt
coltish
columbine
column
columnar
columnist
coma
  (unconsciousness)
  comas *pl*
comatose
comb
combat
  combated
  combating
combatant
combative
combe, coomb

  (valley)
combinable
combination
combine
  combined
  combining
combustible
combustion
come
  came
  comes
  coming
comedian
comedienne
comedy
  comedies *pl*
comeliness
comely (pretty)
  comelier
  comeliest
comestible
comet
comeuppance
comfit (sweetmeat)
comfort
comfortable
comfortably
comforter
comic
comical
comicality

comicalities *pl*
comically
comity (friendship)
  comities *pl*
comma (punctuation
  mark)
  commas *pl*
command
commandant
commandeer
  commandeered
  commandeering
commander
commandment
commando
  commandos *pl*
commemorate
  commemorated
  commemorating
commemoration
commemorative
commence
  commenced
  commencing
commencement
commend
commendable
commendably
commendation
commensurable
commensurate

commensurately
comment
commentary
  commentaries *pl*
commentator
commerce
commercial
commercialism
commercialization
commercialize
  commercialized
  commercializing
commercially
commiserate
  commiserated
  commiserating
commiseration
commissar
commissariat
commission
commissioner
commit
  commits
  committed
  committing
commitment
committal
committee (group)
commode
commodious
commodity

commodities *pl*
commodore
common
Common Market
commoner
commonplace
commonwealth
commotion
communal
communally
commune
  communed
  communing
communicable
communicant
communicate
  communicated
  communicating
communication
communicative
communion
communiqué
communism
communist
community
  communities *pl*
commutable
commutation
commutator
commute
  commuted

commuting
commuter
compact
companion
companionable
company
  companies *pl*
comparable
comparably
comparative
comparatively
compare (to liken)
  compared
  comparing
comparison
compartment
compartmentalization
compartmentalize
  compartmentalized
  compartmentalizing
compass
  compasses *pl*
compassion
compassionate
compassionately
compatibility
compatible
compatibly
compatriot
compel
  compelled

compelling
compels
compendious
compendium
  compendiums,
  compendia *pl*
compensate
  compensated
  compensating
compensation
compensator
compensatory
compete
  competed
  competing
competence
competent
competently
competition
competitive
competitively
competitor
compilation
compile
  compiled
  compiling
compiler
complacency
complacent (smug)
complacently
complain

complained
complaining
complainant
complainer
complaint
complaisance
complaisant (willing)
complement (to add
  to)
  complemented
  complementing
complementary
complete
  completed
  completing
completely
completion
complex
complexion
complexity
  complexities *pl*
compliance
compliant
complicacy
complicate
  complicated
  complicating
complication
complicity
compliment (praise)
complimentary

compline (church service)
comply
 complied
 complies
 complying
component
comport
comportment
compose
 composed
 composing
compos mentis
composer (of music)
composition
compositor (in printing)
compost
composure (calmness)
compote (of fruit)
compound
comprehend
comprehensibility
comprehensible
comprehensibly
comprehension
comprehensive
comprehensively
compress
compressibility
compressible

compression
compressor
comprise
 comprised
 comprising
compromise
 compromised
 compromising
compulsion
compulsive
compulsively
compulsorily
compulsory
compunction
computable
computation
compute
 computed
 computing
computer
computerization
computerize
 computerized
 computerizing
computing
comrade
comradely
comradeship
con
 conned
 conning

cons
concave
concavity
 concavities *pl*
conceal
 concealed
 concealing
concealment
concede
 conceded
 conceding
conceit
conceited
conceivable
conceivably
conceive
 conceived
 conceiving
concentrate
 concentrated
 concentrating
concentration
concentrator
concentric
concentrically
concentricity
concept
conception
conceptual
conceptualize
 conceptualized

conceptualizing

concern

concert

concertina

  concertinas *pl*

concerto

  concertos *pl*

concession

concessionaire

concessionary

concierge

conciliate

  conciliated

  conciliating

conciliation

conciliator

conciliatory

concise

concisely

conciseness

conclave

conclude

  concluded

  concluding

conclusion

conclusive

conclusively

concoct

concoction

concomitance

concomitant

concord

concordance

concordant

concourse

concrete

concretely

concreteness

concubinage

concubine

concur

  concurred

  concurring

  concurs

concurrence

concurrent

concuss

  concussed

concussion

condemn

  condemned

  condemning

condemnation

condemnatory

condensation

condense

  condensed

  condensing

condenser

condescend

condescension

condign

condignly

condiment

condition

conditional

conditionally

condolatory

condole

  condoled

  condoling

condolence

condoler

condom

condone (to forgive)

  condoned

  condoning

conduce

  conduced

  conducing

conducive

conduct

conductance

conductivity

conductor

conduit

cone

coney (rabbit)

  coneys *pl*

confabulate

  confabulated

  confabulating

confabulation

confection
confectioner
confectionery
confederacy
  confederacies *pl*
confederate
  confederated
  confederating
confederation
confer
  conferred
  conferring
  confers
conference
conferment
confess
confessional
confessor
confetti
confidant (person)
confidante (female)
confide
  confided
  confiding
confidence
confident (self-
  assured)
confidential
confidentiality
confidentially
confidently

configuration
confine
  confined
  confining
confinement
confirm
confirmable
confirmation
confirmative
confirmatory
confiscate
  confiscated
  confiscating
confiscation
confiscator
confiscatory
conflagration
conflict
conform
conformable
conformance
conformation
conformity
confound
confrere, confrère
confront
confrontation
confuse
  confused
  confusing
confusion

confutation
confute
  confuted
  confuting
conga (dance)
congeal
  congealed
  congealing
congelation
congenial
congeniality
congenially
congenital
congenitally
conger
conger-eel
congest
congestion
congestive
conglomerate
  conglomerated
  conglomerating
conglomeration
congratulate
  congratulated
  congratulating
congratulation
congratulatory
congregate
  congregated
  congregating

congregation
congregational
congress
  congresses *pl*
congressional
congruence
congruent
congruity
congruous
conic
conical
conically
conifer
coniferous
conjecturable
conjecturably
conjectural
conjecture
conjoin
  conjoined
  conjoining
conjoint
conjointly
conjugal
conjugate
  conjugated
  conjugating
conjugation
conjunction
conjunctival
conjunctive

conjunctivitis
conjure
  conjured
  conjuring
conjuror
conker (chestnut)
connect
connection
connective
connector, connecter
conning-tower
connivance
connive
  connived
  conniving
connoisseur
connotation
connote
  connoted
  connoting
connubial
connubially
conquer (to win)
  conquered
  conquering
conquerable
conqueror
conquest
consanguineous
consanguinity
conscience

conscientious
conscientiously
conscientiousness
conscious
consciously
consciousness
conscript
conscription
consecrate
  consecrated
  consecrating
consecration
consecutive
consecutively
consensus
consent
consequence
consequential
consequently
conservancy
conservation
conservatism
conservative
conservatory
  conservatories *pl*
conserve
  conserved
  conserving
consider
  considered
  considering

considerable
considerably
considerate
considerately
considerateness
consideration
consign
  consigned
  consigning
consignee
consignment
consignor
consist
consistence
consistency
  consistencies *pl*
consistent
consolable
consolation
consolatory
console (to comfort,
  control panel)
  consoled
  consoling
consoler
consolidate
  consolidated
  consolidating
consolidation
consommé
consonant

consort
consortium
  consortia *pl*
conspicuous
conspicuously
conspicuousness
conspiracy
  conspiracies *pl*
conspirator
conspiratorial
conspire
  conspired
  conspiring
constable
constabulary
  constabularies *pl*
constancy
constant
constantly
constellation
consternation
constipate
  constipated
  constipating
constipation
constituency
  constituencies *pl*
constituent
constitute
  constituted
  constituting

constitution
constitutional
constitutionally
constrain
  constrained
  constraining
constraint
constrict
constriction
constrictive
constrictor
construct
construction
constructional
constructive
constructively
constructor
construe
  construed
  construing
consul (official)
consular
consulate
consult
consultant
consultation
consultative
consumable
consume
  consumed
  consuming

consumer
consummate
  consummated
  consummating
consummately
consummation
consumption
consumptive
contact
contactor
contagion
contagious
contain
  contained
  containing
container
containerization
containerize
  containerized
  containerizing
containment
contaminant
contaminate
  contaminated
  contaminating
contamination
contemplate
  contemplated
  contemplating
contemplation
contemplative

contemplatively
contemporaneous
contemporary
  contemporaries *pl*
contempt
contemptible
contemptibly
contemptuous
contemptuously
contend
content
contention
contentious
contentment
contest
contestable
contestant
context
contiguity
contiguous
contiguously
continence
continent
continental
contingency
  contingencies *pl*
contingent
continual
continually
continuance
continuation

continue
  continued
  continuing
continuity
continuous
continuously
contort
contortion
contortionist
contour
contraband
contraception
contraceptive
contract
contraction
contractor
contractual
contractually
contradict
contradiction
contradictory
contralto
  contraltos *pl*
contraption
contrarily
contrariness
contrary
contrast
contravene
  contravened
  contravening

contravention
contretemps
contribute
　contributed
　contributing
contribution
contributor
contributory
contrite
contritely
contrition
contrivance
contrive
　contrived
　contriving
control
　controlled
　controlling
　controls
controllable
controller
controversial
controversially
controversy
　controversies *pl*
controvert
controvertible
contumacious
contumacy
contumely
contuse

contusion
conundrum
　conundrums *pl*
conurbation
convalesce
　convalesced
　convalescing
convalescence
convalescent
convection
convector
convene
　convened
　convening
convener
convenience
convenient
conveniently
convent
convention
conventional
conventionality
conventionally
converge
　converged
　converging
convergence
convergent
conversant
conversation
conversational

conversationalist
conversationally
converse
　conversed
　conversing
conversely
conversion
convert
converter, convertor
convertibility
convertible
convex
convexity
convey
　conveyed
　conveying
　conveys
conveyance
conveyancer
conveyancing
conveyor belt
conveyor, conveyer
convict
conviction
convince
　convinced
　convincing
convincingly
convivial
conviviality
convivially

convocation
convoke
  convoked
  convoking
convoluted
convolution
convolvulus
  convolvuluses *pl*
convoy
  convoys *pl*
convulse
  convulsed
  convulsing
convulsion
convulsive
convulsively
coo (bird sound)
  cooed
  cooing
  coos
cook
  cooked
  cooking
cooker
cookery
cool
  cooled
  cooling
coolant
cooler
coolheaded

coolie (laborer)
coolly
coolness
coomb, combe
  (valley)
coop (to enclose)
co-op
cooperate
  cooperated
  cooperating
cooperation
cooperative
cooperator
co-opt
co-option
coordinate
  coordinated
  coordinating
coordination
cop (policeman)
cope (to manage)
  coped
  coping
copeck, kopeck,
  kopek
copier
copilot
copious
copiously
copper
copperplate

coppice, copse
copra
copulate
  copulated
  copulating
copulation
copy
  copies *pl*
  copied
  copies
  copying
copyright
copyrighted
coquetry
coquette
coquettish
coral (in sea)
cord (thin rope)
cordage
cordial
cordiality
cordially
cordite
cordon
cordon bleu
cords (trousers)
corduroy
core (center)
  cored
  coring
corespondent (in

divorce case)
coriander
cork
corkage
corkscrew
corm
cormorant
corn
cornea
  corneas *pl*
corneal
cornelian
corner
  cornered
  cornering
cornet
cornflower (blue
  flower)
cornice
cornstarch
cornucopia
corny
  cornier
  corniest
corollary
  corollaries *pl*
corona
  coronae, coronas *pl*
coronary
  coronaries *pl*
coronation

coroner
coronet
coroneted
corporal
corporal punishment
corporate
corporation
corporeal (not
  spiritual)
corps (group)
corps de ballet
corpse (dead body)
corpulence
corpulent
corpuscle
corpuscular
corral (to enclose
  cattle)
  corralled
  corralling
  corrals
correct
correction
corrective
correctly
correctness
corrector
correlate
  correlated
  correlating
correlation

correlative
correlativity
correspond
correspondence
correspondent
  (writer)
corridor
corrigendum
  corrigenda *pl*
corroborate
  corroborated
  corroborating
corroboration
corroborative
corrode
  corroded
  corroding
corrodible
corrosion
corrosive
corrugate
  corrugated
  corrugating
corrugation
corrupt
corrupter
corruptibility
corruptible
corruption
corruptive
corruptly

corruptness
corsage
corset
  corseted
  corseting
cortege, cortège
cortex
  cortices *pl*
cortical
cortisone
corundum
corvée
corvette
cosecant
cosignatory
  cosignatories *pl*
cosine (maths.)
cosmetic
cosmetician
cosmic
cosmically
cosmonaut
cosmopolitan
cosmos
cossack
cosset
  cosseted
  cosseting
costar
cost (apple)
costive (constipated)

costlier
costly
costume
costumier
cot
cotangent (maths)
coterie
cottage
cottager
cotton
cotton wool
cotyledon (botany)
couch
couch grass
cough
could (*from* can)
couldn't
council
councillor
counsel (lawyer or
  advice)
  counsels
  counseled
  counseling
counselor
count
countdown
countenance
counter
counteract
counteraction

counterbalance
counterbalancing
counterclockwise
counterfeit
counterfoil
counterirritant
countermand
countermine
counterpane
counterpart
counterpoint
counterpoise
countersign
  countersigned
  countersigning
countersink
  countersinking
  countersinks
  countersunk
counterweight
countess
countless
countrify
  countrified
  countrifies
  countrifying
country
  countries *pl*
countryman
  countrymen *pl*
county

counties *pl*

coup

coup d'état

coup de grace

couple

  coupled

  coupling

couplet

coupon

courage

courageous

courageously

courgette

courier

course

  coursed

  coursing

court (law; to woo)

  courted

  courting

courtesan

courtesy

  courtesies *pl*

courteous

courteously

courtier

courtly (polite)

court-martial

  court-martials,

  courts-martial *pl*

  court-martialed

  court-martialing

courtship

courtyard

cousin

cousinly

couture

couturier

couturière

cove

coven

covenant

cover

  covered

  covering

coverage

coverlet

covert

covertly

cover-up

covet

  coveted

  coveting

covetous

covey

  coveys *pl*

cow

cowboy

  cowboys *pl*

cowherd

cowhide

cowman

cowmen *pl*

coward (scared

cowardice

cowardliness

cowardly

cower (to cringe)

  cowered

  cowering

  cowers

cowl

cowrie, cowry

  cowries *pl*

cowslip

cox

coxcomb

coxswain

coy

coyly

coyness

cozen (to cheat)

  cozened

  cozening

cozenage

cozily

coziness

cozy

  cozies *pl*

  cozier

  coziest

crab

crabbed

crabby

crack

cracker

crackle
  crackled
  crackling

cradle
  cradled
  cradling

craft

craftsman
  craftsmen *pl*

craftsmanship

crafty
  craftier
  craftiest

crag

craggy

crake

cram
  crammed
  cramming
  crams

crammer

cramp

cranberry
  cranberries *pl*

crane
  craned
  craning

cranial

cranium
  craniums *pl*

crank

crankcase

crankiness

crankshaft

cranky
  crankier
  crankiest

cranny
  crannies *pl*

crape (black crêpe)

crapulous

crash

crash-land

crass

crate

crater

cravat

crave
  craved
  craving

craven

crawfish, crayfish

crawl

crawler

crayon

craze

crazed

crazily

craziness

crazy
  crazier
  craziest

creak (to squeak)
  creaked
  creaking

creaky

cream

creamery
  creameries *pl*

creaminess

creamy
  creamier
  creamiest

crease
  creased
  creasing

create
  created
  creating

creation

creative

creatively

creativity

creator

creature

crèche

credence

credential

credibility

credible

credibly

credit

  credited

  crediting

creditable

creditably

creditor

credo

  credos *pl*

credulity

credulous

creed

creek (small stream)

creep

  creeping

  creeps

  crept

creeper

creepily

creepiness

creepy

  creepier

  creepiest

cremate

  cremated

  cremating

cremation

crematorium

  crematoria,

  crematoriums *pl*

crematory

  crematories

Creole

creosote

crêpe

crepitate

  crepitated

  crepitating

crepitation

crept (*from* creep)

crepuscular

crescendo

  crescendos *pl*

crescent

cress

crest

crestfallen

cretin

cretinism

cretinous

crevasse (in glacier)

crevice (crack)

crew

crib

  cribbed

  cribbing

  cribs

cribbage

cribber

crick

cricket

cricketer

cried (*from* cry)

crier

cries (*from* cry)

crime

criminal

criminally

criminologist

criminology

crimson

cringe

  cringed

  cringing

crinkle

  crinkled

  crinkling

crinkly

crinoline

cripple

  crippled

  crippling

crisis

  crises *pl*

crisp

crispness

crisscross

  crisscrossed

  crisscrossing

criterion

  criteria *pl*

critic

critical

critically
criticism
criticize
  criticized
  criticizing
critique (critical
  essay)
croak
crochet (knitting)
  crocheted
  crocheting
crock
crockery
crocodile
crocus
  crocuses *pl*
croissant
crony
  cronies *pl*
crook
crooked
crookedly
croon
crooner
crop
  cropped
  cropping
  crops
cropper
croquet (game)
crore

crosier
cross
crossbreed
  crossbred
  crossbreeding
  crossbreeds
cross-examination
cross-examine
  cross-examined
  cross-examining
cross-examiner
cross-eyed
cross-legged
crossly
crossness
cross-purpose
cross-question
  cross-questioned
  cross-questioning
cross-questioner
cross-reference
  cross-referenced
  cross-referencing
crossroad
crosssection
crossword
crotch
crotchet (music)
crouch
croup
croupier

crouton
crow
crowbar
crowd
  crowded
  crowding
crown
  crowned
  crowning
crucial
crucially
crucible
crucifix
  crucifixes *pl*
crucifixion
crucify
  crucified
  crucifies
  crucifying
crude
crudely
crudity
  crudities *pl*
cruel
  crueler
  cruelest
cruelly
cruelty
  cruelties *pl*
cruet
cruise (on a ship)

cruised
cruising
cruiser
crumb
crumble
  crumbled
  crumbling
crumbly
crumpet
crumple
  crumpled
  crumpling
crunch
crunchy
  crunchier
  crunchiest
crupper
crusade
crusader
crush
crushed
crust
crustacean
crustaceous
crustily
crusty
crutch
  crutches *pl*
crux
  cruxes, cruces *pl*

cry
  cries *pl*
  cried
  cries
  crying
cryogenics
crypt
cryptic (obscure)
cryptically
cryptogam (plant)
cryptogram (code)
cryptograph
cryptographic
cryptography
crystal
crystalline
crystallization
crystallize
  crystallized
  crystallizing
crystallographer
crystallography
cut
  cuts
  cutting
cubbyhole
cube
cubed
cubic
cubicle
cuckold

cuckoo
cucumber
cuddle
  cuddled
  cuddling
cuddly
cudgels
  cudgeled
  cudgeling
cue (signal; hint;
  billiards)
cuff
cuisine
cul-de-sac
  cul-de-sacs *pl*
culinary
cull
culminate
  culminated
  culminating
culmination
culottes
culpability
culpable
culpably
culprit
cult
cultivate
  cultivated
  cultivating
cultivatable

cultivation
cultivator
cultural
culturally
culture
  cultured
  culturing
culver
cumbersome
cummerbund
cumulative
cumulatively
cumulus
cunning
cunningly
cup
  cupped
  cupping
  cups
cupboard
cupful
  cupfuls *pl*
cupidity
cupola
  cupolas *pl*
cur
curaçao
curacy
  curacies *pl*
curate
curator

curb (to restrain; road
  edge)
curbstone
curd
curdle
  curdled
  curdling
curability
curable
curative
cure
  cured
  curing
curé (priest)
curette (knife)
curfew
curio
  curios *pl*
curiosity
  curiosities *pl*
curious
curiously
curl
curler
curly
  curlier
  curliest
curlew
curmudgeon
currant (fruit)
currency

currencies *pl*
current (flow)
currently
curriculum
  curricula,
    curriculums *pl*
curriculum vitae
  curricula vitae *pl*
currish
curry
  curried
  curries
  currying
currycomb
curse
  cursed
  cursing
cursive
cursor
cursorily
cursory
curt
curtail
  curtailed
  curtailing
  curtailment
curtain
  curtained
  curtaining
curtly
curtness

curtsy, curtsey
  curtsied, curtseyed
  curtsies, curtseys
  curtsying, curtseying
curvature
curve
  curved
  curving
cushion
cuss
cussedness
custard
custodial
custodian
custody
custom
customarily
customary
custom-built
customization
customize
  customized
  customizing
customer
custom-made
customs
cut
  cutter
  cutting
  cuts
cutaneous

cutback
cute
  cuter
  cutest
cutely
cuteness
cuticle
cutlass
  cutlasses *pl*
cutler
cutlery
cutlet
cuttlefish
cyanide
cyanosis
cybernetics
cyberspace
cyclamen
cycle
  cycled
  cycling
cyclic
cyclical
cyclically
cyclists
cyclometer
cyclone
cyclonic
cygnet
cylinder
cylindrical

cylindrically
cymbal (gong)
cymbalist
cynic
cynical
cynically
cynicism
cynosure
cyst
cystic fibrosis
cystitis
cytology
Czech

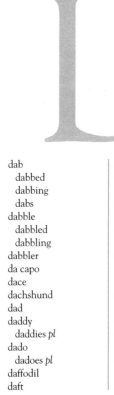

dab
  dabbed
  dabbing
  dabs
dabble
  dabbled
  dabbling
dabbler
da capo
dace
dachshund
dad
daddy
  daddies *pl*
dado
  dadoes *pl*
daffodil
daft

dagger
dahlia
  dahlias *pl*
daily
  dailies *pl*
daintily
daintiness
dainty
  daintier
  daintiest
dairy (milk)
  dairies *pl*
dairymaid
dais (platform)
  daises *pl*
daisy
  daisies *pl*
dale (valley)

dalliance
dally (to dawdle)
  dallied
  dallies
  dallying
Dalmatian
dam (barrier)
  dammed
  damming
  dams
damage
  damaged
  damaging
damageable
damask
dame
damn (to condemn,
  curse)
  damned
  damning
damnable
damnably
damnation
damp
dampen
  dampened
  dampening
damper
dampness
damsel
damson

dance
 danced
 dancing
dancer
dandelion
dandified
dandle
 dandled
 dandling
dandruff
dandy *pl*
 dandies
danger
dangerous
dangerously
dangle
 dangled
 dangling
dank
dankness
dapper
dapple
 dappled
 dappling
dare
 dared
 daring
daredevil
dark
darken
darker

darkly
darkness
darling
darn
dart
dash
dashboard
dastardly
data
date
 dated
 dating
dateless
dative
daub
 daubed
 daubing
dauber
daughter
daughter-in-law
 daughters-in-law *pl*
daunt
dauntless
dauntlessly
dauphin
davit
dawdle
 dawdled
 dawdling
dawdler
dawn

day
 days *pl*
daybreak
daylight
daze (to stun)
 dazed
 dazing
dazzle
 dazzled
 dazzling
deacon
deaconess
dead
deaden
 deadened
 deadening
deadline
deadliness
deadlock
deadlocked
deadly
 deadlier
 deadliest
deaf
deafen
 deafened
 deafening
deafeningly
deafer
deafness
deal

dealing
dealt
dealer
dean
deanery
  deaneries *pl*
dear (loved)
  dearer
  dearest
dearly
dearness
dearth
death
deathless
deathlike
deathly
deathrate
debacle
debar
  debarred
  debarring
debark
debarkation
debase
  debased
  debasing
debasement
debatable
debatably
debate
  debated

debating
debauch
debauchee
debaucher
debauchery
  debaucheries *pl*
debenture
debilitate
  debilitated
  debilitating
debilitation
debility
  debilities *pl*
debit
  debited
  debiting
debitable
debonair
debouch (to emerge)
debouchment
debrief
  debriefed
  debriefing
  debriefs
debris
debt
debtor
debunk
debut
  debutant *m*
  debutante *f*

decade
decadence
decadent
decaffeinated
decamp
decant
decanter
decapitate
  decapitated
  decapitating
decapitation
decarbonize
  decarbonized
  decarbonizing
decathlon
decay
  decayed
  decaying
  decays
decease
deceased
deceit
deceitful
deceitfully
deceive
  deceived
  deceiving
deceiver
decelerate
  decelerated
  decelerating

deceleration
decency
  decencies pl
decent (respectable)
decently
decentralization
decentralize
  decentralized
  decentralizing
deception
deceptive
deceptively
decibel
decide
  decided
  deciding
decidedly
deciduous
decimal
decimalization
decimalize
  decimalized
  decimalizing
decimate
  decimated
  decimating
decimation
decipher
  deciphered
  deciphering
decipherment

decision
decisive
decisively
deck
declaim
  declaimed
  declaiming
declamation
declamatory
declaration
declare
  declared
  declaring
declassification
declassify
  declassified
  declassifies
  declassifying
declension
declinable
declination
decline
  declined
  declining
declivity
  declivities pl
decoction
decode
  decoded
  decoding
decoder

décolletage
décolleté
decomposable
decompose
  decomposed
  decomposing
decomposition
decompress
decompression
decompressor
decongestant
decontaminate
  decontaminated
  decontaminating
decontamination
decontrol
  decontrolled
  decontrolling
decorate
  decorated
  decorating
decoration
decorative
decorator
decorous
decorously
decorum
decor
decoy
  decoys pl
decrease

decreased
decreasing
decree
  decreed
  decreeing
decrement
decrepit
decrepitude
decry
  decried
  decries
  decrying
dedicate
  dedicated
  dedicating
dedication
dedicatory
deduce (to infer)
  deduced
  deducing
deducible
deduct (to subtract)
deductible
deduction
deed
deem
  deemed
  deeming
deep
deepen
  deepened

deepening
deeper
deep-freeze
  deep-freezing
  deep-frozen
deep-freezer
deep-fry
  deep-fried
  deep-fries
  deep-frying
deeply
deep-seated
deer (animal)
de-escalate
  de-escalated
  de-escalating
  de-escalation
deface
  defaced
  defacing
de facto
defamation
defamatory
defame
  defamed
  defaming
default
defaulter
defeat
  defeated
  defeating

defeatism
defeatist
defecate
  defecated
  defecating
defecation
defect
defection
defective
defector
defend
defendant
defender
defense
defenseless
defensibility
defensible
defensibly
defensive
defer
  deferred
  deferring
  defers
deference
deferential
deferentially
deferment
defiance
defiant
defiantly
deficiency

deficiencies *pl*
deficient
deficit
defied
defier
defies (*from* defy)
defile
  defiled
  defiling
defilement
definable
define
  defined
  defining
definite
definitely
definition
definitive
definitively
deflate
  deflated
  deflating
deflation
deflationary
deflect
deflection
deflector
deflower
  deflowered
  deflowering
defoliant

defoliate
  defoliated
  defoliating
defoliation
defoliator
deform
deformation
deformity
  deformities *pl*
defraud
defray
  defrayed
  defraying
  defrays
defrayable
defrayal
defreeze
  defreezing
  defrozen
defrost
deft
deftly
deftness
defunct
defuse
  defused
  defusing
defy
  defied
  defies
  defying

dégagé
degeneracy
degenerate
  degenerated
  degenerating
degeneration
degenerative
degradation
degrade
  degraded
  degrading
degree
dehydrate
  dehydrated
  dehydrating
dehydration
de-ice
  de-iced
  de-icing
de-icer
deification
deify
  deified
  deifies
  deifying
deign
  deigned
  deigning
deism
deity
  deities *pl*

dejected
dejection
de jure
delay
  delayed
  delaying
  delays
delectable
delegacy
  delegacies *pl*
delegate
  delegated
  delegating
delegation
delete
  deleted
  deleting
deleterious
deletion
deliberate
  deliberated
  deliberating
deliberately
deliberation
delicacy
  delicacies *pl*
delicate
delicately
delicatessen
delicious
deliciously

delight
  delighted
  delighting
delightful
delightfully
delimit
  delimited
  delimiting
delimitation
delineate
  delineated
  delineating
delineation
delineator
delinquency
  delinquencies *pl*
delinquent
deliquesce
deliquescence
deliquescent
delirious
delirium
deliver
  delivered
  delivering
deliverance
deliverer
delivery
  deliveries *pl*
delouse
  deloused

delousing
delta
  deltas *pl*
delude
  deluded
  deluding
deluge
  deluged
  deluging
delusion
delusive
deluxe
delve
  delved
  delving
demagnetization
demagnetize
  demagnetized
  demagnetizing
demagogic
demagogue
demagoguery
demagogy
demand
demarcate
  demarcated
  demarcating
demarcation
démarche
demean
  demeans

demeaned
demeanor
demented
dementia
demerara (sugar)
demesne
demilitarize
  demilitarized
  demilitarizing
demise
  demised
  demising
demitasse
demobilization
demobilize
  demobilized
  demobilizing
democracy
  democracies *pl*
democratic
democratically
democratization
democratize
  democratized
  democratizing
demolish
demolition
demon
demonic
demonstrable
demonstrate

demonstrated
demonstrating
demonstration
demonstrative
demonstrator
demoralization
demoralize
  demoralized
  demoralizing
demote
  demoted
  demoting
demotion
demount
demur (to object)
  demurred
  demurring
  demurs
demure (modest)
demurely
demurrage
demurred
den
denationalization
denationalize
  denationalized
  denationalizing
denaturalize
  denaturalized
  denaturalizing
dengue (fever)

denial
denied (*from* deny)
denier (thread
  thickness)
denigrate
  denigrated
  denigrating
denigration
denigrator
denim
denizen
denominate
  denominated
  denominating
denomination
denominational
denominator
denote
  denoted
  denoting
dénouement
denounce
  denounced
  denouncing
denouncement
denouncer
de nouveau
de novo
dense
densely
denseness

denser
density
  densities *pl*
dent
dental
dentifrice
dentine
dentist
dentistry
dentition
denture
denudation
denude
  denuded
  denuding
denunciate
  denunciated
  denunciating
denunciator
deny
  denied
  denies
  denying
deodorant
deodorization
deodorize
  deodorized
  deodorizing
depart
department
departmental

departmentalize
  departmentalized
  departmentalizing
departmentally
departure
depend
dependable
dependence
  dependencies *pl*
dependent (rely on)
depersonalize
  depersonalized
  depersonalizing
depict
depiction
depilatory
  depilatories *pl*
deplete
  depleted
  depleting
depletion
deplorable
deplorably
deplore
  deplored
  deploring
deploy
  deployed
  deploying
  deploys
deployment

depopulate
  depopulated
  depopulating
depopulation
deport
deportation
deportee
deportment
  (behavior)
depose
  deposed
  deposing
deposit
  deposited
  depositing
deposition
depositor
depository
  depositories *pl*
depot
  depots *pl*
deprave (to corrupt)
  depraved
  depraving
depravity
deprecate
  deprecated
  deprecating
deprecation
deprecator
deprecatory

depreciate
  depreciated
  depreciating
depreciation
depredation
  (plundering)
depredator
depress
depressant
depressed
depression
depressive
depressurization
depressurize
  depressurized
  depressurizing
deprival
deprivation
deprive
  deprived
  depriving
depth
deputation
depute
  deputed
  deputing
deputize
  deputized
  deputizing
deputy
  deputies *pl*

derail
  derailed
  derailing
derailment
derange
  deranged
  deranging
derangement
derelict
dereliction
deride
  derided
  deriding
de rigueur
derision
derisive
derisory
derivation
derivative
derive
  derived
  deriving
dermatitis
dermatologist
dermatology
derogate
  derogated
  derogating
derogation
derogatorily
derogatory

derrick
dervish
descant
descendant
descent (going down)
descend
describable
describe
  described
  describing
description
descriptive
desecrate
  desecrated
  desecrating
desecrater
desecration
desecrator
desegregate
  desegregated
  desegregating
desegregation
desensitize
  desensitized
  desensitizing
desert (barren region)
deserts (rewards)
deserve
  deserved
  deserving
deservedly

deshabille
desiccate
  desiccated
  desiccating
desiccation
desiccator
desideratum
  desiderata *pl*
design
designate
  designated
  designating
designation
designer
desirability
desirable
desirably
desire
  desired
  desiring
desirous
desist
desk
desolate
desolated
desolation
despair
  despaired
  despairing
desperado
  desperadoes *pl*

desperate
desperately
desperation
despicable
despicably
despise
  despised
  despising
despite
despoil
despoiler
despoliation
despond
despondency
despondent
despondently
despot
despotic
despotically
despotism
dessert (fruit or sweet)
destination
destine
destiny
  destinies *pl*
destitute
destitution
destroy
  destroyed
  destroying
  destroys

destroyer
destruction
destructive
destructiveness
destructor
desultorily
desultoriness
desultory
detach
detachable
detachment
detail
  detailed
  detailing
detain
  detained
  detaining
detect
detectable
detection
detective
detector
détente
detention
deter
  deterred
  deterring
  deters
detergent
deteriorate
  deteriorated

deteriorating
deterioration
determinable
determinant
determination
determine
determined
determining
determinism
deterrent
detest
detestable
detestation
dethrone
dethroned
dethroning
dethronement
detonate
detonated
detonating
detonation
detonator
detour
detract
detraction
detractor
detriment
detrimental
detrimentally
deuce
devaluation

devalue
devalued
devaluing
devastate
devastated
devastating
devastator
develop
developed
developing
developer
development
developmental
deviant
deviate
deviated
deviating
deviation
device (thing)
devil
deviled
deviling
devils
devilish
devilishly
devilment
devilry
devious
deviously
deviousness
devise (plan)

devised
devising
devoid
devolution
devolve
devolved
devolving
devote
devoted
devoting
devotee
devotion
devour
devoured
devouring
devoutly
devoutness
dew (water)
dewy
dexterity
dexterous, dextrous
dexterously,
dextrously
dextrose (kind of
glucose)
diabetes
diabetic
diabolic
diabolical
diabolically
diadem

diaeresis
diagnose
  diagnosed
  diagnosing
diagnosis
  diagnoses *pl*
diagnostic
diagnostician
diagonal
diagonally
diagram
diagrammatic
diagrammatically
dial
  dialed
  dialing
  dials
dialect
dialectic
dialer
dialogue
diameter
diametric
diametrical
diametrically
diamond
diapason
diaper
diaphanous
diaphragm
diarchy

diarchies *pl*
diarist
diarrhea
diary (daily notes)
  diaries *pl*
diastolic
diastone (heart
  function)
diathermy
diatom
diatomic
diatribe
dibber
dibble
dice
  dice *pl*
  diced
  dicing
dicey
dichotomy
dicker
  dickered
  dickering
dicotyledon
dictaphone
dictate
  dictated
  dictating
dictation
dictator
dictatorial

dictatorially
diction
dictionary
  dictionaries *pl*
didactic
didactically
didacticism
diddle
  diddled
  diddling
didn't (did not)
die (tool)
  dies *pl*
die (to cease living)
  died
  dies
  dying
diehard
dielectric
diesel
diet
  dieted
  dieting
dietary
dietician
differ
  differed
  differing
difference
different
differential

differentially
differentiate
  differentiated
  differentiating
differentiation
difficult
difficulty
  difficulties *pl*
diffidence
diffident
diffidently
diffract
diffraction
diffuse
  diffused
  diffusing
diffuser
diffusion
diffusive
dig
  digging
  digs
  dug
digest
digestibility
digestible
digestion
digestive
digger
digit
digital

digitalin
digitalis
dignify
  dignified
  dignifying
  dignifies
dignitary
  dignitaries *pl*
dignity
digress
digression
digressive
dike, dyke
dilapidate
  dilapidated
  dilapidating
dilapidation
dilatability
dilatable
dilatation
dilate
  dilated
  dilating
dilation
dilator
dilatorily
dilatoriness
dilatory (delaying)
dilemma
  dilemmas *pl*
dilettante

dilettanti,
  dilettantes *pl*
diligence
diligent
diligently
dill
dilly-dally
  dilly-dallied
  dilly-dallies
  dilly-dallying
diluent
dilute
  diluted
  diluting
dilution
diluvial
dim
  dimmed
  dimming
  dims
dime (coin)
dimension
dimensional
diminish
diminuendo
  diminuendos *pl*
diminution
diminutive
dimity
  dimities *pl*
dimly

dimple
  dimpled
  dimpling
din
dinar (currency)
dine (to eat)
  dined
  dining
diner (person; café)
dinghy (boat)
  dinghies pl
dingily
dinginess
dingy (dark)
  dingier
  dingiest
dinner
dinosaur
dint
diocesan
diocese
  dioceses pl
diode
diorama
  dioramas pl
dioxide
dip
  dipped
  dipping
  dips
diphtheria

diphthong
diploma
  diplomas pl
diplomacy
  diplomacies pl
diplomat
diplomatic
diplomatically
diplomatist
dipper
dipsomania
dipsomaniac
dire
  direr
  direst
direct
  directed
  directing
direction
directional
directive
director
directorate
directory
  directories pl
direful
dirge
dirigible
dirndl
dirt
dirtily

dirtiness
dirty
  dirtied
  dirties
  dirtying
disability
  disabilities pl
disable
  disabled
  disabling
disablement
disabuse
  disabused
  disabusing
disadvantage
  disadvantaged
  disadvantaging
disadvantageous
disaffected
disaffection
disagree
  disagreed
  disagreeing
disagreeable
disagreeably
disagreement
disallow
disappear
  disappeared
  disappearing
disappearance

disappoint
  disappointed
  disappointing
disappointment
disapproval
disapprove
  disapproved
  disapproving
disarm
disarmament
disarrange
  disarranged
  disarranging
disarrangement
disarray
disassociate
  disassociated
  disassociating
disassociation
disaster
disastrous
disastrously
disband
disbandment
disbar
  disbarred
  disbarring
  disbars
disbelief
disbelieve
  disbelieved

disbelieving
disbeliever
disburden
  disburdened
  disburdening
disburse
  disbursed
  disbursing
disbursement
disc
discard
discern
discernible
discernment
discharge
  discharged
  discharging
disciple
disciplinarian
disciplinary
discipline
  disciplined
  disciplining
disc jockey
  disc jockeys pl
disclaim
  disclaimed
  disclaiming
disclaimer
disclose
  disclosed

disclosing
disclosure
disco
  discos pl
discolor
  discolored
  discoloring
discoloration
discomfit (to thwart)
  discomfits
  discomfited
  discomfiting
discomfiture
discomfort (pain)
discompose
  discomposed
  discomposing
disconcert
disconnect
disconnection
disconsolate
disconsolately
discontent
discontinuance
discontinue
  discontinued
  discontinuing
discontinuity
  discontinuities pl
discontinuous
discord

discordance
discordant
discotheque
discount
discourage
  discouraged
  discouraging
discouragement
discourse
  discoursed
  discoursing
discourteous
discourteously
discourtesy
  discourtesies *pl*
discover
  discovered
  discovering
discoverer
discovery
  discoveries *pl*
discredit
  discredited
  discrediting
discreet (prudent)
discreetly
discrepancy
  discrepancies *pl*
discrepant
discrete (separate)
discretely

discretion
discriminate
  discriminated
  discriminating
discriminatory
discursive
discus (heavy disc)
  discuses *pl*
discuss
discussion
disdain
disdainful
disdainfully
disease
diseased
disembark
disembarkation
disembodied
disembodiment
disembody
  disembodied
  disembodies
  disembodying
disembowel
  disembowelled
  disembowelling
  disembowels
disenchant
disenchantment
disengage
  disengaged

  disengaging
disengagement
disentangle
  disentangled
  disentangling
disentanglement
disestablish
disestablishment
disfavor
disfavored
disfigure
  disfigured
  disfiguring
disfigurement
disgorge
  disgorged
  disgorging
disgrace
  disgraced
  disgracing
disgraceful
disgracefully
disgruntled
disguise
  disguised
  disguising
disgust
dish
  dishes *pl*
dishabille, déshabillé
dishearten

disheartened
disheartening
disheveled
dishonest
dishonestly
dishonesty
dishonor
dishonored
dishonoring
dishonorable
dishonorably
dishonored
dishwasher
disillusion
disincentive
disinclination
disinclined
disinfect
disinfectant
disinfection
disinherit
disinherited
disinheriting
disinheritance
disintegrate
disintegrated
disintegrating
disintegration
disintegrator
disinter
disinterred

disinterring
disinters
disinterested
disinterment
disjointed
disk
dislikable
dislike
disliked
disliking
dislocate
dislocated
dislocating
dislocation
dislodge
dislodged
dislodging
dislodgment,
dislodgement,
disloyal
disloyally
disloyalty
dismal
dismally
dismantle
dismantled
dismantling
dismay
dismayed
dismember
dismembered

dismembering
dismemberment
dismiss
dismissal
dismount
disobedience
disobedient
disobediently
disobey
disobeyed
disobeying
disoblige
disobliging
disorder
disordered
disorderliness
disorderly
disorganization
disorganize
disorganized
disorganizing
disorientate
disorientated
disorientating
disorientation
disown
disparage
disparaged
disparaging
disparagement
disparate (different)

disparity
  disparities *pl*
dispassionate
dispassionately
dispatch, despatch
dispatcher
dispel
  dispelled
  dispelling
  dispels
dispensary
  dispensaries *pl*
dispensation
dispense
  dispensed
  dispensing
dispenser
dispersal
disperse
  dispersed
  dispersing
dispersion
dispirit
  dispirited
  dispiriting
displace
  displaced
  displacing
displacement
display
  displayed

displaying
displays
displease
  displeased
  displeasing
displeasure
disport
disposable
disposal
dispose
  disposed
  disposing
disposition
dispossess
dispossession (taking
  away)
disproportion
disproportionate
disproportionately
disprove
  disproved
  disproving
disputable
disputably
disputant
dispute
  disputed
  disputing
disqualification
disqualify
  disqualified

disqualifies
disqualifying
disquiet
  disquieted
  disquieting
disquietude
disquisition
disregard
disrepair
disreputable
disreputably
disrepute
disrespect
disrespectful
disrespectfully
disrobe
  disrobed
  disrobing
disrupt
disruption
disruptive
dissatisfaction
dissatisfy
  dissatisfied
  dissatisfies
  dissatisfying
dissect
dissection
dissector
dissemble
  dissembled

dissembling
dissembler
disseminate
  disseminated
  disseminating
dissemination
disseminator
dissension
dissent (difference)
dissenter
dissertation
disservice
dissidence
  (disagreement)
dissident
dissimilar
dissimilarity
  dissimilarities *pl*
dissimulate
  dissimulated
  dissimulating
dissimulation
dissimulator
dissipate
  dissipated
  dissipating
dissipation
dissociate
  dissociated
  dissociating
dissociation

dissoluble
dissolute
dissolutely
dissoluteness
dissolution
dissolve
  dissolved
  dissolving
dissolvent
dissonance
dissonant
dissuade
  dissuaded
  dissuading
dissuasion
dissuasive
distaff
  distaffs *pl*
distance
  distanced
  distancing
distant
distantly
distaste
distasteful
distastefully
distemper
  distempered
  distempering
distend
distensible

distension
distill
  distilled
  distilling
  distills
distillation
distiller
distillery
  distilleries *pl*
distinct
distinction
distinctive
distinctly
distingué
distinguish
distinguishable
distort
distortion
distortionless
distract
distraction
distrain
distraint
distrait
distraught
distress
distribute
  distributed
  distributing
distribution
distributive

distributor
district
distrust
distrustful
disturb
disturbance
disturber
disunion
disunite
  disunited
  disuniting
disunity
disuse
  disused
ditch
  ditches *pl*
ditcher
dither
  dithered
  dithering
dithery
ditto
ditty
  ditties *pl*
diureses
diuretic
diurnal (in a day)
diurnally
diva (prima donna)
  divas *pl*
divagate

divagated
divagating
divagation
divan
dive
  dived
  diving
  dove
diver
diverge
  diverged
  diverging
divergence
divergent
divers (various)
diverse (different)
diversely
diversification
diversify
  diversified
  diversifies
  diversifying
diversion
diversity
  diversities *pl*
divert
divertissement
divest
divide
  divided
  dividing

dividend
divider
divination
divine
  divined
  divining
divinely
diviner
diving (*from* dive)
divinities *pl*
divinity
divisible
division
divisional
divisive
divisor
divorce
  divorced
  divorcing
divorcee
divot
divulge
  divulged
  divulging
dizzily
dizziness
dizzy
  dizzier
  dizziest
do
  did

does
doing
done
docile
docilely
docility
dock
docker
docket
  docketed
  docketing
doctor
  doctored
  doctoring
doctorate
doctrinaire
doctrinal
doctrine
document
documentary
  documentaries *pl*
documentation
dodder
dodderer
doddery
dodge
  dodged
  dodging
dodgy
  dodgier
  dodgiest

dodo
  dodos *pl*
doe (deer)
  does *pl*
doer
does (*from* do)
doesn't
doff
dog
  dogged
  dogging
  dogs
dog-ear
dog-eared
dogged (stubborn)
doggedly
doggerel
doggy, doggie,
dogma
  dogmas *pl*
dogmatic
dogmatically
dogmatism
dogmatize
  dogmatized
  dogmatizing
do-gooder
doily
  doilies *pl*
doing (*from* do)
doldrums

dole (pay)
  doled
  doling
doleful
dolefully
doll (toy)
dollar
dolled
dollop
dolly
  dollies *pl*
dolor (sorrow)
dolorous
dolphin
dolt
domain
dome (round roof)
domed
domestic
domestically
domesticate
  domesticated
  domesticating
domesticity
domicile
domiciliary
dominance
dominant
dominantly
dominate
  dominated

dominating
domination
domineer
  domineered
  domineering
dominical
dominion
domino
  dominoes *pl*
don
  donned
  donning
  dons
don't
donate
  donated
  donating
donation
done (*from* do)
donkey
  donkeys *pl*
donnish
donor (giver)
doodle
  doodled
  doodling
doodler
doom
  doomed
  dooming
door

dope
  doped
  doping
dopey
dormancy
dormant
dormer
dormitory
  dormitories *pl*
dormouse
  dormice *pl*
dorsal
dorsally
dory
  dories *pl*
dosage
dose
  dosed
  dosing
dosimeter
dossier
dot
  dots
  dotted
  dotting
dotage
dotard
dote
  doted
  doting
dottily

dotty
  dottier
  dottiest
double
  doubled
  doubling
double entendre
double-barreled
double-breasted
doubly
doubt
doubter
doubtful
doubtfully
doubtfulness
doubtless
douche
  douched
  douching
dough (bread)
doughnut
doughtily
doughtiness
doughty
  doughtier
  doughtiest
doughy
  doughier
  doughiest
dour
dourly

dourness

douse (drench)

  doused

  dousing

dove

dovecot

dovecote

dovetail

  dovetailed

  dovetailing

dowager

dowdily

dowdiness

dowdy

  dowdier

  dowdiest

dowel

dower

down

downcast

downfall

downfallen

downhearted

downpour

downright

downstairs

downtrodden

downward

dowry

  dowries pl

dowse (search for

  water)

  dowsed

  dowsing

dowser

doyen

doze

  dozed

  dozing

dozen

drab

drachma (Greek

  money)

  drachmas pl

draconian

draft (preliminary

  writing)

draftsman

  draftsmen pl

drafty

  draftier

  draftiest

drag

  dragged

  dragging

  drags

dragoman

  dragomans,

  dragomen pl

dragon

dragonfly

  dragonflies pl

dragoon

  dragooned

  dragooning

drain

  drained

  draining

drainage

drama

  dramas pl

dramatic

dramatically

dramatis personae

dramatist

dramatization

dramatize

  dramatized

  dramatizing

drank (from drink)

drape

  draped

  draping

draper

drapery

  draperies pl

drastic

drastically

draw

  drawing

  drawn

  drew

drawback

drawer
drawing room
drawl
dread
  dreaded
  dreading
dreadful
dreadfully
dreadness
dreadnought
dream
  dreamed, dreamt
  dreaming
dreamer
dreamily
dreamless
dreamy
  dreamier
  dreamiest
drearily
dreariness
dreary
dredge
  dredged
  dredging
dredger
dregs
drench
drenched
dress
  dresses *pl*

dressage
dressed
dresser
dressmaker
dressy
drew
dribble
  dribbled
  dribbling
dribbler
driblet
dried (*from* dry)
drier, dryer (drying
  machine)
dries (*from* dry)
drift
drill
drily (*from* dry)
drink
  drank
  drinking
  drunk
drinker
drip
  dripped
  dripping
  drips
drip-dry
  drip-dried
  drip-dries
  drip-drying

drive
  driven
  driving
  drove
drivel
  drivels
  driveled
  driveling
driveler
driven (*from* drive)
driver
driving
drizzle
  drizzled
  drizzling
drizzly
drogue
droll
drollery
  drolleries *pl*
drolly
drollness
dromedary
  dromedaries *pl*
drone
  droned
  droning
droop
  drooped
  drooping
drop

dropped
dropping
drops
droplet
dropout
  dropouts *pl*
dropper
dropsical
dropsy
dross
drought
drove (*from* drive)
drover
droves
drown
drowse
  drowsed
  drowsing
drowsier
drowsily
drowsiness
drowsy
  drowsier
  drowsiest
drudge
drudgery
drug
  drugged
  drugging
  drugs
drugget (fabric)

druggist
drugstore
druid
drum
  drummed
  drumming
  drums
drum-major
drummer
drunk
drunkard
drunken
drunkenly
drunkenness
dry
  dried
  dries
  drying
  drier
  driest
dry-clean
  dry-cleaned
  dry-cleaning
dryer, drier (drying
  machine)
dryly
dryness
dual (double)
dualism
dual-purpose
dub

dubbed
dubbing
dubs
dubbin, dubbing
  (grease)
dubious
dubiously
ducal
ducat
duchess
  duchesses *pl*
duchy
  duchies *pl*
duck
duckling
duct
ductile
ductility
ductless
dud
dudgeon
due (payable)
duel (fight)
  duels
  dueled
  dueling
duelist
duenna
  duennas *pl*
duet
  dueted

dueting

duffel, duffle (cloth, coat)

duffer

dug (*from* dig)

dugout
  dugouts *pl*

duke

dukery
  dukeries *pl*

dulcet

dull

dullard

dullness

dully

duly (*from* due)

dumb

dumbbell

dumbfound

dumbly

dumbness

dumfound
  dumfounded
  dumfounding

dummy
  dummies *pl*

dump

dumpiness

dumpling

dumpy
  dumpier

dumpiest

dun (demand)
  dunned
  dunning
  duns

dunce

dune

dung

dungarees

dungeon

dunghill

duodecimal

duodecimo

duodenal

duodenum
  duodenums *pl*

duologue

dupe
  duped
  duping

dupery

duplex
  duplexes *pl*

duplicate
  duplicated
  duplicating

duplication

duplicator

duplicity

durability

durable

durably

durance

duration

duress

during

dusk

dust

duster

dustiness

dusty
  dustier
  dustiest

dutiable

dutiful

dutifully

duty
  duties *pl*

duty-free

duvet

dwarf
  dwarfs, dwarves *pl*
  dwarfed
  dwarfing
  dwarfs

dwell
  dwelled, dwelt
  dwelling

dweller

dwelling

dwindle
  dwindled

dwindling
dye (to color)
  dyed
  dyeing
  dyes
dyer
dying (*from* die)
dyke, dike
dynamic
dynamically
dynamite
  dynamited
  dynamiting
dynamo
  dynamos *pl*
dynamometer
dynasty
  dynasties *pl*
dyne (unit)
dysentery
dyslexia
dyslexic
dyspepsia
dyspeptic

each
eager
eagerly
eagerness
eagle
eagle-eyed
eaglet
ear
earache
earful
earl
earldom
earliness
early
  earlier
  earliest
earmark
earn (money)

earner
earnest
earnestly
earnestness
earphone
earring
earth
earthed
earthenware
earthly
earthquake
earwig
ease
  eased
  easing
easel
easily
easiness

east
Easter
easterly
eastern
eastward
eastwards
easy
  easier
  easiest
easygoing
eat
  ate
  eaten
  eating
eatable
eater
eats
eaves
eavesdrop
  eavesdropped
  eavesdropping
  eavesdrops
eavesdropper
ebb
  ebbed
  ebbing
ebbtide
ebonite
ebony
ebullience
ebullient

ebulliently

eccentric

eccentrically

eccentricity

  eccentricities *pl*

ecclesiastic

ecclesiastical

ecclesiastically

echelon

echo

  echoes *pl*

  echoed

  echoes

  echoing

eclair

eclat

eclectic

eclecticism

eclipse

  eclipsed

  eclipsing

ecliptic

eclogue

ecological

ecologically

ecologist

ecology

  ecologies *pl*

economic

economical

economically

economist

economize

  economized

  economizing

economy

  economies *pl*

ecstasy

  ecstasies *pl*

ecstatic

ecstatically

ecumenical

ecumenically

eczema

eddy

  eddies *pl*

  eddied

  eddies

  eddying

edelweiss

edema

  edemas

edge

  edged

  edging

edgeways

edgily

edginess

edgy

  edgier

  edgiest

edibility

edible

edict

edification

  (instruction)

edifice (building)

edify

  edified

  edifies

  edifying

edit

  edited

  editing

edition (book)

editor

editorial

editorially

educability

educable

educatability

educatable

educate

  educated

  educating

education

educational

educationalist

educationally

educationist

educative

educator

educe (to develop,

infer)
educed
educing
educible
eduction
eel
eerie (creepy)
 eerier
 eeriest
eerily
eeriness
efface
 effaced
 effacing
effaceable
effacement
effect (to accomplish)
effective (useful)
effectively
effectiveness
effectual (actual)
effeminacy
effeminate
effeminately
effervesce
 effervesced
 effervescing
effervescence
effervescent
effete
efficacious

efficaciously
efficacy
efficiency
efficient
efficiently
effigy
 effigies pl
efflorescence
efflorescent
effluent
effluvium
 effluvia pl
efflux
effort
effortless
effortlessly
effusion
effusive
effusively
effusiveness
egalitarian
egg
 egged
 egging
eggy
ego
egocentric
egocentricity
egoism
egoist
egoistic

egoistically
egotism (conceit)
egotist
egotistic
egotistical
egotistically
egregious
egregiously
egregiousness
egress
eiderdown
Eiffel (tower)
eight
eighteen
eighteenth
eighth
eightieth
eighty
 eighties pl
eisteddfod
either
ejaculate
 ejaculated
 ejaculating
ejaculation
ejaculatory
eject
ejection
ejector
eke
 eked

eking
elaborate
  elaborated
  elaborating
elaborately
elaborateness
elaboration
elapse
  elapsed
  elapsing
elastic
elastically
elasticity
elated
elation
elbow
  elbowed
  elbowing
elder
elderly
eldest
elect
election
electioneering
elective
elector
electoral
electorate
electric
electrical
electrically

electrician
electricity
electrification
electrified
electrify
  electrified
  electrifies
  electrifying
electrocardiogram
  (E.C.G.)
electrocardiograph
electrocardiography
electrocute
  electrocuted
  electrocuting
electrocution
electrode
electrodynamic
electrodynamically
electrolysis
electrolyte
electrolytic
electromagnet
electromagnetic
electrometer
electrometric
electromotive
electromotive force
  (E.M.F.)
electron
electronic

electronically
electroplate
electroplating
electrostatic
electrotechnical
eleemosynary
  (charitable)
elegance
elegant
elegantly
elegiac
elegy
  elegies pl
element
elemental
elementarily
elementary
elephant
elephantine
elevate
  elevated
  elevating
elevation
elevator
eleven
eleventh
elf
  elves pl
elfin
elfish
elicit (to evoke)

elicited
eliciting
elide
elided
eliding
eligibility
eligible
eliminate
eliminated
eliminating
elimination
eliminator
elision
elite
elitism
elitist
elixir
Elizabethan
ellipse
elliptic
elliptical
elliptically
elm
elocution
elocutionist
elongate
elongated
elongating
elongation
elope
eloped

eloping
elopement
eloquence
eloquent
eloquently
else
elsewhere
elucidate
elucidated
elucidating
elucidation
elude (to evade)
eluded
eluding
elusion (evasion)
elusive
elusiveness
elver
elysian
emaciate
emaciated
emaciating
emaciation
e-mail
emancipate
emancipated
emancipating
emancipation
emancipator
emasculate
emasculated

emasculating
emasculation
embalm
embalmer
embalmment
embankment
embargo
embargoes *pl*
embargoed
embargoes
embargoing
embark
embarkation
embarrass
embarrassed
embarrassment
embassy
embassies *pl*
embattle
embattled
embattling
embed
embedded
embedding
embeds
embellish
embellishment
ember
embezzle
embezzled
embezzling

embezzlement
embezzler
embitter
  embittered
  embittering
embitterment
emblazon
  emblazoned
  emblazoning
emblem
emblematic
emblematically
embodiment
embody
  embodied
  embodies
  embodying
embolism
embonpoint
emboss
embossment
embrace
  embraced
  embracing
embrasure
embrocation
embroider
embroidered
embroidery
  embroideries *pl*
embroil

embroiled
embroiling
embroilment
embryo
embryologist
embryology
embryonic
emend (to remove
  errors)
  emended
  emending
emendation
emerald
emerge
  emerged
  emerging
emergence
emergency
  emergencies *pl*
emergent
emergently
emeritus
emersion
  (reappearance)
emery
emetic
emigrant
emigrate (to leave
  country)
  emigrated
  emigrating

emigration
émigré
  émigrés *pl*
eminence
eminent (famous)
eminently
emissary
  emissaries *pl*
emission
emit (to send out)
  emits
  emitted
  emitting
emitter
emollient (softening)
emolument (pay)
emotion
emotional
emotionally
emotive
empathize
  empathized
  empathizing
empathy
emperor
emphasis
  emphases *pl*
emphasize
  emphasized
  emphasizing
emphatic

emphatically

emphysema (lung
  disease)

empire

empirical
  (experiment)

empirically

emplacement

employ
  employed
  employing
  employs

employability

employable

employee

employer

employment

emporium
  emporiums,
  emporia, *pl*

empower
  empowered
  empowering

empress
  empresses *pl*

emptily

emptiness

empty
  empties *pl*
  emptied
  empties

emptying
  emptier
  emptiest

emu
  emus *pl*

emulate
  emulated
  emulating

emulation

emulative

emulator

emulsification

emulsifier

emulsify
  emulsified
  emulsifies
  emulsifying

emulsion

enable
  enabled
  enabling

enablement

enact

enactment

enamel
  enamels
  enameled
  enameling

enameler

enamor
  enamored

en bloc

encampment

encase
  encased
  encasing

enceinte

encephalitis

enchant
  enchanted
  enchanting

enchanter

enchantment

enchantress

encircle
  encircled
  encircling

encirclement

enclave

enclose
  enclosed
  enclosing

enclosure

encode
  encoded
  encoding

encompass

encore
  encored
  encoring

encounter
  encountered

encountering

encourage
  encouraged
  encouraging
encouragement
encroach
encroachment
encumber
  encumbered
  encumbering
encumbrance
encyclical
encyclopedia,
    encyclopaedia
encyclopedias,
    encyclopaedias *pl*
encyclopedic,
  encyclopaedic
end
  ended
  ending
endanger
  endangered
  endangering
endear
  endeared
  endearing
endearment
endeavor
  endeavored
  endeavoring

endemic
endemically
endive
endless
endlessly
endocrine
endorse
  endorsed
  endorsing
endorsement
endorser
endow
  endowed
  endowing
endowment
endurable
endurance
endure
  endured
  enduring
enema
  enemas *pl*
enemy
  enemies *pl*
energetic
energetically
energize
  energized
  energizing
energizer
energy

energies *pl*
enervate
  enervated
  enervating
enervation
en famille
enfeeble
  enfeebled
  enfeebling
enfeeblement
enforce
  enforced
  enforcing
enforceability
enforceable
enforcement
enfranchise
  enfranchised
  enfranchising
enfranchisement
engage
  engaged
  engaging
engagement
engender
  engendered
  engendering
engine
engineer
  engineered
  engineering

engorge
  engorged
  engorging
engrained
engrave
  engraved
  engraving
engraver
engross
engrossment
engulf
  engulfed
  engulfing
enhance
  enhanced
  enhancing
enhancement
enigma
  enigmas *pl*
enigmatic
enigmatically
enjoin
  enjoined
  enjoining
enjoy
  enjoyed
  enjoying
  enjoys
enjoyable
enjoyably
enjoyment

enlarge
  enlarged
  enlarging
enlargeable
enlargement
enlarger
enlighten
  enlightened
  enlightening
enlightenment
enlist
  enlisted
  enlisting
enlistment
en masse
enmity
  enmities *pl*
ennoble
  ennobled
  ennobling
ennoblement
ennui (boredom)
enormity
  enormities *pl*
enormous
enormously
enough
en passant
enquire (to ask)
  enquired
  enquiring

enquiry
  enquiries *pl*
enrage
  enraged
  enraging
enrapture
  enraptured
  enrapturing
enrich
enrichment
enroll
  enrolled
  enrolling
  enrolls
enrollment
en route
ensconce
  ensconced
  ensconcing
ensemble
enshrine
  enshrined
  enshrining
ensign
enslave
  enslaved
  enslaving
enslavement
ensue (to follow)
  ensued
  ensuing

ensure (to make sure)
  ensured
  ensuring
entail
  entailed
  entailing
entailment
entangle
  entangled
  entangling
entanglement
entente
enter
  entered
  entering
enteric
enteritis
enterprise
enterprising
entertain
  entertained
  entertaining
entertainer
entertainment
enthrall
  enthralled
  enthralling
  enthralls
enthrallment
enthrone
  enthroned

enthroning
enthronement
enthuse
  enthused
  enthusing
enthusiasm
enthusiast
enthusiastic
enthusiastically
entice
  enticed
  enticing
enticement
entire
  entired
  entiring
entirely
entirety
entitle
  entitled
  entitling
entitlement
entity
  entities *pl*
entomb
  entombed
  entombing
entombment
entomological
entomologist
entomology

entourage
entrails
entrance
  entranced
  entrancing
entrancement
entrant
entrap
  entrapped
  entrapping
  entraps
entreat
  entreated
  entreating
entreaty
  entreaties *pl*
entrée
  entrées *pl*
entrench
entrenchment
entrepôt
entrepreneur
entrepreneurial
entropy
entrust
entry
  entries *pl*
entwine
  entwined
  entwining
enumerate

enumerated
enumerating
enumeration
enumerator
enunciate
  enunciated
  enunciating
enunciation
enunciator
envelop (to cover)
  enveloped
  enveloping
envelope (covering)
envelopment
envenom
  envenomed
  envenoming
enviable
envious
enviously
environ
environment
environmental
environmentally
envisage
  envisaged
  envisaging
envoy
  envoys *pl*
envy
  envied

envies
  envying
enwrap
  enwrapped
  enwrapping
  enwraps
enzyme
eolith (ancient flint)
epaulet, epaulette
ephemera (insect)
  ephemerae *pl*
ephemeral (short-
  lived)
ephemerally
ephemeron (printed
  item)
  ephemera *pl*
epic
epical
epically
epicene (both sexes)
epicenter
epicure
epicurean
epicureanism
epicycle
epicyclic
epidemic
epidermal
epidermis
epidiascope

epigastric
epiglottis
epigram (clever
  saying)
epigrammatic
epigraph (inscription)
epilepsy
epileptic
epilogue
epiphany
episcopacy
episcopal
episcopalian
episcopate
episode
episodic
epistle
epistolary
epitaph (inscription
  on tomb)
epithet (adjective)
epitome
  epitomes *pl*
epitomize
  epitomized
  epitomizing
epoch
epochal
eponym
eponymous
epsilon

equability
equable
equably
equal
  equals
  equaled
  equaling
equality
  equalities *pl*
equalize
  equalized
  equalizing
equalizer
equally
equanimity
equate
  equated
  equating
equation
equator
equatorial
equerry
  equerries *pl*
equestrian
equestrianism
equidistant
equilateral
equilibrate
  equilibrated
  equilibrating
equilibration

equilibrium
  equilibria,
  equilibriums *pl*
equine
equinoctial
equinox
  equinoxes *pl*
equip
  equipped
  equipping
  equips
equipage
equipment
equipoise
equitable
equitably
equity
  equities *pl*
equivalence
equivalent
equivocal
equivocally
equivocate
  equivocated
  equivocating
equivocation
equivocator
era
  eras *pl*
eradicable
eradicate

  eradicated
  eradicating
eradication
erasable
erase
  erased
  erasing
eraser
erasure
ere (before)
erect
  erected
  erecting
erection
erector
erg (unit)
ergo (therefore)
ergonomics
ergotism (disease)
ermine
erode
  eroded
  eroding
erogenous
erosion
erosive
erotic
erotica
erotically
eroticism
err

erred
erring
errs
errand
errand (short journey)
errant (wandering)
errantry
errata
erratic
erratically
erroneous
erroneously
error
ersatz
erstwhile
eructate (to belch)
  eructated
  eructating
eructation
erudite (learned)
eruditely
erudition
erupt
  erupted
  erupting
eruption
eruptive
eruptively
erysipelas
escalade (to climb
  over)

escaladed
escalading
escalate (to increase)
  escalated
  escalating
escalation
escalator
escallop, scallop
  (shellfish)
escalope (slice of
  veal)
escapade
escape
  escaped
  escaping
escapement (of a
  clock)
escaper
escapism
escapologist
escargot (snail)
escarpment (of a hill)
eschatological
eschatology
eschew
  eschewed
  eschewing
escort
  escorted
  escorting
escutcheon

Eskimo
  Eskimos, Eskimo pl
esophageal
esophagus
esoteric
esoterical
esoterically
esotericism
espadrilles
espalier
especial
especially
Esperanto
espionage
esplanade
espousal
espouse
  espoused
  espousing
espresso
  espressos pl
esprit de corps
espy
  espied
  espies
  espying
esquire
essay (try)
  essays pl
  essayed
  essaying

essays

essayist

essence

essential

essentially

establish

establishable

establishment

estate

esteem

esteemed

esthete

esthetic

esthetically

estheticism

esthetics

estimable

estimate

  estimated

  estimating

estimation

estimator

estranged

estrangement

estuary

  estuaries *pl*

et cetera, etc.

etch

etcher

eternal

eternally

eternity

  eternities *pl*

ether

ethereal

ethereally

ethic

ethical

ethically

ethics

ethnic

ethnically

ethnological

ethnology

ethos

ethyl

ethylene

etiolate

  etiolated

  etiolating

etiolation

etiology

etiquette

etude

etymological

etymologically

etymologist

etymology

eucalyptus

  eucalypti,

  eucalyptuses *pl*

Eucharist

euclidean

eugenic

eugenically

eugenics

eulogistic

eulogistically

eulogize

  eulogized

  eulogizing

eulogy

  eulogies *pl*

eunuch

euphemism

euphemistic

euphemistically

euphonious

euphony (pleasant
  sound)

  euphonies *pl*

euphoria

euphoric

euphuism (affected
  style of speech)

euphuistic

Eurasian

eureka

eurhythmics

Europe

European

eustachian

euthanasia

evacuate
  evacuated
  evacuating
evacuation
evacuee
evade
  evaded
  evading
evaluate
  evaluated
  evaluating
evaluation
evanesce
  evanesced
  evanescing
evanescent
evangelical
evangelism
evangelist
evangelize
  evangelized
  evangelizing
evaporate
  evaporated
  evaporating
evaporation
evaporator
evasion
evasive
evasively
evasiveness

eve
even
  evened
  evening
evening
evenly
evenness
event
eventful
eventfully
eventide
eventual
eventuality
  eventualities *pl*
eventually
eventuate
  eventuated
  eventuating
ever
everlasting
evermore
every
everybody
everyone
everywhere
evict
  evicted
  evicting
eviction
evidence
evident

evidently
evil
evilly
evince
  evinced
  evincing
eviscerate
  eviscerated
  eviscerating
evisceration
evocation
evocative
evoke
  evoked
  evoking
evolution
evolutionary
evolutionism
evolutionist
evolve
  evolved
  evolving
ewe
ewer
ex officio
exacerbate
  exacerbated
  exacerbating
exacerbation
exact
  exacted

exacting
exactitude
exactly
exactness
exaggerate
  exaggerated
  exaggerating
exaggeration
exaggerator
exalt
  exalted
  exalting
exaltation
exam
examination
examine
  examined
  examining
examiner
example
exasperate
  exasperated
  exasperating
exasperation
excavate
  excavated
  excavating
excavation
excavator
exceed (surpass)
  exceeded

exceeding
exceedingly
excel
  excelled
  excelling
  excels
excellence
Excellency
  Excellencies pl
excellent
excellently
except
  excepted
  excepting
exception
exceptional
exceptionally
excerpt
excess
  excesses pl
excessive
excessively
exchange
  exchanged
  exchanging
exchangeable
exchanger
exchequer
excisable
excise
  excised

excising
excision
excitability
excitable
excitation
excite
  excited
  exciting
excitement
exciter
exclaim
  exclaimed
  exclaiming
exclamation
exclamatory
exclude
  excluded
  excluding
exclusion
exclusive
exclusively
exclusiveness
exclusivity
excommunicate
  excommunicated
  excommunicating
excommunication
excrement
excrescence
excreta
excrete

excreted

excreting

excretion

excruciate

excruciating

excruciatingly

exculpate

exculpated

exculpating

exculpation

excursion

excusable

excusably

excuse

excused

excusing

execrable

execrably

execrate

execrated

execrating

execration

executant (performer)

execute

executed

executing

execution

executioner

executive

executor (of a will)

executrix (female

executor)

executrices *pl*

exemplarily

exemplary

exemplification

exemplify

exemplified

exemplifies

exemplifying

exempt

exempted

exempting

exemption

exercise (to keep fit)

exercised

exercising

exert

exerted

exerting

exertion

exeunt

exhalation

exhale

exhaled

exhaling

exhaust

exhausted

exhausting

exhaustible

exhaustion

exhaustive

exhaustively

exhibit

exhibited

exhibiting

exhibition

exhibitioner

exhibitionism

exhibitionist

exhibitor

exhilarant

exhilarate

exhilarated

exhilarating

exhilaration

exhort

exhorted

exhorting

exhortation

exhumation

exhume

exhumed

exhuming

exigency

exigencies *pl*

exigent

exigently

exiguity

exiguous

exile

exiled

exiling

exist
  existed
  existing
existence
existent
existential
existentialism
exit
  exited
  exiting
exodus
  exoduses *pl*
exonerate
  exonerated
  exonerating
exoneration
exorbitance
exorbitant
exorbitantly
exorcise (to free from
  evil)
  exorcised
  exorcising
exorcism
exorcist
exorcize
  exorcized
  exorcizing
exotic
exotica
exotically

expand
expandable
expanse
expansible
expansion
expansive
expansively
expatiate (to talk at
  length)
  expatiated
  expatiating
expatriate
  expatriated
  expatriating
expatriation
expect
  expected
  expecting
expectancy
expectant
expectation
expectorant
expectorate
  expectorated
  expectorating
expectoration
expediency
  expediencies *pl*
expedient
expedite
  expedited

  expediting
expedition
expeditionary
expeditious
expeditiously
expel
  expelled
  expelling
  expels
expend
expendability
expendable
expenditure
expense
expensive
experience
  experienced
  experiencing
experiment
  experimented
  experimenting
experimental
experimentally
experimentation
experimenter
expert
expertise
expertly
expertness
expiate
  expiated

expiating
expiation
expiration
expiratory
expire
expired
expiring
expiry
explain
explained
explaining
explainable
explanation
explanatory
expletive
explicable
explicate (to explain)
explicated
explicating
explicit
explicitly
explicitness
explode
exploded
exploding
exploit
exploited
exploiting
exploitation
exploiter
exploration

exploratory
explore
explored
exploring
explorer
explosion
explosive
explosively
exponent
exponential
export
exported
exporting
exportable
exportation
exporter
expose
exposed
exposing
exposé (detailed
  description)
exposition
expostulate
expostulated
expostulating
expostulation
exposure
expound
expounded
expounding
express

expressible
expression
expressionless
expressive
expressively
expressly
expropriate
expropriated
expropriating
expropriation
expropriator
expulsion
expunction
expunge
expunged
expunging
expurgate
expurgated
expurgating
expurgation
expurgatory
exquisite
exquisitely
extant
extemporaneous
extemporaneously
extempore
extemporization
extemporize
extemporized
extemporizing

extend

extendible

extensible

extension

extensive

extensively

extent

extenuate

  extenuated

  extenuating

extenuation

exterior

exterminate

  exterminated

  exterminating

extermination

exterminator

external

externally

extinct

extinction

extinguish

extinguisher

extirpate

  extirpated

  extirpating

extirpation

extirpator

extol

  extolled

  extolling

  extols

extort

extortion

extortionate

extortioner

extra

  extras *pl*

extract

  extracted

  extracting

extractable

extraction

extractive

extractor

extracurricular

extraditable

extradite

  extradited

  extraditing

extradition

extramarital

extramural

extraneous

extraneously

extraordinarily

extraordinary

extrapolate

  extrapolated

  extrapolating

extrapolation

extrasensory

extrasystole (heart-
  beat)

extrasystolic

extraterrestrial

extraterritorial

extraterritoriality

extravagance

extravagant

extravagantly

extravaganza

  extravaganzas *pl*

extreme

extremely

extremist

extremity

  extremities *pl*

extricable

extricate

  extricated

  extricating

extrication

extrinsic

extrinsically

extroversion

extrovert

extrude

  extruded

  extruding

extruder

extrusion

exuberance

exuberant
exuberantly
exudation
exude
  exuded
  exuding
exult
  exulted
  exulting
exultant
exultation
eye
  eyes *pl*
  eyed
  eyeing
eyeball
eyebrow
eyeful
eyelash
  eyelashes *pl*
eyelid
eye-opener
eyepiece
eyesight
eyesore
eyewash
eyewitness
eyrie (eagle's nest)

fable
fabled
fabric
fabricate
  fabricated
  fabricating
fabrication
fabricator
fabulous
fabulously
facade
face
  faced
  facing
faceless
facet
faceted
facetious

facetiously
facetiousness
facia (panel)
facial
facially
facile
facilitate
  facilitated
  facilitating
facilitation
facility
  facilities *pl*
facsimile
fact
faction
factious
factitious
factor

factored
  factoring
factorial
factorization
factorize
  factorized
  factorizing
factory
  factories *pl*
factotum
  factotums *pl*
factual
factually
facultative (optional)
faculty
  faculties *pl*
fad
faddish
faddy
fade
  faded
  fading
fag
  fagged
  fagging
  fags
fag-end
Fahrenheit
faience
fail
  failed

failing
fails
failure
fain (gladly)
faint (weak)
fainter
fainthearted
faintly
faintness
fair (clear; light-
　colored; outdoor
　entertainment;
　satisfactory)
fairer
fair-haired
fairly
fairness
fairway
　fairways *pl*
fairy
　fairies *pl*
fairy tale
fait accompli
faith
faithful
faithfully
faithfulness
faithless
faithlessly
faithlessness
fake

faked
faking
faker (fraud)
fakir (Indian holy
　man)
falcon
falconer
falconry
fall
　fallen
　falling
　falls
fallacious
fallacy
　fallacies *pl*
fallibility
fallible
fallout
fallow
false
falsehood
falsely
falseness
falsetto
　falsettos *pl*
falsification
falsify
　falsified
　falsifies
　falsifying
falsity

falter
　faltered
　faltering
fame
familiar
familiarity
familiarization
familiarize
　familiarized
　familiarizing
familiarly
family
　families *pl*
famine
famished
famous
famously
fan
　fanned
　fanning
　fans
fanatic
fanatically
fanaticism
fancier
fanciful
fancifully
fancy
　fancies *pl*
　fancied
　fancies

fancying
fancy-free
fanfare
fantasize
fantasized
fantasizing
fantastic
fantastically
fantasy
fantasies *pl*
far
farther, further
farthest, furthest
farad
faraway
farce
farceur
farcical
farcically
fare (money; food; to manage)
fared
faring
farewell
far-fetched
farinaceous
farm
farmer
farmhouse
farmyard
far-reached

far-reaching
farrier
far-seeing
far-sighted
farthing
fascia (band)
fascicle
fascinate
fascinated
fascinating
fascination
fascinator
fascism
fascist
fascistic
fashion
fashioned
fashioning
fashionable
fashionably
fast
fasten
fastened
fastening
fastener
faster
fastidious
fastidiously
fastidiousness
fat
fatter

fattest
fatal
fatalism
fatalist
fatalistic
fatalistically
fatality
fatalities *pl*
fatally
fathead
fate
fateful
fatefully
father
fathered
fathering
father-in-law
fathers-in-law *pl*
fatherland
fatherless
fatherly
fathom
fatigue
fatigued
fatiguing
fatness
fatten
fattened
fattening
fatuity
fatuous

fatuously
fatwa
  fatwas *pl*
faucet
fault
  faulted
  faulting
faultfinding
faultless
faulty
  faultier
  faultiest
faun (deity)
fauna (animals)
faux pas
favor
  favored
  favoring
favorable
favorably
favorite
favoritism
fawn (color; deer;
  to flatter)
  fawned
  fawning
fax
  faxed
  faxing
fay
fealty

  fealties *pl*
fear
  feared
  fearing
fearful
fearfully
fearless
fearlessness
fearsome
feasibility
feasible
feasibly
feast
  feasted
  feasting
feat (achievement)
feather
  feathered
  feathering
featherbed
featherbedding
featherweight
feathery
feature
  featured
  featuring
featureless
febrile
February
fecal
feces

feckless
fecund
fecundity
fed (*from* feed)
federal
federalism
federalist
federalization
federalize
  federalized
  federalizing
federally
federate
  federated
  federating
federation
fed-up
fee
feeble
feebler
feebly
feed
  fed
  feeding
  feeds
feedback
feel
  feeling
  feels
  felt
feeler

feelingly

feet (pl. of foot)

feign (to pretend)

feint (pretense)

felicitate
  felicitated
  felicitating

felicitation

felicitous

felicitously

felicity (happiness)
  felicities *pl*

feline

felinity

fell

fellow

fellowship

felon

felonious

felony
  felonies *pl*

felt

female

feminine

femininity

feminism

feminist

femme fatale
  femmes fatales *pl*

femoral

femur (thigh bone)

fence
  fenced
  fencing

fencer

fend
  fended
  fending

fender

fennel

feral

ferment (to turn to
    alcohol)
  fermented
  fermenting

fermentation

fern

fernery

ferocious

ferociously

ferociousness

ferocity

ferret
  ferreted
  ferreting

ferric

ferrous

ferrule

ferry
  ferries *pl*
  ferried
  ferries

ferrying

fertile

fertility

fertilization

fertilize
  fertilized
  fertilizing

fertilizer

fervency

fervent

fervently

fervid

fervor

festal

fester
  festered
  festering

festival

festive

festively

festivity
  festivities *pl*

festoon

feta (cheese)

fetal

fetch

fete (fair)
  feted
  feting

fetid (smelly)

fetish

fetishism
fetlock
fetter (chain)
fettered
fettle
fetus
  fetuses pl
feud
feudal
feudalism
fever
fevered
feverish
feverishly
few
fez
  fezzes pl
fiancé m
  fiancés pl
fiancée f
  fiancées pl
fiasco
  fiascos pl
fiat
fib
  fibbed
  fibbing
  fibs
fibber
fiber
fibroid

fibrositis
fibrous
fickle
fickleness
fickly
fiction
fictional
fictitious
fictitiously
fiddle
  fiddled
  fiddling
fiddler
fidelity
  fidelities pl
fidget
  fidgeted
  fidgeting
fidgety
field
fiend
fiendish
fiendishly
fierce
  fiercer
  fiercest
fiercely
fierceness
fierily
fieriness
fiery

fierier
fieriest
fiesta
  fiestas pl
fife
fifteen
fifteenth
fifth
fifthly
fiftieth
fifty
  fifties pl
fig
fight
  fighting
  fights
  fought
fighter
fig-leaf
figment
figurative
figuratively
figure
  figured
  figuring
figurehead
figurine
filament
filbert
filch
file (paper)

filed
filing
filial
filibuster
filigree
fill
filled
filler
fillet
  filleted
  filleting
fillip (stimulus)
filly (young horse)
  fillies *pl*
film
filter
  filtered
  filtering
filth
filthily
filthiness
filthy
  filthier
  filthiest
filtrate
filtration
fin
final (end)
finale (end in music)
finalist
finality

finalize
  finalized
  finalizing
finally
finance
  financed
  financing
financial
financially
financier
finch
  finches *pl*
find
  finding
  finds
  found
finder
fine
  fined
  fining
  finer
  finest
finely
fineness
finery
finesse (subtlety)
finger
  fingered
  fingering
fingernail
fingerprint

finical
finically
finicky
finis (end)
finish
finite
finitely
finny
fiord, fjord
fir (tree)
fire
  fired
  firing
firearm
fire engine
fire escape
fire extinguisher
firefly
  fireflies *pl*
fireplace
firework
firm
firmament
firmly
firmness
first
first aid
firstly
first-rate
firth
fiscal

fiscally

fish
  fish, fishes *pl*

fisher (catches fish)

fishery
  fisheries *pl*

fishily

fishmonger

fishy

fissile

fission

fissionable

fissure (crack)

fist

fisticuffs

fit
  fits
  fitted
  fitting

fitter

fittest

fitful

fitfully

fitness

five

fivefold

fiver

fix
  fixes *pl*

fixation

fixative

fixedly

fixture

fizz

fizziness

fizzle
  fizzled
  fizzling

fizzy
  fizzier
  fizziest

fjord, fiord

flabbergast
  flabbergasted
  flabbergasting

flabbily

flabbiness

flabby
  flabbier
  flabbiest

flaccid

flaccidly

flag
  flagged
  flagging
  flags

flagellate (to flog)
  flagellated
  flagellating

flagellation

flageolet (bean)

flagon

flagrancy

flagrant

flagrantly

flail (stick for
  threshing)
  flailed
  flailing

flair (aptitude)

flake
  flaked
  flaking

flaky
  flakier
  flakiest

flambé
  flambéed
  flambéing
  flambés

flamboyance

flamboyant

flamboyantly

flame
  flamed
  flaming

flamenco
  flamencos *pl*

flamingo
  flamingos *pl*

flammable

flange

flank

flannel

flap
  flapped
  flapping
  flaps
flapper (girl)
flare (blaze)
  flared
  flaring
flash
flashy
  flashier
  flashiest
flask
flat
flatly
flatten
  flattened
  flattening
flatter
  flattered
  flattering
flatterer
flattery
flatulence
flatulent
flaunt
  flaunted
  flaunting
flautist
flavor

  flavored
  flavoring
flavorless
flaw (fault)
flawless
flawlessly
flax
flaxen
flay
  flayed
  flaying
  flays
flea (insect)
fled (*from* flee)
fledgling
flee (to run away)
  fled
  fleeing
  flees
fleece
  fleeced
  fleecing
fleecy
  fleecier
  fleeciest
fleet
fleeting
flesh
fleshiness
fleshy
  fleshier

  fleshiest
fleur-de-lis
flew (*from* fly)
flex (to bend; cable)
flexibility
flexible
flick
flicker
  flickered
  flickering
flier, flyer
flight
flight attendant
flightiness
flighty
flimsily
flimsiness
flimsy
  flimsier
  flimsiest
flinch
fling
  flinging
  flings
  flung
flint
flippancy
flippant
flippantly
flipper
flirt

flirted
flirting
flirtation
flirtatious
flit
  flits
  flitted
  flitting
float
  floated
  floating
flock (group)
floe (floating ice)
flog
  flogged
  flogging
  flogs
flood
  flooded
  flooding
floodgate
floodlight
  floodlighting
  floodlights
  floodlit
floor
  floored
  flooring
flop
  flopped
  flopping

flops
floppy
flora
floral
florid
florist
floss
flossy
  flossier
  flossiest
flotation
flotilla
  flotillas *pl*
flotsam
flounce
  flounced
  flouncing
flounder
  floundered
  floundering
flour (for bread)
flourish
floury
flout
  flouted
  flouting
flow
flower (of a plant)
  flowered
  flowering
flowery

flown (*from* fly)
flu (influenza)
fluctuate
  fluctuated
  fluctuating
fluctuation
flue (chimney)
fluency
fluent
fluently
fluff
fluffiness
fluffy
  fluffier
  fluffiest
fluid
fluidity
fluke
  fluked
  fluking
flummox
flummoxed
flung (*from* fling)
flunkey, flunky
  flunkeys, flunkies *pl*
fluoresce
  fluoresced
  fluorescing
fluorescence
fluorescent
fluoridation

fluoride
fluorine
flurry
  flurries *pl*
flush
fluster
  flustered
  flustering
flute
flutist
flutter
  fluttered
  fluttering
fluvial
flux
fly
  flies *pl*
  flew
  flies
  flown
  flying
fly-by-night
flyer, flier
flyleaf
  flyleaves *pl*
fly-post
fly-posting
flyweight
flywheel
foal
foam

fob
  fobbed
  fobbing
  fobs
focal
focus
  foci, focuses *pl*
  focused, focussed
  focuses, focusses
  focusing, focussing
fodder
foe
  foes *pl*
fog
  fogged
  fogging
  fogs
fogbound
fogey, fogy
  fogeys, fogies *pl*
foggily
fogginess
foggy
  foggier
  foggiest
foghorn
foible
foil
  foiled
  foiling
foist

fold
foldaway
folder
foliage
folio
  folios *pl*
folk
folklore
follicle
follicular
follow
  followed
  following
follower
followthrough
folly
  follies *pl*
foment (to stir up)
  fomented
  fomenting
fomentation
fond
fondant
fonder
fondle
  fondled
  fondling
fondly
fondness
fondue
font

food
foodstuff
fool
  fooled
  fooling
foolery
foolhardiness
foolhardy
foolish
foolishly
foolproof
foolscap
foot
  footed
  footing
footage
football
footballer
footlight
footling
footnote
footsore
footstool
footwear
fop
foppish
forage
  foraged
  foraging
forager
foray

forays *pl*
forbade (*from* forbid)
  (to abstain)
forbear
  forbearing
  forbears
  forbore
  forborne
forbearance
forbearing
forbears
forbid
  forbade
  forbidden
  forbidding
  forbids
forbore (*from* forbear)
forborne (*from*
  forbear)
force
  forced
  forcing
force majeure
forceful
forcefully
forcefulness
forceps
forcible
forcibly
ford
fore (before, in

front of)
forearm
forebear (ancestor)
forebode
foreboding
forecast
forecaster
forecastle
foreclose
  foreclosed
  foreclosing
foreclosure
forecourt
forefather
forefinger
forefront
forego (to go before)
  foregoes
  foregoing
  foregone
  forewent
foreground
forehead
foreign
foreigner
foreignness
foreknowledge
forelock
foreman
  foremen *pl*
foremost

forenoon
forensic
forerunner
foresee
  foresaw
  foreseeing
  foreseen
  foresees
foreseeable
foreshadow
foreshore
foreshorten
  foreshortened
  foreshortening
foresight
foreskin
forest
forestall
forester
forestry
foretaste
foretell
  foretelling
  foretells
  foretold
forethought
forever
forewarn
  forewarned
  forewarning
forewent (*from*

  forego)
forewoman
  forewomen *pl*
foreword
forfeit
  forfeited
  forfeiting
forfeiture
forgave (*from* forgive)
forge
  forged
  forging
forger
forgery
  forgeries *pl*
forget
  forgets
  forgetting
  forgot
  forgotten
forgetful
forgetfulness
forget-me-not
forgettable
forgivable
forgive
  forgave
  forgiven
  forgives
  forgiving
forgiveness

forgo (to give up)
  forgoes
  forgoing
  forgone
  forwent
forgot (*from* forget)
fork
forklift
forlorn
forlornly
form
  formed
  forming
formal
formality
  formalities *pl*
formalization
formalize
  formalized
  formalizing
formally (properly)
format
  formats
  formatted
  formatting
formation
formative
former
formerly
formidable
formidably

formula
  formulas,
  formulae *pl*
formulate
  formulated
  formulating
formulation
fornicate
  fornicated
  fornicating
fornication
fornicator
forsake
  forsaken
  forsakes
  forsaking
  forsook
forsooth
forsythia
  forsythias *pl*
fort
forte (loud; special
  skill)
forth (forward)
forthcoming
forthright
forthwith
fortieth
fortification
fortify
  fortified

fortifies
  fortifying
fortissimo
  fortissimos,
  fortissimi *pl*
fortitude
fortress
  fortresses *pl*
fortuitous
fortuitously
fortuity
fortunate
fortunately
fortune
fortune-teller
fortune-telling
forty
  forties *pl*
forum
  forums, fora *pl*
forward
forwards
forwent (*from* forgo)
fossil
fossilization
fossilize
  fossilized
  fossilizing
foster
  fostered
  fostering

fought (*from* fight)
foul (filthy; unfair)
  fouled
  fouling
fouler
foully
foul-mouthed
foulness
found (to establish)
  founded
  founding
foundation
founder
foundling
foundry
  foundries *pl*
fount
fountain
four
fourfold
four score
foursome
fourteen
fourteenth
fourth
fourthly
fowl (bird)
fox
foxhound
foyer
fracas

fraction
fractional
fractionally
fractious
fracture
  fractured
  fracturing
fragile
fragilely
fragility
fragment
fragmentary
fragmentation
fragrance
fragrant (sweet-
  smelling)
fragrantly
frail
frailer
frailty
  frailties pl
frame
  framed
  framing
frame-up
framework
franc (money)
franchise
frank (open-hearted)
frankfurter
frankincense

frankly
frankness
frantic
frantically
fraternal
fraternally
fraternity
  fraternities pl
fraternization
fraternize
  fraternized
  fraternizing
fraud
fraudulence
fraudulent
fraudulently
fraught
fray
  frayed
  fraying
  frays
freak
freakish
freckle
free
  freed
  freeing
  freer
  freest
free-for-all
freedom

freehold
freeholder
freelance
freelancing
freely
freemason
freemasonry
free-wheel
  free-wheeled
  free-wheeling
freeze
  freezes
  freezing
  froze
  frozen
freezer
freight (cargo)
freightage
freighter
French fries
frenetic
frenzied
frenzy
  frenzies pl
frequency
  frequencies pl
frequent
  frequented
  frequenting
frequently
fresco

frescoes *pl*

fresh

freshen

  freshened

  freshening

fresher

freshly

freshman

  freshmen *pl*

freshness

fret

  frets

  fretted

  fretting

fretful

fretsaw

fretwork

Freudian

friability

friable

friar (monk)

friary

  friaries *pl*

fricassee

friction

frictional

Friday

  Fridays *pl*

fridge

fried

friend

friendlier

friendliness

friendly

friendship

frier, fryer (person or
  thing that fries)

fries

frieze

frigate

fright

frighten

  frightened

  frightening

frightful

frightfully

frightfulness

frigid

frigidity

frigidly

frill

fringe

  fringed

  fringing

fringe benefit

frisk

friskiness

frisky

  friskier

  friskiest

fritter

  frittered

frittering

frivolity

  frivolities *pl*

frivolous

frivolously

frizzle

  frizzled

  frizzling

frock

frog

frogman

  frogmen *pl*

frolic

  frolicked

  frolicking

  frolics

frolicsome

front

frontage

frontal

frontally

frontier

frontispiece

frost

frostbite

frostbitten

frostily

frosty

  frostier

  frostiest

froth

frothy
  frothier
  frothiest
froward
frowardness
frown
  frowned
  frowning
frowziness
frowzy
  frowzier
  frowzier
froze (*from* freeze)
frozen (*from* freeze)
frugal
frugality
frugally
fruit
fruiterer
fruitful
fruitfully
fruitfulness
fruitiness
fruition
fruitless
fruitlessly
fruity
  fruitier
  fruitiest
frump
frumpish

frustrate
  frustrated
  frustrating
frustration
fry
  fried
  fries
  frying
fryer, frier (person or
  thing that fries)
fuchsia (flower)
  fuchsias *pl*
fuddle
  fuddled
  fuddling
fudge
  fudged
  fudging
fuel
  fuels
  fueled
  fueling
fugal
fugitive
fugue
fulcrum
fulfill
  fulfilled
  fulfilling
  fulfills
fulfillment

full
full-blooded
fully
fulminate
  fulminated
  fulminating
fulmination
fulsome
fulsomely
fulsomeness
fumble
  fumbled
  fumbling
fume
  fumed
  fuming
fumigate
  fumigated
  fumigating
fumigation
fumigator
fun
function
  functioned
  functioning
functional
functionally
functionary
  functionaries *pl*
fund
  funded

funding
fundamental
fundamentally
funeral
funerary
funereal (gloomy)
fungicidal
fungicide
fungoid
fungus
  fungi, funguses *pl*
funicular
funk
funky
  funkier
  funkiest
funnel
  funnels
  funneled
  funneling
funnily
funny
  funnier
  funniest
fur (pelt)
  furred
  furring
  furs
furbelow
furbish
furbished

furious
furiously
furl
furled
furlong
furlough
furnace
furnish
furnisher
furniture
furor
furred
furrier (fur dealer)
furrow
furry
  furrier
  furriest
further, farther
furtherance
furthered
furthering
furthermore
furthermost
furthest, farthest
furtive
furtively
furtiveness
fury
  furies *pl*
furze
fuse

fused
fusing
fuselage
fusible
fusilier
fusillade
fusion
fuss
fussily
fussiness
fussy
  fussier
  fussiest
fusty
futile
futilely
futility
future
futurism
futurist
futuristic
futurologist
futurology
fuzz
fuzzbox
fuzzily
fuzziness
fuzzy
  fuzzier
  fuzziest

gab
gabardine
gabble (talk)
  gabbled
  gabbling
gabbler
gable (roof)
gabled
gad
  gadded
  gadding
gadabout
gadfly
  gadflies *pl*
gadget
gadgetry
gads
Gaelic

gaff (hook)
gaffe (mistake)
gag
  gagged
  gagging
  gags
gaga
gage
  gaged
  gaging
gaggle
gaiety
gaily
gain
  gained
  gaining
gainer
gainful

gainfully
gainsay
  gainsaid
  gainsaying
  gainsays
gait (walk)
gaiter
gaitered
gala
  galas *pl*
galactic
galah (bird)
galaxy
  galaxies *pl*
gale
gall
gallant
gallantry
gallbladder
galleon
gallery
  galleries *pl*
galley
  galleys *pl*
galling
gallivant
gallon
gallop (pace)
  galloped
  galloping
galloper

gallows
gallstone
galore
galosh
  galoshes *pl*
galumph
galvanic
galvanism
galvanization
galvanize
  galvanized
  galvanizing
galvanometer
gambit
gamble
  gambled
  gambling
gambler
gambol
  gambols
  gamboled
  gamboling
game
gamekeeper
gamely
gamesmanship
gamin (urchin) *m*
gamine (urchin) *f*
gaming room
gamma
gammon (ham)

gamut
gamy
gander
gang
  ganged
  ganging
gangling
ganglion
  ganglia, ganglions *pl*
gangplank
gangrene
gangrenous
gangster
gangway
  gangways *pl*
gannet
gantry
  gantries *pl*
gap
gape
  gaped
  gaping
garage
  garaged
  garaging
garb
garbage
garble
  garbled
  garbling
garçon

garçons *pl*
garden
  gardened
  gardening
gardener
gardenia
  gardenias *pl*
gardens
gargantuan
gargle
  gargled
  gargling
gargoyle
garish
garland
garlic
garlicky
garment
garner (to collect)
  garnered
  garnering
garnet (gem stone)
garnish
  garnished
garret (attic room)
garrison
  garrisoned
  garrisoning
garrote
  garroted
  garroting

garrulity
garrulous
garrulously
garter
gas
  gases
  gassed
  gassing
gaseous
gash
gashed
gasket
gaslight
gasoline
gasometer
gasp
gassiness
gassy
  gassier
  gassiest
gastric
gastritis
gastroenteritis
gastronome
gastronomic
gastronomical
gastronomy
gastropod
  gastropods,
  gastropoda *pl*
gate (entrance)

gateau
  gateaus, gateaux *pl*
gateway
  gateways *pl*
gather
  gathered
  gathering
gauche
gaucheness
gaucherie
gaudily
gaudiness
gaudy
  gaudier
  gaudiest
gauge
  gauged
  gauging
gaunt
gauntlet
gauss (unit of
  magnetism)
gauze
gave (*from* give)
gavel
gavotte
gawkiness
gawky
  gawkier
  gawkiest
gay

gays *pl*
gayer
gayest
gaze (stare)
  gazed
  gazing
gazebo
  gazebos, gazeboes *pl*
gazelle
gazette
  gazetted
  gazetting
gazetteer
gear
  geared
  gearing
gearbox
gearless
gecko
  geckos *pl*
geek
geese (pl. of goose)
geezer
Geiger counter
geisha
  geishas *pl*
gel (to turn to jelly)
  gelled
  gelling
  gels
gelatine, gelatin

gelatinous
geld
gelding
gelid (very cold)
relignite
gem
gendarme
gendarmerie,
  gendarmery
gender
gene
genealogical
genealogically
genealogist
genealogy
genera (*pl* of genus)
general
generality
  generalities *pl*
generalization
generalize
  generalized
  generalizing
generally
generate
  generated
  generating
generation
generative
generator
generic

generically
generosity
generous
generously
Genesis
genetic
genetically
genial
geniality
genially
genie
  genies, genii *pl*
genital
genitive
genius
  geniuses *pl*
genocide
genome
genre
gent
  gents *pl*
genteel (well bred)
genteelism
genteelly
gentian (plant)
gentile (non-Jew)
gentility
gentle
  gentler
  gentlest
gentleman

  gentlemen *pl*
gentlemanly
gentleness
gentlewoman
  gentlewomen *pl*
gently
gentry
gents
genuflect
genuflection,
  genuflexion
genuine
genuinely
genuineness
genus (biological
  family)
  genera *pl*
geographer
geographic
geographical
geographically
geography
geological
geologically
geologist
geology
geometric
geometrical
geometrically
geometrician
geometry

geophysical

geophysicist

geophysics

Georgian

geranium

  geraniums *pl*

gerbil

geriatrician

geriatrics

germ

germane

germicidal

germicide

germinate

  germinated

  germinating

germination

gerontocracy

  gerontocracies *pl*

gerontology

gerrymander

gerund

gerundive

gestate

  gestated

  gestating

gestation

gesticulate

  gesticulated

  gesticulating

gesticulation

gesture

  gestured

  gesturing

get

  gets

  getting

  got

  gotten

getaway

geyser (hot spring)

ghastliness

ghastly

  ghastlier

  ghastliest

gherkin

ghetto

  ghettos *pl*

ghost

ghostly

ghoul

ghoulish

giant

gibber (to speak

    unclearly)

  gibbered

  gibbering

gibberish

gibbet

gibbon

gibbous

gibe (to mock)

gibed

gibing

giblets

giddily

giddiness

giddy

  giddier

  giddiest

gift

gift wrap

  gift wrapped

  gift wrapping

  gift wraps

gig

gigabyte

gigantic

gigantically

giggle

  giggled

  giggling

giggler

gigolo

  gigolos *pl*

gild (to cover with

    gold)

  gilded

  gilding

gill

gilled

gillie

gillyflower

gilt (gold)
gilt-edged
gimcrack
gimlet
gimmick
gimmickry
gimmicky
gin
ginger
gingerbread
gingerly
gingham
gingival
gingivitis
giraffe
gird
  girded
  girding
girder
girdle
girl
girlish
girlishness
giro
  giros *pl*
girt
girth
gist
give
  gave
  given

gives
giving
giver
gizmo
  gizmos *pl*
gizzard
glacé
glacial
glaciation
glacier
glad
gladden
  gladdened
  gladdening
gladder
glade
gladiator
gladiolus
  gladioli, gladioluses *pl*
gladsome
glamorization
glamorize
  glamorized
  glamorizing
glamorous
glamorously
glamour
glance
  glanced
  glancing

gland
glandular
glare
  glared
  glaring
glass
  glasses *pl*
glassily
glassware
glassy
  glassier
  glassiest
glaucoma
glaucous
glaze
  glazed
  glazing
glazier
gleam
  gleamed
  gleaming
glean
  gleaned
  gleaning
gleaner
glebe
glee
gleeful
gleefully
glen
glengarry

glib
glibly
glibness
glide
  glided
  gliding
glider
glimmer
  glimmered
  glimmering
glimpse
  glimpsed
  glimpsing
glint
  glinted
  glinting
glisten
  glistened
  glistening
glitter
  glittered
  glittering
glitterati
gloaming
gloat
  gloated
  gloating
global
globally
globe
globe-trotter

globe-trotting
globular
globule
gloom
gloomily
gloominess
gloomy
  gloomier
  gloomiest
glorious
gloriously
glory
  glories *pl*
  gloried
  glories
  glorying
gloss
glossary
  glossaries *pl*
glossiness
glossy
  glossier
  glossiest
glottal
glottis
glove
glover
glow
glower
  glowered
  glowering

glowworm
glucose
glue
  glued
  gluing
gluey
glum
  glummer
  glummest
glumly
glumness
glut
gluten
glutenous (having
  gluten)
glutinous (gluey)
glutted
glutton
gluttonous
gluttony
glycerin
gnarled
gnash
gnat
gnaw (nibble)
  gnawed
  gnawing
  gnaws
gnocchi
gnome
gnu

go
goes
going
gone
went
goad
goaded
goading
goal
goalkeeper
goalless
goat
goatee
gob
gobble
gobbled
gobbling
gobbledegook,
gobbledygook
go-between
goblet
goblin
gobsmacked
god
godchild
godchildren *pl*
goddess
goddesses *pl*
God-fearing
God-forsaken
godliness

godly
godparent
godsend
godspeed
goer
goggle
goggled
goggling
goiter
goitrous
gold
golden
goldfinch
goldfinches *pl*
goldsmith
golf
golf course
golfer
golf links
Goliath
golliwog
gondola
gondolas *pl*
gondolier
gone (*from* go)
goner
gong
gonorrhea
goo
good
goodbye

good-humored
good-looking
goodly
goodness
goodness' sake
goodnight
goodwill
goody
goodies *pl*
gooey
goon
goose
geese *pl*
gooseberry
gooseberries *pl*
goose-flesh
goosestep
goosestepped
goosestepping
goosesteps
gopher
gore
gored
goring
gorge
gorged
gorging
gorgeous
gorgeously
Gorgonzola
gorilla

gorillas *pl*
gorse
gory
  gorier
  goriest
gosling
gospel
gospeler
gossamer
gossip
  gossiped
  gossiping
gossiper
got (*from* get)
gotten (*from* get)
gouache
gouge
  gouged
  gouging
goulash
gourd
gourmand
gourmandism
gourmet
gout
gouty
govern
  governed
  governing
governable
governance

governess
government
governmental
governor
gown
grab
  grabbed
  grabbing
  grabs
grace
  graced
  gracing
graceful
gracefully
gracious
graciously
graciousness
gradation
grade
  graded
  grading
gradient
gradual
gradualism
gradually
graduate
  graduated
  graduating
graduation
graduator
graffiti

graft
  grafted
  grafting
grail
grain
gram
grammar
grammarian
grammatical
grammatically
gramophone
granary
  granaries *pl*
grand
Grand Prix
grandchild
  grandchildren *pl*
granddaughter
grandee
grandeur
grandfather
grandiloquence
grandiloquent
grandiloquently
grandiose
grandiosely
grandiosity
grandma
grandmother
grandpa
grandson

grange
granite
granny, grannie
  grannies *pl*
grant
granular
granularity
granulate
  granulated
  granulating
granulation
granule
grape
grapefruit
graph
graphic
graphical
graphically
graphite
graphologist
graphology
grapnel
grapple
  grappled
  grappling
grasp
grass
grasshopper
grassy
grate (fireplace; to
  scrape)

grated
grating
grateful
gratefully
grater (scraper)
graticule
gratification
gratify
  gratified
  gratifies
  gratifying
gratin
gratis
gratitude
gratuitous
gratuitously
gratuity
  gratuities *pl*
grave
  graver
  gravest
gravel
graveled
gravely
graveyard
gravitate
  gravitated
  gravitating
gravitation
gravitational
gravity

gravy
gray
  grayed
  graying
  grays
  grayer
  grayest
grayish
grayling
grayness
graze
  grazed
  grazing
grease (oil)
  greased
  greasing
greaser
greasepaint
greasily
greasiness
greasy
  greasier
  greasiest
great
  greater
  greatest
greatly
greatness
greed
greedily
greediness

greedy
greedier
greediest
green
greener
greenest
greenback
greenery
greenfield
greengage
greengrocer
greenness
greet
greeted
greeting
gregarious
gregariousness
gremlin
grenade
grenadier
grew (*from* grow)
greyhound
grid
griddle
gridiron
grief
grievance
grieve
grieved
grieving
grievous

grievously
griffin (fabulous
  beast)
griffon (dog; vulture)
grill (to cook)
grille (grating)
grilled
grillroom
grim
grimmer
grimmest
grimace
grimaced
grimacing
grime
griminess
grimly
grimness
grimy
grimier
grimiest
grin
grinned
grinning
grins
grind
grinder
grip
gripped
gripping
grips

gripe
griped
griping
grippe (influenza)
grisly
grist
gristle
gristly
grit
grits
gritted
gritting
gritty
grizzle
grizzled
grizzling
grizzly
grizzly bear
groan
groaned
groaning
groats
grocer
grocery
groceries *pl*
grog
grogginess
groggy
groggier
groggiest
groin (body)

grommet, grummet
groom
groove
groovy
  groovier
  grooviest
grope
  groped
  groping
gross
grosser
grossly
grossness
grotesque
grotesquely
grotesqueness
grotto
  grottoes *pl*
grouchy
ground
groundless
groundlessly
group
grouse
  groused
  grousing
grouser
grout
grove
grovel
  grovels

groveled
groveling
groveler
grow
  grew
  growing
  grown
grower
growl
grown-up
growth
groyne (breakwater)
grub
grubbily
grubbiness
grubby
  grubbier
  grubbiest
grudge
  grudged
  grudging
grudgingly
gruel
grueling
gruesome
gruesomely
gruesomeness
gruff
gruffly
gruffness
grumble

grumbled
grumbling
grumbler
grummet, grommet
grumpily
grumpiness
grumpy
  grumpier
  grumpiest
grunt
gruyère
guano
guarantee
  guaranteed
  guaranteeing
  guarantees
guarantor
guaranty
guard
guardian
guardianship
guard-room
guava
  guavas *pl*
gubernatorial
Guernsey
guerrilla, guerilla
  (fighter)
  guerrillas, guerillas
  pl
guess

177

guesswork

guest

guffaw

guffawing

guidance

guide

  guided

  guiding

guild (society)

guilder (Dutch money)

guildhall

guile

guileless

guillotine

  guillotined

  guillotining

guilt (emotion)

guiltily

guiltiness

guilty

  guiltier

  guiltiest

guinea

guinea-pig

guise

guitar

guitarist

gulf

Gulf Stream

gull

gulled

gullet

gullibility

gullible

gully

  gullies *pl*

gulp

  gulped

  gulping

gum

  gummed

  gumming

  gums

gumboil

gumminess

gummy

  gummier

  gummiest

gumption

gun

  gunned

  gunning

  guns

gunnel, gunwale

gunner

gunnery

gunpowder

gurgle

  gurgled

  gurgling

Gurkha

  Gurkhas *pl*

guru

gush

gusset

gust

  gusted

  gusting

gusto

gusty

gut

  guts

  gutted

  gutting

  guts

gutsy

  gutsier

  gutsiest

gutter

guttering

guttersnipe

guttural

gutturally

guy

guzzle

  guzzled

  guzzling

guzzler

gybe (in sailing)

  gybed

  gybing

gym

gymkhana
  gymkhanas *pl*
gymnasium
  gymnasiums,
    gymnasia *pl*
gymnast
gymnastic
gynaecology
gynecological
gynecologist
gynecology
gypsum
gypsy
  gypsies *pl*
gyrate
  gyrated
  gyrating
gyration
gyratory
gyroscope
gyroscopic

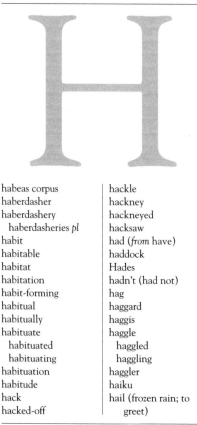

habeas corpus
haberdasher
haberdashery
  haberdasheries *pl*
habit
habitable
habitat
habitation
habit-forming
habitual
habitually
habituate
  habituated
  habituating
habituation
habitude
hack
hacked-off

hackle
hackney
hackneyed
hacksaw
had (*from* have)
haddock
Hades
hadn't (had not)
hag
haggard
haggis
haggle
  haggled
  haggling
haggler
haiku
hail (frozen rain; to
  greet)

  hailed
  hailing
hailer
hair (*eg* on head)
hairbreadth
hairiness
hairless
hairpiece
hairpin
hairy
  hairier
  hairiest
hair's breadth
hake
halcyon
hale (robust)
half
  halves *pl*
half-caste
half-hearted
halfway
halibut
halitosis
hall
hallelujah, halleluiah,
  alleluia
hallmark
hallmarked
hallo, hello, hullo
hallow (make sacred)
Halloween,

Hallowe'en
hallowed
hallucinate
  hallucinated
  hallucinating
hallucination
hallucinatory
hallucinogen
halo (circle of light)
  haloes, halos *pl*
halt
halter
haltingly
halve
  halves *pl*
  halved
  halving
halyard, halliard
ham
hamburger
hamlet
hammer
  hammered
  hammering
hammock
hamper
  hampered
  hampering
hamster
hamstring
  hamstringing

hamstrings
hamstrung
hand
  handed
  handing
handcuff
  handcuffed
  handcuffing
handcuffs
handful
  handfuls *pl*
handicap
  handicapped
  handicapping
  handicaps
handicraft
handily
handiness
handiwork
handkerchief
handkerchiefs,
  handkerchieves *pl*
handle
  handled
  handling
handlebar
handler
handmade (article)
handmaid (girl)
hand-me-down
handout

handsome
handsomely
handsomeness
handwriting
handwritten
handy
  handier
  handiest
handyman
  handymen *pl*
hang
  hanging
  hangs
  hanged (criminal)
  hung
hangar (for aircraft)
hanger (for clothes)
hanger-on
hang-gliding
hangman
hangover
hang-up
hank
hanker
  hankered
  hankering
hanky, hankie
hanky-panky
hansom (cab)
haphazard
hapless

happen
  happened
  happening
happily
happiness
happy
  happier
  happiest
happy-go-lucky
harangue
  harangued
  haranguing
harass
harassed
harassment
harbinger
harbor
  harbored
  harboring
harborage
hard
harden
  hardened
  hardening
hardener
harder
hardheaded
hard-hearted
hardily (boldly)
hardly (barely)
hardness

hardship
hardware
hardy
  hardier
  hardiest
hare (animal; to run)
  hared
  haring
harebell
hare-brained
harelip
harem
haricot
hark
harken
harlequin
harlequinade
harlot
harlotry
harm
harmful
harmfully
harmless
harmlessly
harmlessness
harmonic
harmonica
  harmonicas *pl*
harmonically
harmonious
harmonium

harmoniums *pl*
harmonization
harmonize
  harmonized
  harmonizing
harmony
  harmonies *pl*
harness
harp
  harped
  harping
harpist
harpoon
  harpooned
  harpooning
harpooner
harpsichord
harpy
  harpies *pl*
harrier
harrow
harrowing
harry
  harried
  harries
  harrying
harsh
harshly
harshness
hart (deer)
hartebeest

harum-scarum
harvest
  harvested
  harvesting
harvester
has (*from* have)
has-been
hash
hashish, hasheesh
hasn't (has not)
hasp
hassle
  hassled
  hassling
hassock
haste
hasten
  hastened
  hastening
hastily
hasty
  hastier
  hastiest
hat
hatch
hatchback
hatchery
  hatcheries *pl*
hatchet
hatchway
  hatchways *pl*

hate
  hated
  hating
hateful
hatred
hatter
haughtily
haughtiness
haughty
  haughtier
  haughtiest
haul (to carry)
  hauled
  hauling
haulage
haulier
haunch
haunt
  haunted
  haunting
hausfrau
haute cuisine
hauteur
Havana
have
  had
  has
  having
haven
haven't (have not)
haversack

havoc
hawk
hawkish
hawser
hawthorn
hay
hay fever
haymaker
hayrick
haystack
hazard
hazardous
hazardously
haze
hazel
hazily
haziness
hazy
  hazier
  haziest
head
  headed
  heading
headache
headachy
header
headless
headline
  headlined
  headlining
headlong

headmaster
headmistress
headquarters
headshrinker
headstrong
headway
heal (health)
  healed
  healing
healer
health
healthily
healthy
  healthier
  healthiest
heap
  heaped
  heaping
hear
  heard
  hearing
  hears
hearer
hearken
  hearkened
  hearkening
hearsay
hearse
heart (body)
heartbreaking
heartbroken

heartbrokenly
hearten
  heartened
  heartening
hearth
heartiness
heartfelt
heartless
heartlessly
heartrending
hearty
  heartier
  heartiest
heat
heater
heath
heathen
heathenism
heather
heatstroke
heatwave
heave
  heaved
  heaving
heaven
heavenly
heavily
heaviness
heavy
  heavier
  heaviest

heavyweight
hebdomadal
Hebraic
Hebrew
hecatomb
heckle
  heckled
  heckling
heckler
hectare (unit of area)
hectic
hectically
hectogram
hectoliter
hector (to bully)
  hectored
  hectoring
he'd (he would)
hedge
  hedged
  hedging
hedgehog
hedger
hedgerow
hedonism
hedonist
heed
  heeded
  heeding
heedful
heedless

heel (of foot)
heftily
heftiness
hefty
  heftier
  heftiest
hegemony
  hegemonies *pl*
heifer
height
heighten
  heightened
  heightening
heinous
heir
heir apparent
heiress
heirloom
held (*from* hold)
helical
helicopter
heliograph
heliotrope
heliport
helium
helix
  helices *pl*
hell
he'll (he will)
hellish
hellishly

hello, hallo, hullo
helm
helmet
helmsman
  helmsmen *pl*
helot
helotry
help
  helped
  helping
helper
helpful
helpfully
helpfulness
helpless
helplessly
helplessness
helpmate
helter-skelter
hem
  hemmed
  hemming
  hems
hematologist
hematology
hematoma
  hematomas
hemiplegia
hemiplegic
hemisphere
hemispherical

hemlock
hemoglobin
hemophilia
hemophiliac
hemorrhage
  hemorrhaged
  hemorrhaging
hemorrhoids
hemp
hempen
hemstitch
hen
hence
henceforth
henchman
  henchmen *pl*
henna
hennaed
henpecked
hepatitis
heptagon
heptarchy
  heptarchies *pl*
her
herald
heraldic
heraldry
herb
herbaceous
herbage
herbal

herbalist
herbicide
herbivore
herbivorous
herculean
herd (of animals)
herdsman
  herdsmen *pl*
here (place)
hereabout
hereafter
hereby
hereditarily
hereditary
heredity
herein
hereof
heresy
  heresies *pl*
heretic
hereto
heretofore
hereunder
herewith
heritable
heritage
hermaphrodite
hermaphroditic
hermetic
hermetically
hermit

hermitage
hernia
  hernias *pl*
hero
  heroes *pl*
heroic
heroically
heroin (drug)
heroine (brave
  woman)
heroism
heron
herpes
herring
herringbone
hers
herself
he's (he is)
hesitancy
hesitant
hesitantly
hesitate
  hesitated
  hesitating
hesitation
hessian
heterodox
heterodoxy
heterodyne
heterogeneity
heterogeneous

heterosexual
heuristic
heuristically
hew (cut)
  hewed
  hewing
  hewn
  hews
hexagon
hexagonal
heyday
  heydays *pl*
hiatus
  hiatuses *pl*
hibernate
  hibernated
  hibernating
hibernation
hibernator
hiccup, hiccough
  hiccuped,
    hiccoughed
  hiccuping,
    hiccoughing
hide
hid
hidden
hides
hiding
hideaway
  hideaways *pl*

hidebound
hideout
hideous
hideously
hierarch
hierarchy
  hierarchies *pl*
hieroglyph
hieroglyphic
hi-fi
  hi-fis *pl*
higgledy-piggledy
high
highfalutin
highland
highlander
highlight
  highlighted
  highlighting
highly
high tech
highness
highway
  highways *pl*
highwayman
  highwaymen *pl*
hijack
hijacked
hijacker
hike
  hiked

hiking
hiker
hilarious
hilarity
hill
hillock
hilly
hilt
him (he)
himself
hind
hinder
  hindered
  hindering
Hindi
hindmost, hindermost
hindrance
hindsight
Hindu
  Hindus *pl*
hinge
  hinged
  hinging
hint
  hinted
  hinting
hinterland
hip
hipped
hippo
  hippos *pl*

hippodrome
hippopotamus
  hippopotamuses,
    hippopotami *pl*
hippy, hippie
  hippies *pl*
hire
  hired
  hiring
hire purchase
hireling
hirsute
his
hiss
  hissed
  hisses
  hissing
histamine
histology
historian
historic
historical
historically
history
  histories *pl*
histrionic
histrionically
hit
  hits
  hitting
hitch

hitchhike
  hitchhiked
  hitchhiking
hitchhiker
hither
hitherto
hitter
hive
  hived
  hiving
hoar (gray)
hoard (to store)
hoarder
hoarding
hoariness
hoarse (husky)
hoarsely
hoarseness
hoarser
hoary
hoax
  hoaxes *pl*
hoaxer
hobble
  hobbled
  hobbling
hobby
  hobbies *pl*
hobbyhorse
hobgoblin
hobnail

hobnob
  hobnobbed
  hobnobbing
  hobnobs
hobo
  hobos, hoboes *pl*
hock
hockey
hocus
  hocused, hocussed
  hocuses, hocusses
  hocusing, hocussing
hocus-pocus
hod
hodgepodge
hoe (tool)
  hoed
  hoeing
hoedown
hog
  hogged
  hogging
  hogs
hoggish
hogshead
hogwash
hoi polloi
hoist
hold
  held
  holding

holds
holder
holdup
hole (opening)
  holed
  holing
holey
holiday
  holidays *pl*
  holidayed
  holidaying
  holidays
holidayer
holiness
hollandaise
hollow
  hollowed
  hollowing
holly (tree)
  hollies *pl*
hollyhock
holocaust
hologram
holograph
holster
holy (sacred)
  holier
  holiest
Holy Ghost
homage
home

homed
homing
homecoming
homeless
homeliness
homely
  homelier
  homeliest
homemade
homeopath
homeopathic
homeopathy
homesick
homesickness
homespun
homestead
homeward
homewards
homework
homicidal
homicide
homily
  homilies *pl*
homogeneity
homogeneous (of
  same type)
homogenize
  homogenized
  homogenizing
homogenous (of same
  descent)

homologous
homonym
homonymic
homophobia
homophobic
homophone
homo sapiens
homosexual
homosexuality
hone
  honed
  honing
honest
honestly
honesty
honey
honeycomb
honeydew
honeyed
honeymoon
honeymooner
honeysuckle
honor
  honored
  honoring
honorable
honorably
honorarium
  honorariums,
  honoraria *pl*
honorary

honorific
hood
hooded
hoodlum
  hoodlums *pl*
hoodwink
hoodwinked
hoof
  hooves, hoofs *pl*
hoofed
hoofing
hoofs
hookah
  hookahs *pl*
hookey
hooligan
hooliganism
hoop
hoop-la
hooray
  hoorays *pl*
hoot
  hooted
  hooting
hooter
hop
  hopped
  hopping
  hops
hope
  hoped

hoping
hopeful
hopefully
hopelessly
hopelessness
hopper
hopscotch
horde (crowd)
horizon
horizontal
horizontally
hormone
horn
horned
hornet
hornpipe
horoscope
horrendous
horrible
horribly
horrid
horrific
horrifically
horrify
  horrified
  horrifies
  horrifying
horror
hors d'oeuvre
  hors d'oeuvres *pl*
horse (animal)

horseback
horsehair
horsepower
horseradish
horseshoe
horsewhip
  horsewhipped
  horsewhipping
  horsewhips
horsy
horticultural
horticulture
horticulturist
hosanna
  hosannas *pl*
hose
  hosed
  hosing
hosiery
hospice
hospitable
hospitably
hospital
hospitality
hospitalization
hospitalize
  hospitalized
  hospitalizing
host
  hosted
  hosting

hostage
hostel
hostelry
  hostelries *pl*
hostess
hostile
hostilely
hostility
  hostilities *pl*
hostler
hot
  hotter
  hottest
hotchpot, hotchpotch
hotel
hotelier
hotheaded
hotly
hound
hour (tie)
houri
  houris *pl*
hourly
house
  housed
  housing
housebreaker
houseful
household
householder
housekeeper

housekeeping
housemaster
housewife
  housewives *pl*
housework
hove
hovel
hover
  hovered
  hovering
hovercraft
how
however
howitzer
howl
howler
howsoever
hoyden
hub
hubbub
huddle
  huddled
  huddling
hue (color; outcry)
huff
huffily
huffy
hug
  hugged
  hugging
  hugs

huge
hugely
Huguenot
hulk
hulking
hull
hullabaloo
  hullabaloos *pl*
hullo, hallo, hello
hum
  hummed
  humming
  hums
human
humane (kind)
humanely
humaneness
humanism
humanist
humanistic
humanitarian
humanitarianism
humanity
  humanities *pl*
humanly
humble
humbleness
humbly
humbug
humdrum
humeral

humerus (arm-bone)
humid
humidifier
humidify
  humidified
  humidifies
  humidifying
humidity
humiliate
  humiliated
  humiliating
humiliation
humility
hummingbird
hummock (mound)
humor
  humored
  humoring
humoresque
humorist
humorous
humorously
hump
humpback
humus (of soil)
hunch
hunchback
hundred
hundredfold
hundredth
hundredweight

hung (*from* hang)
hunger
  hungered
  hungering
hungrily
hungry
  hungrier
  hungriest
hunk
hunt
hunter
huntress
huntsman
  huntsmen *pl*
hurdle
  hurdled
  hurdling
hurdy-gurdy
  hurdy-gurdies *pl*
hurl
  hurled
  hurling
hurly-burly
hurrah, hurray
hurricane
hurriedly
hurry
  hurried
  hurries
  hurrying
hurt

hurtle
  hurtled
  hurtling
husband
husbandry
hush
husk
huskily
huskiness
husky
  huskies *pl*
hussar
hussy
  hussies *pl*
hustings
hustle
  hustled
  hustling
hustler
hut
hutch
hutment
hyacinth
hybrid
hydra
  hydras *pl*
hydrangea
  hydrangeas *pl*
hydrant
hydrate
  hydrated

hydrating
hydration
hydraulic
hydraulically
hydrocarbon
hydrocephalic
hydrocephalus
hydrochloric
hydrodynamic
hydroelectric
hydrofoil
hydrogen
hydrology
hydrolysis
hydrolytic
hydrometer
hydrometric
hydrometry
hydropath
hydropathic
hydrophobia
hydroplane
hydroponics
hydrostatic
hydrotherapeutic
hydrotherapy
hydroxide
hyena, hyaena
  hyenas, hyaenas *pl*
hygiene
hygienic

hygienically
hygienist
hygrometer
hygrometric
hygroscope
hygroscopic
hymen
hymeneal
hymn (song)
hymnal
hype
  hyped
  hyping
hyperbola (curve)
  hyperbolas *pl*
hyperbole
  (exaggeration)
hyperbolic
hyperbolical
hypercritical (over-
  critical)
hyperglycemia
  (excess sugar)
hypermarket
hypersensitive
hypertension
hypertensive
hyperthyroidism
hyphen
hyphenated
hypnosis

hypnotic
hypnotism
hypnotist
hypnotize
  hypnotized
  hypnotizing
hypoallergenic
hypochondria
hypochondriac
hypocrisy
hypocrite
hypocritical
hypocritically
hypodermic
hypodermically
hypoglycemia
  (sugar deficiency)
hypoglycemic
hypotenuse
hypothermia
hypothesis
  hypotheses *pl*
hypothetical
hypothetically
hysterectomy
  hysterectomies *pl*
hysteresis
hysteria
hysterical
hysterically
hysterics

I
ibex
  ibexes *pl*
ibis
  ibises *pl*
ice
  iced
  icing
iceberg
ice cap
icebreaker
ice cream
ice hockey
ichthyologist
ichthyology
icicle
icing
icily

icon
iconoclasm
iconoclast
icy
  icier
  iciest
I'd (I would)
idea
  ideas *pl*
idealism
idealist
idealization
idealize
  idealized
  idealizing
ideally
idée fixe
idem

identical
identically
identifiable
identification
identify
  identified
  identifies
  identifying
identity
  identities *pl*
ideological
ideologically
ideology
  ideologies *pl*
idiocy
idiom
idiomatic
idiomatically
idiosyncrasy
  idiosyncrasies *pl*
idiosyncratic
idiosyncratically
idiot
idiotic
idiotically
idle (lazy)
  idled
  idling
idleness
idler
idly

idol (image)

idolater

idolatrous

idolatry

idolization

idolize

  idolized

  idolizing

idyll (poem)

idyllic

igloo

  igloos pl

igneous

ignitable

ignite

  ignited

  igniting

igniter

ignition

ignoble

ignobly

ignominious

ignominiously

ignominy

  ignominies pl

ignoramus

  ignoramuses pl

ignorance

ignorant

ignorantly

ignore

  ignored

  ignoring

I'll (I will)

ilk

ill

ill-advised

ill-assorted

ill-bred

ill defined

illegal

illegality

  illegalities pl

illegally

illegibility

illegible

illegibly

illegitimacy

illegitimate

illegitimately

ill-fated

ill-gotten

illicit (unlawful)

illicitly

illimitable

illiteracy

illiterate

(ill-mannered)

illness

illogical

illogicality

illogicalities pl

illogically

ill-treated

illuminate

  illuminated

  illuminating

illumination

illusion (apparence)

illusionist

illusive

illusory

illustrate

  illustrated

  illustrating

illustration

illustrative

illustrator

illustrious

illustriously

illustriousness

I'm (I am)

image

imagery

imaginable

imaginary

imagination

imaginative

imaginatively

imagine

  imagined

  imagining

imam
imbalance
imbecile
imbecility
imbibe
  imbibed
  imbibing
imbroglio
  imbroglios *pl*
imbue
  imbued
  imbuing
imitate
  imitated
  imitating
imitation
imitative
imitator
immaculacy
immaculate
immaculately
immanence
immanency
immanent (inherent)
immaterial
immaterially
immature
immaturely
immaturity
immeasurable
immeasurably

immediacy
immediate
immediately
immemorial
immense
immensely
immensity
immerse
  immersed
  immersing
immersion
immigrant
immigrate (to come as
  settler)
  immigrated
  immigrating
immigration
immigrator
imminence
imminent (happening
  soon)
imminently
immiscible
immobile
immobility
immobilization
immobilize
  immobilized
  immobilizing
immoderate
immoderately

immodest
immodestly
immodesty
immoral
immorality
immorally
immortal
immortality
immortalization
immortalize
  immortalized
  immortalizing
immortally
immovable
immovably
immune
immunity
immunization
immunize
  immunized
  immunizing
immunodeficiency
immunology
immure
  immured
  immuring
immutability
immutable
immutably
imp
impact

impair
  impaired
  impairing
impairment
impale
  impaled
  impaling
impalpable
impalpably
impart
impartial
impartiality
impartially
impassable (*eg* road)
impasse
impassioned
impassive
impassively
impassivity
impatience
impatient
impatiently
impeach
impeachable
impeachment
impeccability
impeccable
impeccably
impecuniosity
impecunious
impedance

impede
  impeded
  impeding
impediment
impedimenta
impel
  impelled
  impelling
  impels
impeller
impend
impending
impenetrability
impenetrable
impenitence
impenitent
impenitently
imperative
imperatively
imperceptible
imperceptibly
imperfect
imperfection
imperfectly
imperial
imperialism
imperialist
imperialistic
imperil
  imperils
  imperiled

  imperiling
imperilment
imperious
imperiously
imperiousness
imperishable
imperishably
impermeability
impermeable
impermissible
impersonal
impersonally
impersonate
  impersonated
  impersonating
impersonation
impersonator
impertinence
impertinent
impertinently
imperturbability
imperturbable
imperturbably
impervious
imperviousness
impetigo
impetuosity
impetuous
impetuously
impetus
  impetuses *pl*

impiety
impinge
  impinged
  impinging
impingement
impious
impish
impishly
impishness
implacability
implacable
implacably
implant
implantation
implausibility
implausible
implausibly
implement
implementation
implicate
  implicated
  implicating
implication
implicit
implicitly
implode
  imploded
  imploding
implore
  implored
  imploring

implosion
implosive
imply
  implied
  implies
  implying
impolite
impolitely
impoliteness
impolitic
impoliticly
imponderability
imponderable
import
  imported
  importing
importance
important
importantly
importation
importunate
importunately
importune
  importuned
  importuning
importunity
impose
  imposed
  imposing
imposition
impossibility

impossible
impossibly
impost
impostor
imposture
impotence
impotent
impotently
impound
impoverish
impoverishment
impracticability
impracticable
impracticably
impractical
imprecate
  imprecated
  imprecating
imprecation
imprecise
imprecisely
imprecision
impregnability
impregnable
impregnably
impregnate
  impregnated
  impregnating
impregnation
impresario
  impresarios *pl*

impress
impressed
impression
impressionable
impressionism
impressive
impressively
impressiveness
imprest (money
  advanced)
imprimatur
imprint
imprison
imprisonment
improbability
improbable
improbably
impromptu
improper
improperly
impropriety
  improprieties *pl*
improvable
improve
  improved
  improving
improvement
improver
improvidence
improvident
improvidently

improvisation
improvise
  improvised
  improvising
improviser
imprudence
imprudent
imprudently
impugn
  impugned
  impugning
impulse
impulsive
impulsively
impunity
impure
impurity
  impurities *pl*
imputable
imputation
impute
  imputed
  imputing
inability
in absentia
inaccessibility
inaccessible
inaccuracy
  inaccuracies *pl*
inaccurate
inaccurately

inaction
inactive
inactively
inactivity
inadequacy
  inadequacies *pl*
inadequate
inadequately
inadmissibility
inadmissible
inadmissibly
inadvertence
inadvertent
inadvertently
inadvisability
inadvisable
inadvisably
inalienability
inalienable
inane
inanely
inanimate
inanity
  inanities *pl*
inapplicable
inappreciable
inappreciably
inappropriate
inappropriately
inappropriateness
inapt

inaptitude
inaptly
inaptness
inarticulate
inarticulately
inarticulateness
inartistic
inartistically
inasmuch
inattention
inattentive
inattentively
inaudibility
inaudible
inaudibly
inaugural
inaugurate
  inaugurated
  inaugurating
inauguration
inaugurator
inauguratory
inauspicious
inauspiciously
inborn
inbreed
  inbred
  inbreeding
  inbreeds
incalculability
incalculable

incalculably
incandescence
incandescent
incantation
incapability
incapable
incapably
incapacitate
  incapacitated
  incapacitating
incapacitation
incapacity
incarcerate
  incarcerated
  incarcerating
incarceration
incarnate
incarnation
incautious
incautiously
incendiarism
incendiary
  incendiaries pl
incense (perfume; to
  anger)
  incensed
  incensing
incentive
inception
incertitude
incessant

incessantly
incest
incestuous
incestuously
inch
incidence
incident
incidental
incidentally
incinerate
  incinerated
  incinerating
incineration
incinerator
incipient
incise
incision
incisive
incisively
incisor
incitation
incite (to urge)
  incited
  inciting
incitement
inciter
incivility
  incivilities pl
inclemency
  inclemencies eg
inclement

inclemently
inclination
incline
  inclined
  inclining
include
  included
  including
inclusion
inclusive
inclusively
incognito
incoherence
incoherent
incoherently
incombustibility
incombustible
income
incomer
incoming
incommensurable
incommensurate
incommode
  incommoded
  incommoding
incommodious
incommunicado
incomparable
incomparably
incompatibility
incompatible

incompetence
incompetent
incompetently
incomplete
incompletely
incompleteness
incomprehensibility
incomprehensible
incomprehensibly
incompressibility
incompressible
inconceivable
inconceivably
inconclusive
inconclusively
incongruity
  incongruities *pl*
incongruous
incongruously
inconsequent
inconsequential
inconsequently
inconsiderable
inconsiderably
inconsiderate
inconsiderately
inconsistency
  inconsistencies *pl*
inconsistent
inconsistently
inconsolable

inconspicuous
inconspicuously
inconspicuousness
inconstancy
inconstant
incontestable
incontestably
incontinence
incontinent
incontrovertible
incontrovertibly
inconvenience
inconvenient
inconveniently
inconvertibility
inconvertible
incorporate
  incorporated
  incorporating
incorporation
incorrect
incorrectly
incorrectness
incorrigibility
incorrigible
incorrigibly
incorruptibility
incorruptible
increase
  increased
  increasing

increasingly
incredibility
incredible
incredibly
incredulity
incredulous
increment
incriminate
  incriminated
  incriminating
incrimination
incriminatory
incubate
  incubated
  incubating
incubation
incubator
incubus
  incubuses, incubi *pl*
inculcate
  inculcated
  inculcating
inculcation
inculpate
  inculpated
  inculpating
inculpation
incumbency
  incumbencies *pl*
incumbent
incur

incurred
incurring
incurs
incurability
incurable
incurably
incurious
incursion
incursive
indebted
indebtedness
indecency
  indecencies *pl*
indecent
indecently
indecipherable
indecision
indecisive
indecisively
indeclinable
indecorous
indecorously
indecorousness
indecorum
indeed
indefatigability
indefatigable
indefatigably
indefensible
indefensibly
indefinable

indefinite
indefinitely
indelible
indelibly
indelicacy
  indelicacies *pl*
indelicate
indelicately
indemnification
indemnify
  indemnified
  indemnifies
  indemnifying
indemnity
  indemnities *pl*
indent
indentation
indented
indenture
independence
independent
independently
indescribable
indescribably
indestructibility
indestructible
indestructibly
indeterminable
indeterminate
indeterminately
index

indexes, indices *pl*
indexation
indicate
  indicated
  indicating
indication
indicative
indicator
indict (to accuse)
indictable
indictment
indifference
indifferent
indifferently
indigence
indigenous
indigent
indigestibility
indigestible
indigestion
indignant
indignantly
indignation
indignity
  indignities *pl*
indigo
indirect
indirectly
indiscernible
indiscipline
indiscreet

indiscreetly
indiscretion
indiscriminate
indiscriminately
indispensability
indispensable
indispensably
indisposed
indisposition
indisputable
indisputably
indistinct
indistinguishable
indite (to write)
  indited
  inditing
individual
individualism
individualist
individualistic
individuality
individualization
individualize
  individualized
  individualizing
individually
indivisible
indivisibility
indivisibly
indoctrinate
  indoctrinated

indoctrinating
indoctrination
indolence
indolent
indolently
indomitable
indomitably
indoor
indoors
indubitable
indubitably
induce
  induced
  inducing
inducement
induct
inductance
induction
inductive
inductively
indulge
  indulged
  indulging
indulgence
indulgent
indulgently
industrial
industrialist
industrialization
industrialize
  industrialized

industrializing
industrially
industrious
industriously
industry
  industries *pl*
inebriated
inebriation
inedibility
inedible
ineducable
ineffable
ineffably
ineffective
ineffectively
ineffectiveness
ineffectual
ineffectually
inefficiency
  inefficiencies *pl*
inefficient
inefficiently
inelastic
inelastically
inelasticity
inelegancy
inelegant
inelegantly
ineligibility
ineligible
inept

ineptitude
ineptly
inequality
  inequalities *pl*
inequitable
inequitably
ineradicable
ineradicably
inert
inertia
inertly
inertness
inescapable
inescapably
inessential
inestimable
inestimably
inevitability
inevitable
inevitably
inexact
inexactitude
inexcusable
inexcusably
inexhaustible
inexhaustibly
inexorable
inexorably
inexpediency
inexpedient
inexpediently

inexpensive
inexpensively
inexperience
inexplicable
inexplicably
inexpressible
inexpressibly
inextinguishable
inextricable
inextricably
infallibility
infallible
infallibly
infamous
infamously
infamy
infancy
infant
infanticide
infantile
infantry
infantryman
  infantrymen *pl*
infatuated
infatuation
infect
  infected
  infecting
infection
infectious
infectiousness

infelicitous
infelicitously
infelicity
  infelicities *pl*
infer
  inferred
  inferring
  infers
inference
inferential
inferior
inferiority
infernal
infernally
inferno
  infernos *pl*
infertile
infertility
infest
infestation
infidel
infidelity
  infidelities *pl*
infighting
infiltrate
  infiltrated
  infiltrating
infiltration
infiltrator
infinite
infinitely

infinitesimal
infinitesimally
infinitival
infinitive
infinitude
infinity
infirm
infirmary
  infirmaries *pl*
infirmity
  infirmities *pl*
inflame
  inflamed
  inflaming
inflammable
inflammation
inflammatory
inflatable
inflate
  inflated
  inflating
inflation
inflationary
inflect
inflection
inflexibility
inflexible
inflexibly
inflexion
inflict
infliction

influence
  influenced
  influencing
influential
influentially
influenza
influx
  influxes *pl*
inform
  informed
  informing
informal
informality
informally
informant
information
informative
informer
infra dig
infraction
infrared
infrastructure
infrequency
infrequent
infrequently
infringe
  infringed
  infringing
infringement
infuriate
  infuriated

infuriating
infuse
  infused
  infusing
infusion
ingenious (clever)
ingeniously
ingénue
ingenuity
ingenuous (naive)
ingenuously
ingenuousness
ingest
ingestion
inglorious
ingloriously
ingoing
ingot
ingrain
  ingrained
  ingraining
ingratiate
  ingratiated
  ingratiating
ingratitude
ingredient
ingress
ingrowing
ingrown
inhabit
  inhabited

inhabiting
inhabitable
inhabitant
inhalant
inhalation
inhale
  inhaled
  inhaling
inherence
inherent
inheritance
inheritor
inhibit
  inhibited
  inhibiting
inhibition
inhibitory
inhospitable
inhospitably
inhuman (barbarous)
inhumane (cruel)
inhumanely
inhumanity
  inhumanities pl
inhumanly
inimical
inimitable
inimitably
iniquitous
iniquitously
iniquity

iniquities pl
initial
  initials
  initialed
  initialing
initially
initiate
  initiated
  initiating
initiation
initiative
initiator
inject
injection
injudicious
injudiciously
injunction
injure
  injured
  injuring
injurious
injuriously
injury
  injuries pl
injustice
ink
inkling
inky
  inkier
  inkiest
inlaid

inland
in-law
inlay
  inlaid
  inlaying
  inlays
inlet
inmate
in memoriam
inmost
inn (hostelry)
innards
innate
innately
inner
innermost
innings
innkeeper
innocence
innocent
innocently
innocuous
innocuously
innovate
  innovated
  innovating
innovation
innovator
innuendo
  innuendoes,
  innuendos *pl*

innumerable
innumerably
inoculate
  inoculated
  inoculating
inoculation
inoffensive
inoffensively
inoffensiveness
inoperable
inoperative
inoperativeness
inopportune
inopportunely
inordinate
inordinately
inorganic
input
  inputs
  inputted
  inputting
inquest
inquire (to
  investigate)
  inquired
  inquiring
inquiry (investigation)
  inquiries *pl*
inquisition
inquisitive
inquisitively

inquisitiveness
inquisitor
inquisitorial
inroad
inrush
insalubrious
insalubrity
insane
insanely
insanitariness
insanitary
insanity
insatiable
insatiably
inscribe
  inscribed
  inscribing
inscription
inscrutability
inscrutable
inscrutably
insect
insecticide
insecure
insecurely
insecurity
inseminate
  inseminated
  inseminating
insemination
insensate

insensibility
insensible
insensibly
insensitive
insensitively
insensitivity
inseparable
inseparably
insert
insertion
inset
  insets
  insetting
inshore
inside
insider
insidious
insidiously
insidiousness
insight
  (understanding)
insignia
insignificance
insignificant
insignificantly
insincere
insincerely
insincerity
insinuate
  insinuated
  insinuating

insinuation
insinuator
insipid
insipidly
insipidness
insist
insistence
insistent
insistently
insobriety
insolence
insolent
insolently
insolubility
insoluble
insolubly
insolvency
insolvent
insomnia
insomniac
insouciance
insouciant
inspect
inspection
inspector
inspectorate
inspiration
inspire
  inspired
  inspiring
instability

install
installation
installment
instance
instant
instantaneous
instantaneously
instantly
instead
instep
instigate
  instigated
  instigating
instigation
instigator
instill
  instilled
  instilling
  instills
instinct
instinctive
instinctively
institute
  instituted
  instituting
institution
institutional
institutionalize
  institutionalized
  institutionalizing
instruct

instruction
instructional
instructive
instructor
instrument
instrumental
instrumentalist
instrumentality
instrumentation
insubordinate
insubordinately
insubordination
insubstantial
insufferable
insufferably
insufficiency
insufficient
insufficiently
insular
insularity
insulate
  insulated
  insulating
insulation
insulator
insulin
insult
insuperable
insuperably
insupportable
insurability

insurable
insurance
insure (protect
  financially)
  insured
  insuring
insurer
insurgence
insurgency
insurgent
insurmountable
insurmountably
insurrection
insurrectionary
intact
intake
intangible
intangibly
integer
integral
integrally
integrate
  integrated
  integrating
integration
integrity
intellect
intellectual
intellectualism
intellectualize
  intellectualized

  intellectualizing
intellectually
intelligence
intelligent
intelligently
intelligentsia
  intelligentsias pl
intelligible
intelligibly
intemperance
intemperate
intemperately
intend
intense
intensely
intensification
intensify
  intensified
  intensifies
  intensifying
intensity
  intensities pl
intensive
intensively
intent (purpose;
  earnest)
intention
intentional
intentionally
intently
inter (bury)

interred
interring
inters
inter alia
interact
interaction
interbreed
interbred
interbreeding
interbreeds
intercalary
intercalate (to insert)
intercalated
intercalating
intercalation
intercede
interceded
interceding
intercept
interception
interceptor
intercession
interchange
interchanged
interchanging
interchangeable
intercommunicate
intercommunicated
intercommunicating
intercommunication
interconnect

interconnection
intercontinental
intercourse
interdenominational
interdepartmental
interdependence
interdependent
interdependently
interdict
interdiction
interdisciplinary
interest
interested
interesting
interface
interfaced
interfacing
interfere
interfered
interfering
interference
interim
interior
interiorly
interject
interjection
interlace
interlaced
interlacing
interleave
interleaved

interleaving
interline
interlined
interlining
interlock
interlope
interloped
interloping
interloper
interlude
intermarriage
intermarry
intermarried
intermarries
intermarrying
intermediary
intermediaries *pl*
intermediate
intermediately
interment (burial)
intermezzo
intermezzos,
intermezzi *pl*
interminable
interminably
intermingle
intermingled
intermingling
intermission
intermittent
intermittently

intern (to confine)
  interned
  interning
intern, interne
  (doctor)
internal
internally
international
internationalism
internationalization
internationalize
  internationalized
  internationalizing
internationally
internecine
internee
Internet
internment
  (confinement)
interpellate (to ask
  questions)
  interpellated
  interpellating
interpellation
  (interrogation)
interplanetary
interpolate (to insert)
  interpolated
  interpolating
interpolation
  (insertion)

interpose
  interposed
  interposing
interposition
interpret
  interpreted
  interpreting
interpretation
interpreter
interracial
interregnum
  interregnums,
    interregna *pl*
interrelate
  interrelated
  interrelating
interrelation
interrogate
  interrogated
  interrogating
interrogation
interrogative
interrogator
interrupt
  interrupted
  interrupting
interrupter
interruption
intersect
  intersected
  intersecting

intersection
intersperse
  interspersed
  interspersing
interspersion
interstellar
interstice
interstitial
interval
intervene
  intervened
  intervening
intervention
interview
  interviewed
  interviewing
interviewee
interviewer
interweave
  interweaves
  interweaving
  interwove
  interwoven
intestacy
intestate
intestinal
intestine
intimacy
intimate
  intimated
  intimating

intimately
intimation
intimidate
  intimidated
  intimidating
intimidation
intolerable
intolerably
intolerance
intolerant
intolerantly
intonation
intone
  intoned
  intoning
intoxicant
intoxicate
  intoxicated
  intoxicating
intoxication
intractability
intractable
intractably
intramuscular
intransigence
intransigent
intransigently
intransitive
intrauterine
intravenous
intrepid

intrepidity
intrepidly
intricacy
  intricacies *pl*
intricate
intricately
intrigue
  intrigued
  intriguing
intrinsic
intrinsically
introduce
  introduced
  introducing
introduction
introductory
introspection
introspective
introversion
introvert
intrude
  intruded
  intruding
intruder
intrusion
intrusive
intuition
intuitive
intuitively
inundate
  inundated

  inundating
inundation
inure
  inured
  inuring
invade
  invaded
  invading
invader
invalid
invalidate
  invalidated
  invalidating
invalidation
invalidism
invaluable (precious)
invariable
invariably
invasion
invective
inveigh (to abuse)
  inveighed
  inveighing
inveigle (to entice)
  inveigled
  inveigling
invent
  invented
  inventing
invention
inventive

inventiveness
inventor
inventory
  inventories *pl*
inverse
inversely
inversion
invert
  inverted
  inverting
invertebrate
inverter
invest
  invested
  investing
investigate
  investigated
  investigating
investigation
investigator
investiture
investment
investor
inveteracy
inveterate
inveterately
invidious (causing
  offence)
invidiously
invidiousness
invigilate

invigilated
invigilating
invigilation
invigilator
invigorate
  invigorated
  invigorating
invigoration
invincibility
invincible
invincibly
inviolable (sacred)
inviolate (unbroken)
invisibility
invisible
invisibly
invitation
invite
  invited
  inviting
invocation
invoice
  invoiced
  invoicing
invoke
  invoked
  invoking
involuntarily
involuntary
involution
involve

involved
  involving
involvement
invulnerability
invulnerable
inward
inwardly
inwardness
inwards
iodide
iodine
ion (atom)
ionic
ionization
ionize
  ionized
  ionizing
ionosphere
iota
  iotas *pl*
ipeca, ipecacuanha
  ipecacuanhas *pl*
ipso facto
irascibility
irascible
irascibly
irate
irately
ire (anger)
ireful
iridescence

iridescent
iris
  irises *pl*
irk
  irked
  irking
irksome
iron (metal)
ironic
ironical
ironically
ironmonger
ironmongery
irony
  ironies *pl*
irradiate
  irradiated
  irradiating
irradiation
irrational
irrationality
irrationally
irreconcilability
irreconcilable
irreconcilably
irrecoverable
irrecoverably
irredeemable
irredeemably
irreducible
irreducibly

irrefutable
irrefutably
irregular
irregularity
  irregularities *pl*
irregularly
irrelevance
irrelevant
irrelevantly
irreligious
irremediable
irremediably
irremissible
irremovable
irremovably
irreparable
irreparably
irreplaceable
irrepressible
irrepressibly
irreproachable
irreproachably
irresistible
irresistibly
irresolute
irresolutely
irrespective
irrespectively
irresponsibility
irresponsible
irresponsibly

irretrievable
irretrievably
irreverence
irreverent
irreverently
irreversibility
irreversible
irreversibly
irrevocability
irrevocable
irrevocably
irrigate
  irrigated
  irrigating
irrigation
irrigator
irritability
irritable
irritably
irritant
irritate
  irritated
  irritating
irritation
irrupt (to break in)
  irrupted
  irrupting
irruption
irruptive
isinglass
island

islander

isle (island)

islet

isn't (is not)

isobar

isochronous

isolate

  isolated

  isolating

isolation

isometric

isometrically

isosceles

isotherm

isothermal

isotope

issuance

issue

  issued

  issuing

isthmus

  isthmuses, isthmi *pl*

italic

italicize

  italicized

  italicizing

itch

  itched

  itching

itchy

  itchier

  itchiest

item

itemize

  itemized

  itemizing

iterate

  iterated

  iterating

iteration

iterative

itinerant

itinerary

  itineraries *pl*

it's (it is)

its

itself

I've (I have)

ivory

  ivories *pl*

ivy

  ivies *pl*

J

jab
  jabbed
  jabbing
  jabs
jabber
  jabbered
  jabbering
jack
jackal
jackanapes
jackass
jackdaw
jacket
jackhammer
jack-in-the-box

jack-in-the-boxes *pl*
jackknife
  jackknives *pl*
  jackknifed
  jackknifes
  jackknifing
jackpot
Jacobean (of James I's
  time)
Jacobin (French
  revolutionary)
Jacobinic
Jacobinical
Jacobite (loyal to
  James II)

jade
  jaded
  jading
jag
jagged
jaguar
jail
  jailed
  jailing
  jailer, jailor
jalopy
  jalopies *pl*
jam (preserve; to stick)
  jammed
  jamming
  jams
jamb (of door)
jamboree
jammy
  jammier
  jammiest
jangle
  jangled
  jangling
janitor
japan (to varnish)
  japanned
  japanning
  japans
japonica
  japonicas *pl*

jar
jarred
jarring
jars
jargon
jasmine, jasmin
jasper
jaundice
jaundiced
jaunt
jauntily
jauntiness
jaunty
jauntier
jauntiest
javelin
jaw
jawbone
jay
jays *pl*
jaywalk
jaywalked
jaywalking
jaywalker
jazz
jazzy
jazzier
jazziest
jealous
jealously
jealousy

jeans (trousers)
jeep
jeer
jeered
jeering
jejune
jellied
jelly
jellies *pl*
jeopardize
jeopardized
jeopardizing
jeopardy
jerk
jerkily
jerkin
jerkiness
jerky
jerkier
jerkiest
jeroboam
jerry-builder
jerry-building
jerry-built
jersey
jerseys *pl*
jest
jester
jet
jets
jetted

jetting
jet-propelled
jetsam
jettison
jettisoned
jettisoning
jetty
jetties *pl*
Jew
jewel (cut gem)
jeweled
jeweler
jewelry
Jewish
Jewry
jib
jibbed
jibbing
jibs
jibe
jibed
jibing
jiffy
jiffies *pl*
jig
jiggered
jigsaw
jilt
jilted
jilting
jingle

jingled
jingling
jingo
  jingoes *pl*
jingoism
jinx
  jinxes *pl*
jitters
jittery
jive
  jived
  jiving
job
jobber
jobbing
jobless
jockey
  jockeys *pl*
jocose (playful)
jocosely
jocosity
jocular
jocularity
jocularly
jocund
jocundity
jocundly
jodhpurs
joey
  joeys *pl*
jog

jogged
jogging
jogs
joggle
  joggled
  joggling
joie de vivre
join
  joined
  joining
joiner
joinery
joint
jointer
jointly
jointure
joist
joke
  joked
  joking
joker
jokingly
jollification
jollify
  jollified
  jollifies
  jollifying
jollily
jollity
jolly
  jollier

jolliest
jolt
  jolted
  jolting
jonquil
jostle
  jostled
  jostling
jot
  jots
  jotted
  jotting
joule (unit of energy)
journal
journalism
journalist
journey
  journeys *pl*
  journeyed
  journeying
  journeys
jovial
joviality
jovially
jowl
joy
  joys *pl*
joyful
joyfully
joyless
joyous

joyously

joyride

joyriding

jubilant

jubilantly

jubilation

jubilee

Judaism

judge

 judged

 judging

judgment, judgement

judicature

judicial

judicially

judiciary

 judiciaries pl

judicious

judiciously

judo

jug

 jugged

 jugging

 jugs

juggernaut

juggle

 juggled

 juggling

juggler

jugular

juice

juiced

juicing

juicily

juiciness

juicy

 juicier

 juiciest

jukebox

julep

julienne

jumble

 jumbled

 jumbling

jumbo

jump

 jumped

 jumping

jumper

jumpiness

jumpy

 jumpier

 jumpiest

junction

juncture

jungle

junior

juniper

junk

junket

 junketed

 junketing

junta

 juntas pl

juridical

jurisdiction

jurisdictional

jurisprudence

jurisprudent

jurist

juror

jury

 juries pl

just

justice

justifiable

justifiably

justification

justify

 justified

 justifies

 justifying

justly

jut

 juts

 jutted

 jutting

jute

juvenile

juxtapose

 juxtaposed

 juxtaposing

juxtaposition

kale (cabbage)
kaleidoscope
kaleidoscopic
kalends, calends
kamikaze
kangaroo
 kangaroos *pl*
kaolin
kapok
karate
kayak
kebab
kedgeree
keel
keen
 keener
 keenest
keenly

keenness
keep
 keeping
 keeps
 kept
keeper
keepsake
keg
kelp
kempt
ken
kennel
 kennels
 kenneled
 kenneling
kerchief
 kerchiefs *pl*
kernel (center)

kerosene, kerosine
kestrel
ketch
ketchup
kettle
kettledrum
key (lock)
 keys *pl*
 keyed
 keying
keyboard
keyhole
keynote
khaki
khan (Oriental title)
kibbutz
 kibbutzim *pl*
kibbutznik
kibosh
kick
kickoff
kid
 kidded
 kidding
 kids
kidnap
 kidnapped
 kidnapping
 kidnaps
 kidnapper
kidney

kidneys *pl*

kids

kill

killer

kiln

kilo

  kilos *pl*

kilocycle

kilogram

kilohertz

kiloliter

kilometer

kiloton

kilotonne (metric)

kilowatt

kilt

kimono

  kimonos *pl*

kin

kind

kindergarten

  kindergartens *pl*

kindhearted

kindle

  kindled

  kindling

kindliness

kindly

kindness

kindred

kinetic

king

kingdom

kink

kinky

kinsfolk

kinship

kinsman

  kinsmen *pl*

kinswoman

  kinswomen *pl*

kiosk

kipper

kippered

kiss

kit

  kits

  kitted

  kitting

kitchen

kitchenette

kite

kith

kitten

kittenish

kitty (fund of money)

kleptomania

kleptomaniac

knack

knapsack

knave

knavery

knavish

knead (to mix dough)

knee

  kneed

  kneeing

kneecap

kneel

  kneeled

  kneeling

knell (sound of bell)

knelt

knew (from know)

knickerbockers

knickers

knickknack

knife

  knives *pl*

  knifed

  knifes

  knifing

knight (chivalric)

  knighted

  knighting

knight-errant

knight-errantry

knighthood

knightly (chivalrous)

knit (handicraft)

  knits

  knitted

  knitting

knitter
knob (*eg* on a door)
knobby
knock
knocker
knock-kneed
knoll (small hill)
knot (*eg* in string
  knots
  knotted
  knotting
knout (to flog)
  knouted
  knouting
know (have the
  knowledge)
  knew
  knowing
  known
  knows
know-how (expertise)
knowledge
knowledgeable
knowledgeably
knuckle
  knuckled
  knuckling
koala
  koalas *pl*
koala bear
kohlrabi

kookaburra
Koran
kosher
kowtow
Krishna
krona (Swedish
  money)
  kronor *pl*
krone (currency)
  kroner *pl*
kudos
kumquat
kung-fu

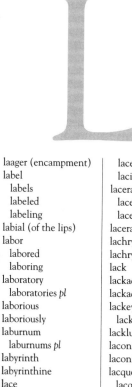

laager (encampment)
label
  labels
  labeled
  labeling
labial (of the lips)
labor
  labored
  laboring
laboratory
  laboratories *pl*
laborious
laboriously
laburnum
  laburnums *pl*
labyrinth
labyrinthine
lace

laced
lacing
lacerate (to tear)
  lacerated
  lacerating
laceration
lachrymal
lachrymose
lack
lackadaisical
lackadaisically
lackey
  lackeys *pl*
lackluster
laconic
laconically
lacquer (varnish)
  lacquered

  lacquering
lacrosse
lactation
lactic
lad
ladder
laddie
laden
lading
ladle
  ladled
  ladling
lady
  ladies *pl*
ladylike
ladyship
lag
  lagged
  lagging
  lags
lager (beer)
laggard
lagoon
laid (*from* lay)
lain (*from* lie)
lair (den)
laird
laissez-faire
laity
lake
lama (priest)

lamb (young sheep)
lambast, lambaste
  lambasted
  lambasting
  lambasts, lambastes
lambda
  lambdas pl
lambent
lambskin
lame
lamely
lameness
lament
lamentable
lamentably
lamentation
lamina
  laminae pl
laminated
lamination
lamp
lamplight
lampoon
  lampooned
  lampooning
lampooner
lamprey
  lampreys pl.)
lance
  lanced
  lancing

lancer (soldier)
lancers (dance)
lancet
land
landfall
landfill
landlady
  landladies pl
landlocked
landlord
landlubber
landmark
landowner
landscape
  landscaped
  landscaping
landslide
lane (track; road)
language
languid
languidly
languidness
languish
languor
languorous
lank
lankiness
lanky
  lankier
  lankiest
lanolin

lantern
lanyard
lap
  lapped
  lapping
  laps
lapdog
lapel
lapidary
  lapidaries pl
lapis lazuli
lapse
  lapsed
  lapsing
larboard
larceny
  larcenies pl
larch
lard
larder
large
largely
largess, largesse
larghetto
  larghettos pl
largish
largo
  largos pl
lark
larva
  larvae pl

larval
laryngeal
laryngitis
larynx
  larynges *pl*
lascivious
lasciviously
lasciviousness
lase (act as a laser)
  lased
  lasing
laser
lash
lass
lassie
lassitude
lasso
  lassos, lassoes *pl*
  lassoed
  lassoes
  lassoing
last
lastly
latch
latchkey
late
  later
  latest
lately
latency
latent

lateral
laterally
latex
lath (strip of wood)
lathe (machine)
lather
  lathered
  lathering
latitude
latrine
latter
latter-day
latterly
lattice
laud (to praise)
laudable
laudably
laudanum
laugh
laughable
laughing stock
laughter
launch
launched
launder
  laundered
  laundering
launderette
laundress *f*
laundry
  laundries *pl*

laureate
laurel
laurel wreath
lava (*from* volcano)
lavatory
  lavatories *pl*
lavender
laver (kind of
  seaweed)
lavish
lavishly
lavishness
law (rule)
law-abiding
lawful
lawfully
lawfulness
lawless
lawlessly
lawlessness
lawn
lawn-mower
lawsuit
lawyer
lax
laxative
laxity
laxly
lay
  laid
  laying

lays

layer
  layered
  layering

layette

layman
  laymen *pl*

layoff

laze
  lazed
  lazing

lazily

laziness

lazy
  lazier
  laziest

lea (meadow)

leach (filter)

lead (to go first;
    metal)
  leading
  leads
  led

leaded

leaden

leader

leadership

leaf (on tree)
  leaves *pl*
  leafed
  leafing

leafs

leafage

leafiness

leafless

leaflet

leafy
  leafier
  leafiest

league

leak (hole *pl* in pipe)

leakage

leaky
  leakier
  leakiest

lean
  leaned
  leaning
  leans
  leant

leaner

leanness

lean-to
  lean-tos *pl*

leap
  leaped
  leaping
  leapt

leapfrog
  leapfrogged
  leapfrogging
  leapfrogs

leapyear

learn
  learned
  learning
  learns
  learnt

lease
  leased
  leasing

leasehold

leash

least

leastways

leastwise

leather

leatherette

leathery

leave (to depart)
  leaves
  leaving
  left

leaven

leavened

lecher

lecherous

lechery

lectern

lecture
  lectured
  lecturing

lecturer

led (*from* lead)
ledge
ledger (book)
lee (shelter)
leech (worm)
leek (vegetable)
leer
  leered
  leering
leery
leeward
leeway
left
left wing
left-handed
leftward
left-winger
leg
  legged
  legging
  legs
legacy
  legacies *pl*
legal
legality
legalization
legalize
  legalized
  legalizing
legally
legate

legation
legato
  legatos *pl*
legend
legendary
leger (stand)
legerdemain
leggings
leggy
legibility
legible
legibly
legion
legionnaire
legionary
  legionaries *pl*
legislate
  legislated
  legislating
legislation
legislator (law maker)
legislature (legal
  assembly)
legitimacy
legitimate
legitimately
legitimation
legitimatize
  legitimatized
  legitimatizing
legitimize

legitimized
  legitimizing
legitimizing
legume
leguminous
Leicester
leisure
leisurely
leitmotiv, leitmotif
lemming
lemon
lemonade
lend
  lending
  lends
  lent
lender
length
lengthen
  lengthened
  lengthening
lengthily
lengthways
lengthwise
lengthy
lenience
leniency
lenient
leniently
lens
lent (*from* lend)

Lent
Lenten
lentil
leonine
leopard
leotard
leper
leprechaun
leprosy
leprous
lesbian
lèse-majesté
lesion
less
lessee
lessen (to reduce)
  lessened
  lessening
lesser
lesson (study)
lessor (granter of
  lease)
let
lethal
lethally
lethargic
lethargically
lethargy
let's (let us)
lettable
letter

  lettered
  lettering
letterhead
lettuce
leucocyte
leukemia
  leukemias pl
level
  levels
  leveled
  leveling
leveler
levelheaded
lever
  levered
  levering
leverage
leviathan
Levis (jeans)
levitate
  levitated
  levitating
levitation
levity (humor)
levy (payment)
  levies pl
  levied
  levies
  levying
lewd
lewdly

lewdness
lexicographer
lexicography
lexicon
liability
  liabilities pl
liable
liaison
liar (person who lies)
libation
libel
  libels
  libeled
  libeling
libeler
libelous
liberal
liberality
liberally
liberate
  liberated
  liberating
liberation
liberator
libertine (licentious
  person)
liberty
  liberties pl
libidinal
libidinous
libido

libidos *pl*
librarian
library
  libraries *pl*
libretto
  librettos, libretti *pl*
lice (*pl* of louse)
license (to grant
    permission;
    permission)
  licensed
  licensing
licensee
licenser
licentiate
licentious
licentiousness
lichen
lick
licorice
lid
lidded
lido
  lidos *pl*
lie (horizontal)
  lain
  lay
  lies
  lying
lie (to fib)
  lied

lies
  lying
lied (German song)
  lieder *pl*
lien (right to
    property)
lieu (instead of)
lieutenancy
lieutenant
life
  lives *pl*
life buoy
lifeguard
lifeless
lifelessly
lifelike
lifelong
life-size
life-sized
lift
liftoff
ligament
ligature
light
  lights
  lighted
  lighting
  lit
lighten
  lightened
  lightening

lighthearted
lightheartedly
lighthouse
lightly
lightness
lightning (in
    thunderstorm)
lightweight
lignite
like
  liked
  liking
likeable, likable
likelihood
likely
liken
  likened
  likening
likeness
likewise
lilac
lilliputian
lilt
lily
  lilies *pl*
lily-livered
limb
limber
  limbered
  limbering
limbless

limbo
  limbos *pl*
lime
limelight
limerick
limit
  limited
  limiting
limitation
limousine
limp
limpet
limpid
limpness
linchpin
linctus
  linctuses *pl*
line
  lined
  lining
lineage
lineal
lineament
linear
linearity
linen
liner
linger
  lingered
  lingering
lingerie

lingo
  lingoes *pl*
lingua franca
  lingua francas *pl*
lingual
linguist
linguistic
liniment
link
linkage
links (golf)
linnet
linocut
linoleum
linotype
linseed
lint
lintel
lion
lioness
  lionesses *pl*
lionhearted
lionization
lionize
  lionized
  lionizing
lip
lipped
lip-read
lip-reader
lipreading

lipstick
liquefaction
liquefy
  liquefied
  liquefies
  liquefying
liquescent
liqueur (strong, sweet
  alcohol)
liquid
liquidate
  liquidated
  liquidating
liquidation
liquidator
liquidity
liquidize
  liquidized
  liquidizing
liquor (liquid)
lira (Italian money)
  lire, liras *pl*
lisle
lisp
lissom, lissome (agile)
list
listen
  listened
  listening
listener
listeria

lit (*from* light)

litany
  litanies *pl*

litchi

liter

literacy

literal (exact)

literally

literary (learned)

literate

literature

lithe

lithograph

lithography

litigant

litigate
  litigated
  litigating

litigation

litigious

litmus

litmus paper

litter
  littered
  littering

little

littoral (near the sea)

liturgical

liturgy
  liturgies *pl*

livable

live
  lived
  living

livelihood

liveliness

lively
  livelier
  liveliest

liven (to cheer up)
  livened
  livening

liver

liverish

livery (costume)
  liveries *pl*

livestock

livid

lizard

llama (animal)

load

loaf
  loaves *pl*
  loafed
  loafing
  loafs

loafer

loam

loamy

loan
  loaned
  loaning

loath, loth
  (unwilling)

loathe (to hate)
  loathed
  loathing

loathsome

lob
  lobbed
  lobbing
  lobs

lobby
  lobbies *pl*
  lobbied
  lobbies
  lobbying

lobe (of the ear)

lobster

local (nearby)

locale (locality of
  events)

locality
  localities *pl*

localization

localize
  localized
  localizing

locally

locate
  located
  locating

location

locative (grammar)
loch (lake)
lock (hair, in door, on canal)
locker
locket
lockjaw
lockout
  lockouts *pl*
locksmith
locomotion
locomotive
locum tenens (substitute)
locus
  loci *pl*
locust
lode (of metal ore)
lodge
  lodged
  lodging
lodgement, lodgment
lodger
loft
loftily
loftiness
lofty
  loftier
  loftiest
log
  logged

  logging
  logs
loganberry
  loganberries *pl*
logarithm
logarithmic
logarithmically
logbook
loggerheads
loggia
  loggias *pl*
logic
logical
logically
logician
logistics
logo, logotype
loin
loiter
  loitered
  loitering
loiterer
loll
lollipop
lone
lonelier
loneliness
lonely
lonesome
long
longer

longevity
longitude
longitudinal
longitudinally
long-suffering
loofah
look
looker-on
  lookers-on *pl*
loom
  loomed
  looming
loop
  looped
  looping
loophole
loose
  loosed
  loosing
loose-leaf
loosely
loosen
  loosened
  loosening
looseness
loot (plunder)
looter
lop
  lopped
  lopping
  lops

lope (to run)
  loped
  loping
lopsided
loquacious
loquaciously
loquaciousness
loquacity
lord
lordship
lordly
lore (tradition)
lorgnette
lorry
  lorries *pl*
lose
  loses
  losing
  lost
loser
loss
lost
lot
loth, loath
  (unwilling)
lothario
  lotharios *pl*
lotion
lottery
  lotteries *pl*
lotus

lotuses *pl*
loud
loudly
loudmouthed
loudness
loudspeaker
lounge
  lounged
  lounging
louse
  lice *pl*
lousy
lout
loutish
louver
love
  loved
  loving
loveable, lovable
lovelier
loveliness
lovelorn
lovely
lover
low
  lowed
  lowing
lower
lower
  lowered
  lowering

lowliness
lowly
lowness
loyal
loyalism
loyalist
loyally
loyalty
  loyalties *pl*
lozenge
lubricant
lubricate
  lubricated
  lubricating
lubrication
lucid
lucidity
lucidly
luck
luckily
lucky
  luckier
  luckiest
lucrative
lucratively
lucre
ludicrous
ludicrously
ludicrousness
luff
lug

lugged

lugging

lugs

luggage

lugger

lugubrious

lugubriously

lukewarm

lull

lullaby

  lullabies *pl*

lumbago

lumbar (part of the
  body)

lumber (timber;
  rubbish)

lumberjack

lumberroom

lumen

luminary

  luminaries *pl*

luminescence

luminescent

luminosity

luminous

lump

lumpiness

lumpy

  lumpier

  lumpiest

lunacy

lunacies *pl*

lunar

lunatic

lunch

luncheon

lung

lunge

  lunged

  lunging

lungfish

lurch

lure

  lured

  luring

lurid

luridly

lurk

luscious

lusciousness

lush

lust

luster

lustful

lustily

lustiness

lustrous

lusty

  lustier

  lustiest

lute (musical
  instrument)

Lutheran

luxuriance

luxuriant

luxuriate

  luxuriated

  luxuriating

luxurious

luxuriously

luxury

  luxuries *pl*

lychee

lying (*from* lie)

lymph

lymphatic

lynx

  lynxes *pl*

lyre (harp)

lyric

lyrical

lyrically

lyricism

lyrics

ma'am (Madame)
macabre
macadam
macadamize
  macadamized
  macadamizing
macaroni
macaroon
macaw
mace
macerate
  macerated
  macerating
maceration
Mach (speed ratio)
machiavellian
machination
machine

machined
  machining
machinery
machinist
mackerel
mackintosh
macramé
macrobiotic
macrocosm
macroscopic
macula (spot on skin)
  maculae pl
mad
  madder
  maddest
madam
madame
  mesdames pl

madden
maddening
madder (plant or red
  dye)
madding
made (from make)
Madeira
mademoiselle
  mesdemoiselles pl
madly
madman
  madmen pl
madness
Madonna
madrigal
maelstrom
maestro
  maestros, maestri pl
Mafia
magazine
magenta
maggot
maggoty
magic
magical
magically
magician
magisterial
magisterially
magistracy
  magistracies pl

magistral

magistrate

magistrature

magnanimity

magnanimous

magnanimously

magnate (great man)

magnesia

magnesium

magnet

magnetic

magnetically

magnetism

magnetizable

magnetization

magnetize

  magnetized

  magnetizing

magneto

  magnetos *pl*

magnification

magnificence

magnificent

magnificently

magnifier

magnify

  magnified

  magnifies

  magnifying

magnitude

magnolia

  magnolias *pl*

magnum

  magnums *pl*

magnum opus

  magna opera *pl*

magpie

maharajah, maharaja

  maharajahs,

    maharajas *pl*

maharani, maharanee

  maharanis,

    maharanees *pl*

mah-jongg

mahogany

maid

maiden

maidenly

mail (letters; armor)

mailbox

maim

  maimed

  maiming

main (principal)

mainly

maintain

  maintained

  maintaining

maintenance

maisonette

maitre d'hotel

maize (corn)

majestic

majestically

majesty

  majesties *pl*

majolica

major

major domo

  major-domos *pl*

majority

  majorities *pl*

make

made

makes

making

make-up

maker

makeshift

makeweight

maladjusted

maladjustment

maladministration

maladroit

maladroitness

malady

  maladies *pl*

malaise

malapropism

malapropos

malaria

malcontent

male (masculine)

malediction
malefaction
malefactor
malevolence
malevolent
malformation
malfunction
malice
malice aforethought
malicious
maliciously
malign
  maligned
  maligning
malignancy
malignant (very bad)
maligner
malignity
malinger
  malingered
  malingering
malingerer
mall (shady walk)
mallard
malleability
malleable
mallet
mallow
malnutrition
malodorous
malpractice

malt
maltreat
  maltreated
  maltreating
maltreatment
mamma, mama
mammal
mammalian
mammary
mammogram
mammon
mammography
mammoth
man
  men pl
  manned
  manning
  mans
manacle
manage
  managed
  managing
manageable
management
manager
managerial
managing
mandarin
mandatary (person)
mandate
  mandated

mandating
mandatory
  (compulsory)
mandible
mandolin (musical
  instrument)
mandoline (vegetable
  slicer)
mandrake
mandrel (part of
  lathe)
mandrill (baboon)
mane (of horse)
manège
maneuver
maneuverable
maneuverability
maneuvering
manful
manfully
manganese
mange
mangel-wurzel
manger
mangle
  mangled
  mangling
mango
  mangoes, mangos pl
mangrove
mangy

manhandle
  manhandled
  manhandling
manhole
manhood
mania
  manias *pl*
maniac
maniacal
manic
manicure
  manicured
  manicuring
manicurist
manifest
manifestation
manifesto
  manifestos,
    manifestoes *pl*
manifold
manikin (little man)
mankind
manliness
manly
manna (miraculous
  food)
mannequin (model)
manner
mannered
mannerism
mannerly

manometer
manor (estate)
manorial
manse
mansion
manslaughter
mantel (shelf)
mantelpiece
mantle (cloak)
manual
manually
manufacture
  manufactured
  manufacturing
manufacturer
manure
manuscript
many
map
  mapped
  mapping
  maps
maple
mar
  marred
  marring
  mars
marathon
maraud
  marauded
  marauding

marauder
marble
marcasite
march
marcher
marchioness
Mardi Gras
mare (horse)
margarine
margin
marginal
marginally
marguerite
marigold
marijuana, marihuana
marina (harbor)
  marinas *pl*
marinade
  marinaded
  marinading
marinate
  marinated
  marinating
marine
mariner
marionette
marital
maritime
marjoram
mark
marked

markedly

marker

market

marketability

marketable

marketeer

marketing

marksman

marl

marlinspike,
  marlinespike

marmalade

marmoreal

marmoset

marmot

maroon
  marooned
  marooning

marquee (large tent)

marquetry

marquis, marquess

marriage

marriageable

marrow

marry
  married
  marries
  marrying

marsh

marshal
  marshals

marshaled
  marshaling

marshmallow

marsupial

mart (market place)

marten (weasel)

martial

martially

Martian

martin (bird)

martinet

martyr

martyrdom

marvel
  marvels
  marveled
  marveling

marvelous

marvelously

Marxism

Marxist

marzipan

mascara

mascot

masculine

masculinity

mash

mask (face cover)

masochism

masochist

mason

masonic

masonry

masque
  (entertainment)

masquerade
  masqueraded
  masquerading

mass

massacre
  massacred
  massacring

massage
  massaged
  massaging

masseur *m*

masseuse *f*

massif (mountain
  tops)

massive (very large)

massively

massiveness

mast

mastectomy
  mastectomies *pl*

master
  mastered
  mastering

masterful

masterfully

masterpiece

mastery

masthead
masticate
  masticated
  masticating
mastication
mastiff
  mastiffs *pl*
mastoid
masturbate
  masturbated
  masturbating
masturbation
mat (rug)
  mats
  matted
  matting
matador
match
matchless
matchmaker
mate
  mated
  mating
material
materialism
materialist
materialization
materialize
  materialized
  materializing
materially

maternal
maternally
maternity
math (mathematics)
mathematical
mathematician
mathematics
maths
matinee
matins
matriarch
matriarchal
matriarchy
  matriarchies *pl*
matriculate
  matriculated
  matriculating
matriculation
matrimonial
matrimony
matrix
  matrices, matrixes *pl*
matron
matt (dull surface)
matter
  mattered
  mattering
matter-of-fact
mattock
mattress
maturation

mature
  matured
  maturing
maturely
maturity
maudlin
maul
  mauled
  mauling
mausoleum
  mausoleums *pl*
mauve
maverick
mawkish
mawkishness
maxim
  maxims *pl*
maximal
maximization
maximize
  maximized
  maximizing
maximum
  maximums,
    maxima *pl*
may
May (month)
maybe
mayday (distress
  signal)
mayhem

mayn't (may not)
mayonnaise
mayor
mayoral
mayoralty
maypole
maze (tangle of paths)
mazurka
  mazurkas *pl*
mead
meadow
meager
meagerly
meagerness
meal
  mealier
  mealiest
mealtime
mealy
mealy-mouthed
mean (to signify;
    average; thrifty)
  meaning
  means
  meant
meander
  meandered
  meandering
meaningful
meaningfully
meaningless

meanly
meanness
means
meant (*from* mean)
meantime
meanwhile
measles
measly
measurable
measurableness
measure
  measured
  measuring
measurement
meat (food)
meatless
mechanic
mechanical
mechanically
mechanician
mechanism
mechanization
mechanize
  mechanized
  mechanizing
medal (*eg* for bravery)
medallion
medalist
meddle (to interfere)
  meddled
  meddling

meddler (person who
  meddles)
meddlesome
media (*eg* newspapers)
mediaeval, medieval
medial
medially
median
mediate
  mediated
  mediating
mediation
mediator
medic (doctor)
medical
medically
medicament
Medicare
medicate
  medicated
  medicating
medication
medicinal
medicinally
medicine
medieval, mediaeval
mediocre
mediocrity
  mediocrities *pl*
meditate
  meditated

meditating

meditation

meditator

Mediterranean

medium (*eg* art)

  media *pl*

medium (spiritualist)

  mediums *pl*

medlar (fruit)

medley

  medleys *pl*

meek

meekly

meekness

meet (contact)

  meeting

  meets

  met

megahertz

megalith

megalithic

megalomania

megalomaniac

megaphone

megastar

megastore

megaton, megatonne

megavolt

megawatt

megohm

melancholia

melancholias *pl*

melancholic

melancholy

mélange

melanoma

  melanomas *pl*

melee

  melees *pl*

meliorate

  meliorated

  meliorating

melioration

mellifluous

mellow

melodic

melodically

melodious

melodrama

  melodramas *pl*

melodramatic

melodramatically

melody

  melodies *pl*

melon

melt

member

membership

membrane

membranous,

  membraneous

memento

mementoes,

  mementos *pl*

memo

  memos *pl*

memoir

memorabilia

memorable

memorably

memorandum

  memoranda,

    memorandums *pl*

memorial

memorize

  memorized

  memorizing

memory

  memories *pl*

memsahib

men (*pl* of man)

menace

  menaced

  menacing

ménage

menagerie

mend

mendacious

mendaciously

mendacity

mendicant

mendicity

menhir

menial
menially
meningitis
menopausal
menopause
menstrual
menstruate
  menstruated
  menstruating
menstruation
mensuration
mental
mentality
mentally
menthol
mention
mentor (adviser)
menu
  menus *pl*
mercantile
mercenary
  mercenaries *pl*
mercerize
  mercerized
  mercerizing
merchandise
merchant
merciful
mercifully
merciless
mercilessly

mercurial
mercury
mercy
  mercies *pl*
mere
merely
merest
meretricious
merge
  merged
  merging
merger
meridian
meridional
meringue
merit
  merited
  meriting
meritocracy
  meritocracies *pl*
meritorious
meritoriously
mermaid
merrier
merrily
merriment
merry
mesdames (*pl* of
  madame)
mesdemoiselles (*pl* of
  mademoiselle)

mesh
mesmerism
mesmerize
  mesmerized
  mesmerizing
mess
message
messenger
Messiah
Messianic
messieurs (*pl* of
  monsieur)
messily
messiness
messrs (messieurs)
messy
  messier
  messiest
met (*from* meet)
metabolic
metabolism
metal (*eg* silver)
metaled
metallic
metallurgical
metallurgist
metallurgy
metamorphose
  metamorphosed
  metamorphosing
metamorphosis

metamorphoses *pl*

metaphor
metaphorical
metaphorically
metaphysical
metaphysically
metaphysics
mete (to apportion)
  meted
  meting
meteor
meteoric
meteorically
meteorite
meteoroid
meteorological
meteorologist
meteorology
meter (to measure, *eg*
  gas)
  metered
  metering
meter (measurement)
methane
methedrine
method
methodical
methodically
methodology
methyl
methylated

meticulous
meticulously
meticulousness
metiér
metric
metricate
  metricated
  metricating
metrication
metricize
  metricized
  metricizing
metronome
metropolis
metropolitan
mettle (temperament)
mews (stables)
mezza voce (softly)
mezzanine
mezzoforte
mezzo-soprano
  mezzo-sopranos *pl*
mezzotint
miaow, miaou
miasma
  miasmata, miasmas
  pl
miasmal
mica
mice (pl. of mouse)
mickle, muckle (large

amount)
microbe
microbial
microbiologist
microbiology
microcosm
microfiche
micrometer
microphone
microscope
microscopic
microscopy
microtome
microwave
micturition
midday
midden
middle
middleman
  middlemen *pl*
middleweight
middling
midge
midget
midi (skirt length)
midnight
midriff
midshipman
  midshipmen *pl*
midst
midsummer

midway

Midwest

Midwesterner

midwife

  midwives *pl*

midwifery

mien (appearance)

miffed

might

mightily

mightiness

mighty

  mightier

  mightiest

mignonette

migraine

migrant

migrate

  migrated

  migrating

migration

migrator

mikado

  mikados *pl*

mike

  miked

  miking

mil

mild

milder

mildew

mildewy

mildly

mildness

mile

mileage

milieu

  milieus, milieux *pl*

militancy

militant

militarily

militarism

militarist

militarization

militarize

  militarized

  militarizing

military

militate

  militated

  militating

militia

  militias *pl*

milk

milker

milkiness

milkmaid

milksop

milky

  milkier

  milkiest

mill (grind)

mille-feuille

millennium

  millenniums,

    millennia *pl*

millipede

miller

millet

milliard

milligram

milliliter

millimeter

milliner

millinery

million

millionaire

millionairess *f*

millionth

millipede

millivolt

milliwatt

millstone

mime

  mimed

  miming

mimic

  mimicked

  mimicking

  mimics

mimicker

mimicry

mimosa

mimosas *pl*
minaret
minatory
mince
  minced
  mincing
mincemeat
mincer
mind (brain; to object)
minder
mindful
mindless
mine
  mined
  mining
miner (person who mines)
mineral
mineralogist
mineralogy
minestrone
mingle
  mingled
  mingling
mingy (stingy)
miniature
minibus
minicab
minim
minimal

minimally
minimize
  minimized
  minimizing
minimum
  minimums, minima *pl*
mining
minion
miniskirt
minister
  ministered
  ministering
ministerial
ministrant
ministration
ministry
  ministries *pl*
mink
minnow
minor (smaller; juvenile)
minority
  minorities *pl*
minstrel
mint
mint sauce
minuet
minus
  minuses *pl*
minuscule

minute
  minuted
  minuting
minutely
minuteness
minutes (notes of meeting)
minutiae
minx
miracle
miraculous
miraculously
mirage
mire
mirror
  mirrored
  mirroring
mirth
mirthful
misadventure
misalliance
misanthrope
misanthropic
misanthropy
misapplication
misapply
  misapplied
  misapplies
  misapplying
misapprehend
misapprehension

misappropriate
  misappropriated
  misappropriating
misappropriation
misbehave
  misbehaved
  misbehaving
misbehavior
miscalculate
  miscalculated
  miscalculating
miscalculation
miscarriage
miscarry
  miscarried
  miscarries
  miscarrying
miscast
miscegenation
miscellaneous
miscellany
  miscellanies *pl*
mischance
mischief
mischievous
mischievously
miscible
misconceive
  misconceived
  misconceiving
misconception

misconduct
misconstruction
misconstrue
  misconstrued
  misconstruing
miscount
miscreant
misdeed
misdemeanor
mise en scène
  mises en scène *pl*
miser
miserable
miserably
miserliness
miserly
misery
  miseries *pl*
misfire
  misfired
  misfiring
misfit
misfortune
misgiving
misgovern
misgovernment
misguidance
misguide
  misguided
  misguiding
mishandle

  mishandled
  mishandling
mishap
mishmash
misinform
misinterpret
  misinterpreted
  misinterpreting
misinterpretation
misjudge
  misjudged
  misjudging
misjudgment,
  misjudgement
mislay
  mislaid
  mislaying
  mislays
mislead
  misleading
  misleads
  misled
mismanage
  mismanaged
  mismanaging
mismanagement
mismatch
misnomer
misogynist
misogyny
misplace

misplaced
misplacing
misplacement
misprint
mispronounce
  mispronounced
  mispronouncing
mispronunciation
misquotation
misquote
  misquoted
  misquoting
misread
  misreading
misrepresent
misrepresentation
misrule
miss
  misses *pl*
Miss
  Misses *pl*
missal (book of
  prayer)
misshapen
missile
missing
mission
missionary
  missionaries *pl*
Mississippi
missive

misspell
  misspelled
  misspelling
  misspells
  misspelt
misspend
  misspending
  misspends
  misspent
misstate
  misstated
  misstating
misstatement
mist (fog)
mistake
  mistaken
  mistakes
  mistaking
  mistook
mistakenly
Mister, Mr.
  Messrs *pl*
mistily
mistime
  mistimed
  mistiming
mistiness
mistletoe
mistral
mistranslate
  mistranslated

mistranslating
mistranslation
mistress
mistrust
mistrustful
misty
  mistier
  mistiest
misunderstand
  misunderstanding
  misunderstands
  misunderstood
misuse
  misused
  misusing
mite (small insect)
miter
mitigate
  mitigated
  mitigating
mitigation
mitten
mix
  mixed
  mixing
mixer
mixture
mizen, mizzen (sail)
mnemonic
moan
  moaned

moaning
moaner
moat (ditch)
moated
mob
  mobbed
  mobbing
  mobs
mobile
mobility
mobilization
mobilize
  mobilized
  mobilizing
moccasin
mocha (coffee)
mock
mockery
mock-heroic
modal
mode
model
  models
  modeled
  modeling
moderate
  moderated
  moderating
moderately
moderation
moderator

modern
modernism
modernity
modernization
modernize
  modernized
  modernizing
modest
modestly
modesty
modicum
modifiable
modification
modify
  modified
  modifies
  modifying
modish
modular
modulate
  modulated
  modulating
modulation
modulator
module (unit of
  measurement)
modulus
  moduli *pl*
modus operandi
  modi operandi *pl*
mogul

mohair
Mohammed,
  Muhammad
Mohammedan,
  Muhammadan
moiety
moist
moisten
  moistened
  moistening
moistness
moisture
moisturize
  moisturized
  moisturizing
molar
molasses
mold
  molded
  molding
molder
  moldered
  moldering
moldiness
moldy
  moldier
  moldiest
mole
molecular
molecule
molehill

moleskin
molest
molestation
mollify
　mollified
　mollifies
　mollifying
mollusk
mollycoddle
　mollycoddled
　mollycoddling
Molotov cocktail
molt
molten
molybdenum
moment
momentarily
momentary
momentous
momentum
monachal (like a
　monk)
monachism
monarch
monarchical
monarchy
　monarchies *pl*
monastery
　monasteries *pl*
monastic
monasticism

Monday
monetarism
monetarist
monetary
money
　moneys, monies *pl*
moneyless
Mongol
Mongolian
mongolism
mongoose
　mongooses *pl*
mongrel
monitor
　monitored
　monitoring
monk
monkey
　monkeys *pl*
monochromatic
monochrome
monocle
monogamist
monogamous
monogamy
monogram
monograph
monolith
monolithic
monologue
monomania

monomaniac
monoplane
monopolist
monopolistic
monopolization
monopolize
　monopolized
　monopolizing
monopoly
　monopolies *pl*
monorail
monosyllabic
monosyllable
monotheism
monotonous
monotonously
monotony
monotype
monoxide
monseigneur
monsieur
　messieurs *pl*
monsoon
monster
monstrosity
　monstrosities *pl*
monstrous
montage
month
monthly
monument

monumental
monumentally
moo
  moos *pl*
  mooed
  mooing
  moos
mooch
mood
moodily
moodiness
moody
  moodier
  moodiest
moon
  mooned
  mooning
moonless
moonlight
moonlighting
moonlit
moonshine
moor (to tether;
  heath)
  moored
  mooring
moorage
moose
moot (undecided)
moot point
mop (to wipe)

  mopped
  mopping
  mops
mope (to feel sad)
  moping
  moped
moped (motorbike)
moral
morale (state of
  mind)
morality
moralize
  moralized
  moralizing
morally
morass
moratorium
  moratoriums,
  moratoria *pl*
morbid
morbidity
morbidness
mordant
more (extra)
moreover
morganatic
morganatically
morgue
moribund
morn (morning)
morning

Morocco
moron
moronic
morose
morosely
moroseness
Morpheus
morphia
morphine
morphological
morphology
  morphologies *pl*
Moroccan
morrow
Morse (code)
morsel
mortal
mortality
mortally
mortar
mortarboard
mortgage
  mortgaged
  mortgaging
mortgagee
mortgagor
mortification
mortify
  mortified
  mortifies
  mortifying

mortise, mortice
mortuary
  mortuaries *pl*
mosaic
Moslem, Muslim
mosque
mosquito
  mosquitoes *pl*
moss
mossy
  mossier
  mossiest
most
mostly
mote (speck)
motel
motet
moth
moth-eaten
mother
  mothered
  mothering
mother tongue
mother-in-law
  mothers-in-law *pl*
mothering
motherless
motherly
motif
  motifs *pl*
motion

motionless
motivate
  motivated
  motivating
motivation
motive
motley
motor
  motored
  motoring
motorboat
motorist
motorize
  motorized
  motorizing
mottled
motto
  mottoes *pl*
moujik, muzhik
  (Russian peasant)
mound
mount
mountain
mountaineer
mountainous
mountebank
mourn (to grieve)
mourner
mournful
mournfully
mourning (for the

dead)
mouse
  mice *pl*
mouser
moussaka
mousse (fruit cream)
moustache
mousy
mouth
mouthed
mouthful
  mouthfuls *pl*
mouthpiece
movable, moveable
move
  moved
  moving
movement
movie
mow
  mowed
  mowing
  mown
mower
Mr.
Mrs.
much
mucilage
mucilaginous
muck
mucky

mucous (slimy)
mucus (phlegm)
mud
muddle
  muddled
  muddling
muddleheaded
muddler
muddy
  muddied
  muddies
  muddying
  muddier
  muddiest
mudslinging
muff
muffin
muffle
  muffled
  muffling
mufti
mug
  mugged
  mugging
  mugs
mugger
muggy
  muggier
  muggiest
mugwump
mulatto

mulattos, mulattoes
  pl
mulberry
  mulberries pl
mulch
mulct
mule
muleteer
mulish
mulligatawny
mullion
multifarious
multiform
multilateral
multilaterally
multiple
multiplex
multiplication
multiplicity
multiplier
multiply
  multiplied
  multiplies
  multiplying
multiracial
multitude
multitudinous
mum (silent)
mumble
  mumbled
  mumbling

mummery
mummified
mummy
  mummies pl
munch
mundane
municipal
municipality
  municipalities pl
munificence
munificent
munition
mural
murder
  murdered
  murdering
murderer
murderess
murderous
murderously
murk
murkily
murkiness
murky
  murkier
  murkiest
murmur
  murmured
  murmuring
murrain
muscat

muscatel
muscle (body)
  muscled
  muscling
muscular
muse (to think)
  mused
  musing
museum
  museums *pl*
mush
mushroom
mushy
  mushier
  mushiest
music
musical
musically
musician
musk
musket
musketry
Muslim, Moslem
muslin
musquash
mussel (mollusc)
must
mustache
mustang
mustard
muster

mustered
mustering
mustn't (must not)
musty
mustiness
mutability
mutable
mutant
mutation
mute
mutely
mutilate
  mutilated
  mutilating
mutilation
mutilator
mutineer
mutinous
mutiny
  mutinies *pl*
  mutinied
  mutinies
  mutinying
mutter
  muttered
  muttering
mutton
mutual
mutually
muzhik
muzzily

muzziness
muzzle
  muzzled
  muzzling
muzzy
my
mycelium
  mycelia *pl*
mycology
myelitis
myocarditis
myocardium
  myocardia *pl*
myopia
myopic
myriad
myrmidon
myrrh
myrtle
myself
mysterious
mysteriously
mystery
  mysteries *pl*
mystic
mystical
mysticism
mystification
mystify
  mystified
  mystifies

mystifying
mystique
myth
mythical
mythological
mythologist
mythology
  mythologies *pl*
myxomatosis

nab
  nabbed
  nabbing
  nabs
nabob
nadir
nag
  nagged
  nagging
  nags
nagger
naiad
nail
naive
naiveté, naivety
naked
nakedly
nakedness

namby-pamby
name
  named
  naming
nameable
name-dropper
nameless
namely
namesake
nanny
  nannies *pl*
nap
  napped
  napping
  naps
napalm
nape (of neck)
naphtha

  naphthas *pl*
naphthalene
napkin
narcissism
narcissus
  narcissus, narcissi,
    narcissuses *pl*
narcosis
narcotic
narrate
  narrated
  narrating
narration
narrative
narrator
narrow
  narrower
  narrowly
narrow-minded
narrowness
nasal
nasally
nascency
nascent
nastily
nastiness
nasturtium
  nasturtiums *pl*
nasty
  nastier
  nastiest

natal	naturalizing	né (born) *m*
natality	naturally	neap (of the tide)
natation	nature	near
nation	naught (nothing)	neared
national	naughtily	nearing
nationalism	naughtiness	nearby
nationalist	naughty	nearer
nationalistic	naughtier	nearly
nationality	naughtiest	nearness
nationalities *pl*	nausea	nearsighted
nationalization	nauseate	neat
nationalize	nauseated	neater
nationalized	nauseating	neatest
nationalizing	nauseous	neatly
nationally	nautical	neatness
native	nautilus	nebula
nativity	nautiluses, nautili *pl*	nebulae, nebulas *pl*
natter	naval (of ships; navy)	nebulosity
nattered	nave (of church)	nebulous
nattering	navel (umbilicus)	necessarily
natterer	navigability	necessary
natty	navigable	necessitate
nattier	navigate	necessitated
nattiest	navigated	necessitating
natural	navigating	necessitous
naturalism	navigation	necessity
naturalist	navigator	necessities *pl*
naturalistic	navy (ships)	neck
naturalization	navies *pl*	neckerchief
naturalize	nay (no)	necklace
naturalized	N.B. (nota bene)	necktie

necromancy
necrosis
nectar
nectarine
née f
need (to require)
needful
needle
  needled
  needling
needless
needlessly
needlework
needy
  needier
  neediest
neep (turnip)
ne'er
ne'er-do-well
nefarious
nefariously
negate
  negated
  negating
negation
negative
negatively
neglect
neglectful
negligee, négligé
negligence

negligent
negligently
negligible
negligibly
negotiable
negotiate
  negotiated
  negotiating
negotiation
negotiator
Negress f
  Negresses pl
Negro
  Negroes pl
Negroid
neigh (horse's cry)
neighbor
neighborhood
neighboring
neighborliness
neighborly
neighing
neither
nemesis
neoclassical
neolithic
neologism
neology
neon
neophyte
nephew

nephritic
nephritis
nepotism
nerve
  nerved
  nerving
nerve-racking
nervous
nervously
nervousness
nervy
  nervier
  nerviest
nest
nestle
  nestled
  nestling
net
  nets
  netted
  netting
net (weight or
  price)
nether (lower)
nettle
network
neural
neuralgia
neurasthenia
neurasthenic
neuritis

neurological
neurologist
neurology
neurosis
  neuroses *pl*
neurotic
neuter
  neutered
  neutering
neutral
neutrality
neutralization
neutralize
  neutralized
  neutralizing
neutron
never
nevermore
nevertheless
new
newborn
newcomer
newel
newfangled
newly
newness
news
newspaper
newsworthy
newt
next

nib
nibble
  nibbled
  nibbling
nice
nicely
niceness
nicety
  niceties *pl*
niche
nick
nickel
nickname
  nicknamed
  nicknaming
nicotine
niece
niggard
niggardly
niggle
  niggled
  niggling
nigh
night (end of day)
nightclub
nightdress
nightfall
nightingale
nightlife
nightlight
nightly

nightmare
nightmarish
nighttime
nihilism
nihilistic
nil
nimble
nimbler
nimbly
nimbus
  nimbi, nimbuses *pl*
nincompoop
nine
nineteen
nineteenth
ninetieth
ninety
  nineties *pl*
ninny
  ninnies *pl*
ninth
ninthly
nip
  nipped
  nipping
  nips
nipple
nirvana
nisi
nit (insect)
niter

nit-picking
nitrate
nitric
nitrite
nitrogen
nitroglycerine,
  nitroglycerin
nitrous
nitty-gritty
no (negative)
  noes *pl*
nitwit
no one
nob
Nobel prize
nobility
noble
nobleman
  noblemen *pl*
nobler
noblesse oblige
nobly
nobody
  nobodies *pl*
nocturnal
nocturnally
nocturne
nod
  nodded
  nodding
  nods

nodal
noddle (head)
node
nodular
nodule (lump)
Noel
noggin (mug)
nogging (brickwork)
nohow (by no means)
noise
noiseless
noiselessly
noisily
noisiness
noisome
noisy
  noisier
  noisiest
nom de plume
nomad
nomadic
nomenclature
nominal
nominally
nominate
  nominated
  nominating
nomination
nominative
  (grammar)
nominator

nominee
nonage
nonagenarian
nonce
nonchalance
nonchalant
nonchalantly
noncombatant
noncommissioned
noncommittally
noncompos mentis
nonconductor
nonconformist
noncontributory
noncooperation
noncooperative
nondescript
none
none the less,
  nonetheless
nonentity
  nonentities *pl*
nonessential
nonesuch, nonsuch
nonetheless
nonexistent
nonflammable
nonpareil
nonplussed
nonsense
nonsensical

nonsensically
non sequitur
  non sequiturs *pl*
nonsuch, nonesuch
noodle
nook
noon
noose
norm
normal
normality
normalization
normalize
  normalized
  normalizing
normally
north
northerly
northern
northward
northwards
nose
  nosed
  nosing
nosegay
  nosegays *pl*
nosey, nosy
  nosier
  nosiest
nosiness
nostalgia

nostalgic
nostril
nostrum
  nostrums *pl*
nosy, nosey
  nosier
  nosiest
notability
  notabilities *pl*
notable
notably
notary
  notaries *pl*
notation
notch
note
  noted
  noting
noteworthiness
noteworthy
nothing
notice
  noticed
  noticing
noticeable
noticeably
notifiable
notification
notify
  notified
  notifies

notifying
notion
notional
notionally
notoriety
notorious
notoriously
notwithstanding
nougat
nought (zero)
noun
nourish
nourishment
nouveau riche
  nouveaux riches *pl*
nouvelle cuisine
novel
novelette
novelist
novelty
  novelties *pl*
novice
noviciate
now
nowadays
nowhere
nowise
noxious
nozzle
nuance
nubile

nubility

nuclear

nucleus

nuclei *pl*

nude

nudge

nudged

nudging

nudism

nudist

nudity

nugatory

nugget

nuisance

null

nullification

nullify

nullified

nullifies

nullifying

numb

number

numbered

numbering

numbness

numeral

numerator

numerical

numerically

numerous

numismatic

numismatist

numskull

nun

nuncio

nuncios *pl*

nunnery

nunneries *pl*

nuptial

nurse

nursed

nursing

nursling

nursemaid

nursery

nurseries *pl*

nurseryman

nurserymen *pl*

nurture

nurtured

nurturing

nut

nutcracker

nutmeg

nutrient

nutriment

nutrition

nutritious

nutritive

nutty

nuttier

nuttiest

nuzzle

nuzzled

nuzzling

nylon

nymph

nymphomania

nymphomaniac

O

oaf
  oafs *pl*
oafish
oak
oaken
oakum
oar (of boat)
oasis
  oases *pl*
oast
oat
oath
oatmeal
obduracy
obdurate
obdurately
obedience
obedient

obediently
obeisance
obelisk
obese
obesity
obey
  obeyed
  obeying
  obeys
obituary
  obituaries *pl*
object
objection
objectionable
objective
objectively
objectivity
objector

objet d'art
  objets d'art *pl*
oblation
obligation
obligatory
oblige
  obliged
  obliging
oblique
obliquely
obliquity
obliterate
  obliterated
  obliterating
obliteration
oblivion
oblivious
oblong
obloquy
  obloquies *pl*
obnoxious
obnoxiousness
oboe
  oboes *pl*
oboist
obscene
obscenely
obscenity
  obscenities *pl*
obscure
  obscured

obscuring
obscurely
obscurity
  obscurities *pl*
obsequious
obsequiously
obsequiousness
observable
observance
observant
observation
observatory
  observatories *pl*
observe
  observed
  observing
observer
obsess
obsessed
obsession
obsessive
obsolescence
obsolescent
obsolete
obstacle
obstetric
obstetrician
obstetrics
obstinacy
obstinate
obstinately

obstreperous
obstreperously
obstreperousness
obstruct
obstruction
obstructive
obstructively
obtain
  obtained
  obtaining
obtainable
obtrude
  obtruded
  obtruding
obtruder
obtrusion
obtrusive
obtuse
obtusely
obtuseness
obverse
obviate
  obviated
  obviating
obvious
obviously
occasion
occasional
occasionally
occident (west)
occidental

occlude
  occluded
  occluding
occlusion
occult
occultation
occupancy
occupant
occupation
occupational
occupier
occupy
  occupied
  occupies
  occupying
occur
  occurred
  occurring
  occurs
occurrence
ocean
oceanic
ocelot
ocher
o'clock
octagon
octagonal
octane
octave
octavo
  octavos *pl*

octet
October
octogenarian
octopus
  octopuses *pl*
octoroon
ocular
oculist
odd
odder
oddity
  oddities *pl*
oddly
oddment
odds
odds-on
ode
odious
odiously
odiousness
odium
odor
odoriferous
odorless
odorous
off
offal
offend
offender
offense
offensive

offensively
offensiveness
offer
  offered
  offering
offertory
offhand
offhanded
offhandedly
offhandedness
office
officer
official
officialese
officially
officiate
  officiated
  officiating
officious
officiously
officiousness
offing
off-peak
offprint
offset
  offsets
  offsetting
offshoot
offside
offspring
oft

often
oftener
ogle
  ogled
  ogling
ogre
ogress
ohm
ohmic
ohmmeter
Ohm's Law
oil
  oiled
  oiling
oily
ointment
OK, O.K., okay
old
old maid
olden
older
old-fashioned
old-maidish
oleaginous
oleander
olfaction
olfactory
oligarch
oligarchy
  oligarchies *pl*
oligopoly

oligopolies *pl*
olive
Olympia
Olympian
Olympic
ombudsman
omega
omelette
omen
ominous
ominously
omission
omit (leave out)
omits
omitted
omitting
omnibus
omnibuses *pl*
omnipotence
omniscience
omniscient
omnivorous
once
once-over
oncoming
one
oneness
onerous
onerousness
oneself
one-up

one-upmanship
ongoing
onion
on-line, online
onlooker
only
onomatopoeia
onomatopoeic
onrush
onset
onslaught
onus
onward, onwards
onyx
oolite
oolitic
ooze
oozed
oozing
opacity
opal
opalescence
opalescent
opaque
opaquely
open
opened
opening
open-and-shut
open-ended
opener

openly
openness
opera
operas *pl*
operability
operable
operate
operated
operating
operatic
operatically
operation
operational
operationally
operative
operator
operetta
operettas *pl*
ophthalmia
ophthalmic
ophthalmologist
ophthalmology
opiate (drug)
opine
opined
opining
opinion
opinionated
opium
opossum
opossums *pl*

opponent
opportune
opportunely
opportuneness
opportunism
opportunist
opportunity
  opportunities *pl*
oppose
  opposed
  opposing
opposer
opposite
opposition
oppress
oppression
oppressive
oppressively
oppressor
opprobrious
opprobrium
opt
optative
optic
optical
optically
optician
optimism
optimist
optimistic
optimistically

optimization
optimize
  optimized
  optimizing
optimum
  optima, optimums *pl*
option
optional
optionally
opulence
opulent
opus
  opuses, opera *pl*
oracle
oracular
oral (by mouth)
orally
orange
orangeade
orangutan
orate
  orated
  orating
oration
orator
oratorio (sacred
    opera)
  oratorios *pl*
oratory
  oratories *pl*
orb

orbit
  orbited
  orbiting
orbital
orchard
orchestra
  orchestras *pl*
orchestrate
  orchestrated
  orchestrating
orchestration
orchestrator
orchid
ordain
  ordained
  ordaining
ordeal
order
  ordered
  ordering
orderliness
orderly
ordinal
ordinance (decree)
ordinarily
ordinary
ordinate
ordination
ordnance (military
    stores)
ordure

ore (mineral)
oregano
organ
organic
organically
organism
organist
organization
organize
  organized
  organizing
organizer
orgasm
orgiastic
orgy
  orgies *pl*
oriel
orient
oriental
orientally
orientate
  orientated
  orientating
orientation
orifice
origami
origin
original
originality
originally
originate

originated
originating
originator
orison
ormolu
ornament
ornamental
ornamentation
ornate
ornately
ornithologist
ornithology
orotund
orphan
orphanage
orphaned
orrery
  orreries *pl*
orthodontics
orthodontist
orthodox
orthodoxy
  orthodoxies *pl*
orthographic
orthography
orthopedic
ortolan
oscillate
  oscillated
  oscillating
oscillation

oscillator
oscillatory
oscillogram
oscillograph
oscilloscope
osculate
  osculated
  osculating
osculation
osier
osmosis
osprey
  ospreys *pl*
osseous
ossification
ossify
  ossified
  ossifies
  ossifying
ossuary
  ossuaries *pl*
ostensible
ostensibly
ostensive
ostensively
ostentation
ostentatious
ostentatiously
osteoarthritis
osteology
osteopath

steopathic
steopathy
stracism
stracize
  ostracized
  ostracizing
strich
  ostriches *pl*
ther
therwise
tiose
titis
tter
ttoman
publiette
pught
pughtn't (ought not)
punce
pur
purs
purself
  ourselves *pl*
put
  outed
  outing
putage
putbid
  outbidding
  outbids
putboard
putbound

outbreak
outburst
outcast
outclass
outclassed
outcome
outcry
  outcries *pl*
outdo
  outdid
  outdoes
  outdoing
  outdone
outdoors
outer
outermost
outfit
outfitter
outfitting
outflank
outflanked
outgoing
outgrow
  outgrew
  outgrowing
  outgrown
  outgrows
outgrowth
outlandish
outlast
outlaw

outlawry
outlay
  outlays *pl*
outlet
outline
  outlined
  outlining
outlive
  outlived
  outliving
outlook
outlying
outmaneuver
  outmaneuvered
  outmaneuvering
outmoded
outmost
outnumber
  outnumbered
  outnumbering
outpatient
outpost
outpouring
output
  outputs
  outputted
  outputting
outrage
  outraged
  outraging
outrageous

outrageously
outran (*from* outrun)
outreach
outrider
outrigger
outright
outrun
  outran
  outrunning
  outruns
outset
outshine
  outshines
  outshining
  outshone
outside
outsider
outsized
outskirts
outsourcing
outspoken
outspokenness
outstanding
outstation
outstay
  outstayed
  outstaying
  outstays
outstretched
outstrip
  outstripped

outstripping
outstrips
outvote
  outvoted
  outvoting
outward
outward-bound
outwardly
outweigh
outwit
  outwits
  outwitted
  outwitting
outworn
ova
oval
ovary
  ovaries *pl*
ovation
oven
over
overact
overall
overarm
overawe
  overawed
  overawing
overbalance
  overbalanced
  overbalancing
overbearing

overboard
overburden
  overburdened
  overburdening
overcame (*from* overcome)
overcast
overcharge
  overcharged
  overcharging
overcoat
overcome
  overcame
  overcomes
  overcoming
overconfident
overcrowded
overdo
  overdid
  overdoes
  overdoing
  overdone
overdose
  overdosed
  overdosing
overdraft
overdraw
  overdrawing
  overdrawn
  overdraws
  overdrew

overdress

overate

overeaten

overeating

overeats

overflow

overflowed

overflowing

overflown

overflows

overground

overgrow

overgrew

overgrowing

overgrown

overgrows

overgrowth

overhand

overhanding

overhaul

overhead

overhear

overhears

overhearing

overheard

overheat

overheated

overheating

overhang

overhanging

overhangs

overhung

overindulgence

overjoyed

overland

overlap

overlapped

overlapping

overlaps

overlay

overlaid

overlaying

overlays

overleaf

overload

overloaded

overloading

overlook

overnight

overpay

overpaid

overpaying

overpays

overpopulated

overpower

overpowered

overpowering

overran (*from*

overrun)

overrate

overrated

overrating

overreact

overreach

override

overridden

overrides

overriding

overrode

overripe

overrule

overruled

overruling

overrun

overran

overrunning

overruns

overseas (abroad)

oversee (supervise)

oversaw

overseeing

overseen

oversees

overseer

oversexed

overshadow

overshadowed

overshoot

overshot

oversight
oversimplification
oversimplify
  oversimplified
  oversimplifies
  oversimplifying
oversleep
  oversleeping
  oversleeps
  overslept
overspend
  overspending
  overspends
  overspent
overstate
  overstated
  overstating
overstatement
overstay
  overstayed
  overstaying
  overstays
overstep
  overstepped
  overstepping
  oversteps
oversubscribed
overt
overtake
  overtakes
  overtaking

  overtook
overtax
  overtaxing
over-the-counter
overthrow
  overthrew
  overthrowing
  overthrown
  overthrows
overtime
overtired
overtly
overtone
overtook (*from*
  overtake)
overture
overturn
overweening
overweight
overwhelm
overwork
overwrought
oviduct
oviparous
ovoid
ovulate
  ovulated
  ovulating
ovulation
ovum (*egg cell*)
  ova *pl*

owe
  owed
  owing
owl
own
  owned
  owning
owner
ox
  oxen *pl*
oxalic
oxalic acid
oxidation
oxide
oxidization
oxidize
  oxidized
  oxidizing
oxtail
oxtongue
oxyacetylene
oxygen
oxygenate
  oxygenated
  oxygenating
oxygenation
oxymoron
  oxymorons *pl*
oyster
ozone

P

pace
  paced
  pacing
pachyderm
pachydermatous
Pacific
pacific (peaceful)
pacifically
pacification
pacifier
pacifism
pacifist
pacify
  pacified
  pacifies
  pacifying
pack
package

packaged
  packaging
packed
packet (parcel)
packhorse
pact (treaty)
pad
  padded
  padding
  pads
paddle
  paddled
  paddling
paddler
paddock
padlock
padlocked
padre

paean
pagan
paganism
page
  paged
  paging
pageant
pageantry
  pageantries *pl*
pagination
pagoda
  pagodas *pl*
paid (from pay)
paid-up
pail (bucket)
pain (discomfort)
pained
painful
painfully
painless
painlessly
painstaking
paint
painter
pair (couple)
  paired
  pairing
paisley
pal (friend)
palace
palatable (tasting

good)
palate (of mouth)
palatial
palaver
  palavered
  palavering
pale (whitish; stake or
  post)
  paled
  paling
palely
paleness
paleographic
paleography
Paleolithic
paleontology
palette (artist's)
palindrome
palisade
pall
Palladium
pallbearer
palled
pallet (tool; mattress)
palliasse
palliate
  palliated
  palliating
palliation
palliative
pallid (pale)

palling
pallor
pally
palpitation
palm
palmist
palmistry
palomino
  palominos *pl*
palpable
palpably
palpate
  palpated
  palpating
palpation
palpitate
  palpitated
  palpitating
palsied
palsy
paltriness
paltry
  paltrier
  paltriest
pamper
  pampered
  pampering
pamphlet
pamphleteer
pan
  panned

panning
pans
Pan (god of nature)
panacea
panache
pancake
panchromatic
pancreas
panda (animal)
  pandas *pl*
pandemic
pandemonium
pander (to indulge)
  pandered
  pandering
pane (glass)
panegyric
panel
  panels
  paneled
  paneling
panelist
pang
panic
  panicked
  panicking
  panics
panicky
panic-stricken
pannier
panoply

panoplies *pl*
panorama
  panoramas *pl*
panoramic
panoramically
pansy
  pansies *pl*
pant
pantaloon
pantechnicon
pantheism
pantheistic
Pantheon
panther
pantile
pantomime
pantry
  pantries *pl*
pants
papacy
  papacies *pl*
papal
paparazzi
paper
  papered
  papering
paperback
paperclip
paperweight
papier-mâché
papist

papistry
paprika
papyrus
  papyri *pl*
par
parable
parabola
  parabolas *pl*
parabolic
parabolically
parachute
  parachuted
  parachuting
parachutist
parade
  paraded
  parading
paradise
paradox
  paradoxes *pl*
paradoxical
paradoxically
paraffin
paragliding
paragon
paragraph
parakeet
parallax
parallel
  paralleled
  paralleling

parallels
parallelepiped
parallelism
parallelogram
paralysis
paralytic
paralyze
  paralyzed
  paralyzing
parameter
paramilitary
  paramilitaries *pl*
paramount
paramour
paranoia
paranoiac
paranoid
parapet
paraphernalia
paraphrase
  paraphrased
  paraphrasing
paraplegia
paraplegic
parasite
parasitic
parasol
paratrooper
paratroops
paratyphoid
parboil

parboiled
parboiling
parcel
  parcels
  parceled
  parceling
parched
parchment
pardon
  pardoned
  pardoning
pardonable
pare (to cut)
  pared
  paring
paregoric
parent
parentage
parental
parentally
parenthesis
  parentheses *pl*
parenthetic
par excellence
pariah
parish
parishioner
Parisian *m*
Parisienne *f*
parity
  parities *pl*

park
parka
  parkas *pl*
parlance
parley
  parleyed
  parleying
  parleys
parliament
parliamentarian
parliamentary
parlor
parlous
Parmesan
parochial
parochialism
parochially
parodist
parody
  parodies *pl*
  parodied
  parodies
  parodying
parole
paroxysm
paroxysmal
parquet
parquetry
parricidal
parricide
parrot

parry
  parried
  parries
  parrying
parse
  parsed
  parsing
parsimonious
parsimony
parsley
parsnip
parson
parsonage
part
partake
  partaken
  partaking
  partook
partaker
parterre
parthenogenesis
parthenogenetic
parthenogenetically
Parthenon
partial
partiality
partially
participant
participate
  participated
  participating

participation
participator
participial
participle
particle
particular
particularity
  particularities *pl*
particularize
  particularized
  particularizing
particularly
partisan
partition
  partitioned
  partitioning
partly
partner
  partnered
  partnering
partnership
partook
partridge
part-time
parturient
parturition
party
  parties *pl*
  partied
  parties
  partying

pass
passable
passably
passage
passé
passed
passenger
passerby
  passersby *pl*
passim
passion
passionate
passionately
passive
passively
passiveness
passivity
passport
password
past
pasta
paste
  pasted
  pasting
pasteboard
pastel (picture)
pasteurization
pasteurize
  pasteurized
  pasteurizing
pastille (lozenge)

pastime
pastor (minister)
pastoral
pastorate
pastry
  pastries *pl*
pasturage
pasture (grazing land)
pasty (pie; paste-like)
  pasties *pl*
pat
  pats
  patted
  patting
patch
patched
patchwork
patchy
pate (head)
pâté
pâté de foie gras
patent
patentable
patentee
patently
paterfamilias
paternal
paternalistic
paternally
paternity
paternoster

path
pathetic
pathetically
pathless
pathogenic
pathological
pathologically
pathologist
pathology
pathos
pathway
patience
patient
patiently
patina
  patinas *pl*
patio
  patios *pl*
patisserie
  patisseries *pl*
patois
patriarch
patriarchal
patriarchy
  patriarchies *pl*
patrician
patricide
patrimonial
patrimony
  patrimonies *pl*
patriot

patriotic
patriotically
patriotism
patrol
  patrolled
  patrolling
  patrols
patron
patronage
patroness
patronize
  patronized
  patronizing
patronizer
patronymic
patten (kind of shoe)
patter
  pattered
  pattering
pattern (design)
patterned
patty
  patties *pl*
paucity
paunch
paunchy
pauper
pauperism
pause
  paused
  pausing

pave
  paved
  paving
pavement
pavilion
Pavlova
  Pavlovas *pl*
paw (animal's foot)
  pawed
  pawing
pawn
pawnbroker
pay
  paid
  paying
  pays
payable
payee
payer
paymaster
payment
payoff
payphone
payroll
pea
  peas *pl*
peace
peaceable
peaceably
peaceful
peacefully

peacefulness
peach
peacock
peahen
peak
  peaked
  peaking
peakload
peaky
peal (of bells)
  pealed
  pealing
peanut
pear (fruit)
pearl
pearly
  pearlies pl
peasant
peasantry
peat
pebble
pebbly
peccadillo
  peccadilloes,
    peccadillos pl
peccant (sinning)
peck
peckish
pectoral
peculation
peculator

peculiar
peculiarity
  peculiarities pl
peculiarly
pecuniary
pedagogue (teacher)
pedagogy
pedal (of bicycle)
  pedals
  pedaled
  pedaling
pedant
pedantic
pedantry
peddle (to sell trifles)
  peddled
  peddling
peddler
pedestal
pedestrian
pediatrician
pediatrics
pedicure
pedigree
pediment
pedometer
peek (to peep)
  peeked
  peeking
peel (to remove skin)
  peeled

peeling
peep
  peeped
  peeping
peer (look)
  peered
  peering
peerage
peeress
peerless
peeved
peevish
peevishness
peewit, pewit
peg
  pegged
  pegging
  pegs
pejorative
pejoratively
Pekinese
pelagic
pelican
pellet
pell-mell
pellucid (clear)
pelmet
pelt
pelvic
pelvis
pen

penned

penning

pens

penal

penalization

penalize

penalized

penalizing

penalty

penalties *pl*

penance

pence

penchant

pencil

pencils

penciled

penciling

pendant (hanging jewel)

pendent (hanging)

pending

pendulous (drooping)

pendulum

pendulums *pl*

penetrability

penetrable

penetrate

penetrated

penetrating

penetration

penetrative

penguin

penicillin

peninsula

peninsulas *pl*

peninsular (of a peninsula)

penis

penises *pl*

penitence

penitent

penitential

penitentiary

penitentiaries *pl*

penknife

penknives *pl*

pennant

penniless

pennilessness

pennon

penny

pennies *pl*

penology

pension

pensionable

pensioner

pensive

pensively

pensiveness

pentagon

pentagonal

pentameter

Pentateuch

pentathlon

penultimate

penultimately

penumbra

penumbrae, penumbras *pl*

penurious

penury

peon

peony (plant)

peonies *pl*

people

peopled

peopling

pep

pepped

pepping

peps

pepper

peppered

peppering

peppercorn

peppermint

peppery

pepsin

peptic

Pepys

Pepysian

peradventure

perambulate

perambulated
perambulating
perambulation
perambulator
per annum
per capita
perceivable
perceive
  perceived
  perceiving
percent
percentage
perceptible
perceptibly
perception
perceptive
perch
perchance
percipience
percipient
percolate
  percolated
  percolating
percolation
percolator
percuss
percussion
percussive
perdition
peregrinate
  peregrinated

  peregrinating
peregrination
peregrine
peremptorily
peremptoriness
peremptory
perennial
perennially
perfect
perfection
perfectionist
perfidious
perfidy
perforate
  perforated
  perforating
perforation
perforator
perforce
perform
performance
performer
perfume
  perfumed
  perfuming
perfumery
  perfumeries *pl*
perfunctorily
perfunctoriness
perfunctory
pergola

  pergolas *pl*
perhaps
pericardial
pericardium
  pericardia *pl*
peril
perilous
perilously
perimeter
period
periodic
periodical
periodically
periodicity
peripatetic
peripheral
periphery
periphrasis
periscope
perish
perishable
peritoneum
  peritonea,
    peritoneums *pl*
peritonitis
periwinkle
perjure
  perjured
  perjuring
perjurer
perjurious

perjury
perk
perkiness
perky
perm
permafrost
permanence
permanency
permanent
permanently
permanganate
permeability
permeable
permeate
  permeated
  permeating
permeation
permissible
permission
permissive
permissiveness
permit
  permits
  permitted
  permitting
permutation
pernicious
perniciously
perniciousness
pernickety
perorate

perorated
perorating
peroration
peroxide
perpendicular
perpendicularity
perpendicularly
perpetrate
  perpetrated
  perpetrating
perpetrator
perpetual
perpetually
perpetuate
  perpetuated
  perpetuating
perpetuity
perplex
perplexity
perquisite
per se
persecute
  persecuted
  persecuting
persecution
persecutor
perseverance
persevere
  persevered
  persevering
persiflage

persimmon
persist
persistence
persistency
persistent
persistently
person
persona grata
persona non grata
personable
personage
personal
personality
  personalities *pl*
personally
personate
  personated
  personating
personation
personator
personification
personify
  personified
  personifies
  personifying
personnel (staff)
perspective
perspicacious
perspicacity
perspicuity
perspicuous

perspiration
perspire
  perspired
  perspiring
persuadable
persuade
  persuaded
  persuading
persuader
persuasion
persuasive
persuasively
pert
pertain
pertinacious
pertinaciously
pertinacity
pertinence
pertinent
pertly
pertness
perturb
perturbation
peruke
perusal
peruse
  perused
  perusing
pervade
  pervaded
  pervading

pervasion
pervasive
pervasively
perverse
perversely
perversion
perversity
pervert
perverter
perverted
pervious
peseta (Spanish
  money)
peso (S. American
  money)
pessary
  pessaries *pl*
pessimism
pessimist
pessimistic
pessimistically
pest
pester
  pestered
  pestering
pesterer
pesticide
pestiferous
pestilence
pestilent
pestilential

pestle
pet
  pets
  petted
  petting
petal
petaled

petard
peter
  petered
  petering
petite
petit four
  petit fours *pl*
petition
petitioner
petit mal
petit point
petrel (sea bird)
petrification
petrify
  petrified
  petrifies
  petrifying
petrol
petroleum
petticoat
pettifog
  pettifogged
  pettifogging

pettifogs

pettifogger

pettifoggery

pettily

pettiness

pettish

petty

  pettier

  pettiest

petulance

petulant

petulantly

pew

pewit, peewit

pewter

pfennig (German money)

phagocyte

phalanx

  phalanges, phalanxes *pl*

phallic

phallus

  phalluses *pl*

phantasm

phantasmagoria

phantasmal

phantasmic

phantom

pharisaic

Pharisee

pharmaceutical

pharmacist

pharmacologist

pharmacology

pharmacopoeia

pharmacy

  pharmacies *pl*

pharyngeal

pharyngitis

pharynx

  pharynxes *pl*

phase

  phased

  phasing

pheasant

phenacetin

phenobarbital

phenobarbitone

phenol (type of benzene)

phenomenal

phenomenally

phenomenon

  phenomena *pl*

phenyl (formed from benzene)

phial, vial

philander

philanderer

philanthropic

philanthropically

philanthropist

philanthropy

philatelist

philately

philharmonic

Philistine

philistinism

philologist

philology

philosopher

philosophical

philosophically

philosophy

  philosophies *pl*

philter (love potion)

phlebitis

phlegm

phlegmatic

phlegmatically

phlox

phobia

  phobias *pl*

phoenix

  phoenixes *pl*

phone (telephone)

  phoned

  phoning

phonetic

phonetically

phonograph

phony (sham)

phonies *pl*
phosgene
phosphate
phosphorescence
phosphorescent
phosphoric
phosphorus
photocopier
photocopy
  photocopies *pl*
  photocopied
  photocopies
  photocopying
photogenic
photograph
photographer
photography
photometer
photometric
photometry
photostat
photosynthesis
phrase
  phrased
  phrasing
phraseology
phrenetic, frenetic
phrenologist
phrenology
phthisical
phthisis

phylactery
  phylacteries *pl*
phylloxera
phylum
  phyla *pl*
physical
physically
physician
physicist
physics
physiognomist
physiognomy
physiological
physiologically
physiologist
physiotherapist
physiotherapy
physique
pianissimo
pianist
piano
  pianos *pl*
pianoforte
pianola
  pianolas *pl*
piaster, piastre
  (Turkish money)
piazza, piazzas *pl*
picador
picaresque
piccalilli

piccalillis *pl*
piccolo
  piccolos *pl*
pick
pickax
picker
picket
  picketed
  picketing
pickle
  pickled
  pickling
pickpocket
  pickpocketed
  pickpocketing
picnic
  picnicked
  picnicking
  picnics
picnicker
picric acid
pictorial
pictorially
picture
  pictured
  picturing
picturesque
picturesquely
picturesqueness
piddle
  piddled

piddling
pidgin English
pie
piebald
piece
  pieced
  piecing
pièce de résistance
piecemeal
piecework
piecing
pied-à-terre
pier (on coast)
pierce
  pierced
  piercing
pier-head
pierrette
pierrot
pietism
pietist
piety
piezoelectric
piezoelectricity
piffle
piffling
pig
pigeon
pigeonhole
  pigeonholed
  pigeonholing

pigeon-toed
piggery
  piggeries *pl*
piggish
piggyback
pigheaded
pigheadedness
pigiron
piglet
pigment
pigmentation
pigsty
  pigsties *pl*
pike
pikestaff
pilaff, pilaf
pilchard
pile
  piled
  piling
pileup
pilfer
  pilfered
  pilfering
pilferage
pilferer
pilgrim
pilgrimage
pill
pillage
  pillaged

pillaging
pillager
pillar
pillar-box
  pillar-boxes *pl*
pillion
pillory
  pilloried
  pillories
  pillorying
pillow
pilot
  piloted
  piloting
pilotage
pimpernel
pimple
pimply
pin
  pinned
  pinning
  pins
pinafore
pince-nez
pincers
pinch
pinched
pinch-hit
  pinch-hits
  pinch-hitting
pinchhitter

pincushion
pine
  pined
  pining
pineapple
ping-pong
pinhead
pinion
  pinioned
  pinioning
pin-up
  pin-ups *pl*
pink
pinnace
pinnacle
pinpoint
pinstripe
pint
pioneer
  pioneered
  pioneering
pious
piously
pip
  pipped
  pipping
  pips
pipe
  piped
  piping
piper

pipette
pippin
pip-squeak
piquancy
piquant
pique
  piqued
  piquing
piquet (card game)
piracy
pirate
piratical
pirating
pirouette
  pirouetted
  pirouetting
piscatorial
piscina (fish pond)
piscine (bathing pool)
pistachio
  pistachios *pl*
pistil (of flower)
pistol (firearm)
piston
pit
  pits
  pitted
  pitting
pitch
pitcher (jug)
piteous

piteously
pitfall
pith
pithily
pithiness
pithy
pitiable
pitiful
pitiless, pitifully
pitilessly
pittance
pituitary
pity
  pities *pl*
  pitied
  pities
  pitying
pivot
  pivoted
  pivoting
pivotal
pixy, pixie
  pixies *pl*
pizza
  pizzas *pl*
pizzeria
  pizzerias *pl*
pizzicato
  pizzicatos *pl*
placability
placable

placard

placate

  placated

  placating

placation

place

  placed

  placing

placebo

  placebos *pl*

placement

placenta

  placentas *pl*

placid

placidity

placidly

placket

plagiarism

plagiarist

plagiarize

  plagiarized

  plagiarizing

plague

  plagued

  plaguing

plaice (fish)

plaid

plain

plainclothes

plainer

plainly

plainness

plainsong

plainspoken

plaint

plaintiff (prosecutor)

plaintive (sad)

plaintively

plaintiveness

plait (of hair)

plan

  planned

  planning

  plans

planchette

plane

  planed

  planing

planet

planetarium

  planetaria,

    planetariums *pl*

planetary

plank

plankton

planner

plant

plantain

plantation

planter

plaque

plasma

plaster

  plastered

  plastering

plasterer

plastic

plastically

plasticine

plasticity

plate

  plated

  plating

plateau

  plateaus, plateaux *pl*

plateful

  platefuls *pl*

platform

platinum

platitude

platitudinous

platonic

platonically

platoon

platter

platypus

  platypuses *pl*

plaudit

plausibility

plausible

plausibly

play

  played

playing

play off

player

playful

playfully

playfulness

playgoer

playgoing

playmate

playwright

plaza

plazas *pl*

plea

pleas *pl*

plead

pleader

pleasant

pleasantly

pleasantness

pleasantry (joke)

pleasantries *pl*

please

pleased

pleasing

pleasurable

pleasurably

pleasure

pleasured

pleasuring

pleat

plebeian

plebiscite

pledge

pledged

pledging

Pleistocene

plenary

plenaries *pl*

plenipotentiary

plenipotentiaries *pl*

plenitude

plenteous

plenteously

plentiful

plentifully

plentifulness

plenty

plethora

plethoric

pleura

pleural

pleurisy

pliability

pliable

pliancy

pliant

plied (*from* ply)

pliers

plies

plight

Plimsoll line

plimsoll

plinth

Pliocene

plod

plodded

plodding

plods

plodder

plonk

plop

plopped

plopping

plops

plot

plots

plotted

plotting

plotter

plover

plow

plowed

plowing

pluck

pluckily

plucky

pluckier

pluckiest

plug

plugged

plugging

plugs

plum

plumage

plumb (to measure
  depth)

plumbago

  plumbagos *pl*

plumber

plumbing

plume

plummet

  plummeted

  plummeting

plummy

plummet

plump

plumper

plumpness

plunder

  plundered

  plundering

plunge

  plunged

  plunging

plunger

pluperfect

plural

pluralism

plurality

plus

  pluses *pl*

plush

plutocracy

plutocracies *pl*

plutocrat

plutocratic

plutonium

ply

  plied

  plies

  plying

plywood

pneumatic

pneumonia

poach

  poached

  poaches

  poaching

poacher

pock

pocket

  pocketed

  pocketing

pocketbook

pockmarked

pockmark

pod

podge

podgy

podium

  podia, podiums *pl*

poem

poesy

poet

poetic

poetical

poetically

poetry

pogrom

poignancy

poignant

poignantly

poinsettia

  poinsettias *pl*

point

point-blank

pointed

pointedly

pointless

pointlessly

poise

poised

poison

  poisoned

  poisoning

poisoner

poisonous

poke

  poked

  poking

poker

poky

polar

polarity

polarization

polarize
  polarized
  polarizing
pole
polemic
polemical
polemically
police
  policed
  policing
policeman
  policemen *pl*
policewoman
  policewomen *pl*
policy
  policies *pl*
poliomyelitis
polish
polite
politely
politeness
politer
politic
political
politically
politician
polity
polka
  polkas *pl*
poll
pollard

pollen
pollinate
  pollinated
  pollinating
pollination
pollinator
pollster
pollutant
pollute
  polluted
  polluting
pollution
polo
polonaise
polonium
polony
  polonies *pl*
poltergeist
poltroon
polyandrous
polyandry
polyanthus
polychromatic
polychrome
polyester
polygamist
polygamous
polygamously
polygamy
polyglot
polygon

polymer
polymerization
polymerize
  polymerized
  polymerizing
polyp
polyphonic
polyphony
polypus
  polypi *pl*
polystyrene
polysyllabic
polytechnic
polythene
polyunsaturated
pomade
pomegranate
pommel (of saddle)
pomp
Pompeian
Pompeii
pomposity
pompous
pompously
poncho
  ponchos *pl*
pond (to consider)
ponder
  pondered
  pondering
ponderous

poniard
pontiff
  pontiffs *pl*
pontifical
pontificate
  pontificated
  pontificating
pontification
pontoon
pony
  ponies *pl*
ponytail
poodle
pooh-pooh
  pooh-poohed
  pooh-poohing
pool
  pooled
  pooling
poop
  pooped
  pooping
pooper scooper
poor (lacking wealth)
poorly
poorness
pop
  popped
  popping
  pops
popcorn

pope
popery
pop-eyed
poplar (tree)
poplin
poppers
poppy
  poppies *pl*
populace
popular
popularity
popularization
popularize
  popularized
  popularizing
popularly
populate
  populated
  populating
population
populous
porcelain
porch
porcupine
pore (of skin; to look,
    think intently)
  pored
  poring
pork
porker
pornographer

pornographic
pornographically
pornography
porosity
porous
porphyry
porpoise
porridge
porringer
port
portability
portable
portal
portcullis
portend
portent
portentous
porter
porterage
portfolio
  portfolios *pl*
porthole
portico
  porticoes, porticos *pl*
portion
portlier
portliness
portly
portmanteau
  portmanteaus,
    portmanteaux *pl*

portrait
portraiture
portray
  portrayed
  portraying
portrayal
Portugal
Portuguese
pose
  posed
  posing
poser
posh
position
  positioned
  positioning
positive
positively
positivism
positivist
positron
posse
possess
possession
possessive
possessively
possessiveness
possessor
possibility
  possibilities *pl*
possible

possibly
post
postage
postal order
postdate
  postdated
  postdating
poste restante
poster
posterior
posterity
postgraduate
posthaste
posthumous
posthumously
Postimpressionism
Postimpressionist
postman
  postmen *pl*
postmark
postmaster
postmortem
postnatal
post office
postpaid
postpone
  postponed
  postponing
postponement
postscript
postulant

postulate
  postulated
  postulating
postulation
postural
posture
  postured
  posturing
posturer
postwoman
  postwomen *pl*
posy
  posies *pl*
pot
  pots
  potted
  potting
potable
potash
potassium
potation
potato
  potatoes *pl*
potbellied
potbelly
  potbellies *pl*
potboiler
potency
potent
potentate
potential

potentiality
potentially
potentiometer
potently
pother
pothole
  potholed
  potholing
potholer
potion
potpourri
pottage
potter
  pottered
  pottering
potterer
pottery
  potteries *pl*
pottily
pouch
pouffe, pouf (cushion)
poulterer
poultice
poultry
pounce
  pounced
  pouncing
pound
poundage
poundal
pour (liquid)

poured
pouring
pout
  pouted
  pouting
pouter
poverty
powder
  powdered
  powdering
powdery
power
  powered
  powering
powerful
powerfully
powerless
powerlessness
powwow
pox
practicability
practicable
practical
practicality
  practicalities *pl*
practically
practice
  practiced
  practicing
practitioner
pragmatic

pragmatical
pragmatically
pragmatism
prairie
praise
  praised
  praising
praiseworthy
praline
pram
prance
  pranced
  prancing
prank
prate
  prated
  prating
prattle
  prattled
  prattling
prattler
prawn
pray (to say prayers)
  prayed
  praying
prayer
preach
preacher
preamble
prearrange
  prearranged

prearranging
prearrangement
prebend
prebendary
  prebendaries *pl*
precarious
precariously
precariousness
precatory
precaution
precautionary
precede (to go before)
  preceded
  preceding
precedence
precedent
precentor
precept
precession
precinct
precious
precipice
precipitant
precipitate
  precipitated
  precipitating
precipitately
precipitation
precipitous
precipitously
précis

precise
precisely
precision
preclude
  precluded
  precluding
preclusive
precocious
precociousness
precocity
precognition
preconceived
preconception
precursor
precursory
predacious
predator
predatory
predecease
  predeceased
  predeceasing
predecessor
predestination
predestine
  predestined
  predestining
predetermined
predicament
predicate
  predicated
  predicating

predication
predict
predictable
predictably
prediction
predigest
predigestion
predilection
predispose
  predisposed
  predisposing
predisposition
predominance
predominant
predominantly
predominate
  predominated
  predominating
preeminence
preeminent
preeminently
preempt
preemption
preemptive
preexist
preexistence
preexistent
preexisting
preen
  preened
  preening

prefab
prefabricate
  prefabricated
  prefabricating
prefabrication
preface
  prefaced
  prefacing
prefect
prefectorial
prefecture
prefer
  preferred
  preferring
  prefers
preferable
preferably
preference
preferential
preferentially
preferment
prefix
  prefixes *pl*
  prefixed
  prefixing
pregnancy
  pregnancies *pl*
pregnant
prehensile
prehension
prehistoric

prehistorically
prehistory
prejudge
  prejudged
  prejudging
prejudice
  prejudiced
  prejudicing
prejudicial
prejudicially
prelacy
  prelacies *pl*
prelate
preliminarily
preliminary
  preliminaries *pl*
prelude
preluding
premarital
premature
prematurely
prematurity
premeditate
  premeditated
  premeditating
premeditation
premier (most
  important; prime
  minister)
premiere (first
  performance)

premiered
premieres
premiering
premiership
premise (logic
  statement)
  premises *pl*
premises (*eg* houses)
premium
  premiums *pl*
premonition
premonitory
prenatal
prentice
  prenticed
  prenticing
preoccupation
preoccupy
  preoccupied
  preoccupies
  preoccupying
prepaid (*from* prepay)
preparation
preparative
preparatorily
preparatory
prepare
  prepared
  preparing
preparedness
prepay

prepaid
prepaying
prepays
prepayable
preponderance
preponderant
preponderantly
preponderate
  preponderated
  preponderating
preposition
prepossess
prepossessing
preposterous
preposterously
prerequisite
prerogative
presage
  presaged
  presaging
presbyter
Presbyterian
prescience
prescient
prescribe (*eg*
  medicine)
  prescribed
  prescribing
prescription
prescriptive
presence

present
presentable
presentation
presentiment
presently
preservation
preservative
preserve
  preserved
  preserving
preserver
preside
  presided
  presiding
presidency
  presidencies *pl*
president
presidential
presidio
  presidios *pl*
presidium
  presidiums *pl*
press
pressed
pressure
pressurization
pressurize
  pressurized
  pressurizing
prestidigitation
prestidigitator

prestige
prestigious
prestissimo
  prestissimos *pl*
presto
prestress
prestressed
presumably
presume
  presumed
  presuming
presumption
presumptive
presumptuous
presuppose
  presupposed
  presupposing
presupposition
pretend
pretender
pretense
pretension
pretentious
pretentiously
preterit
preternatural
pretext
prettily
prettiness
pretty
  prettier

prettiest
pretzel
prevail
  prevailed
  prevailing
prevalence
prevalent
prevaricate
  prevaricated
  prevaricating
prevarication
prevaricator
prevent
preventable
preventative
prevention
preventive
preview
previous
previously
prewar
prey (plunder)
  preyed
  preying
price
  priced
  pricing
priceless
prick
pricker
prickle

prickled
  prickling
prickly
pride
  prided
  priding
pried (*from* pry)
pries (*from* pry)
priest
priesthood
priestly
prig
priggish
prim
  primmer
  primmest
prima donna
  prima donnas *pl*
prima facie
primacy
primarily
primary
  primaries *pl*
primate
prime
  primed
  priming
prime minister
primeval
primitive
primitively

primly
primogenitor (earliest
  ancestor)
primogeniture (being
  first born)
primordial
primordially
primrose
primula
  primulas *pl*
prince
princely
princess
principal (chief)
principality
  principalities *pl*
principally
principle (moral
  code)
print
printable
printer
prior
prioress
priority
  priorities *pl*
priory
  priories *pl*
prism
prismatic
prison

prisoner
pristine
privacy
private
privateer
privately
privation
privative
privet (hedge)
privilege
privileged
privy
prize
  prized
  prizing
prizefight
prizefighter
proactive
probability
probable
probably
probate
probation
probationer
probe
  probed
  probing
probity
problem
problematic
problematical

problematically
proboscis
  proboscises,
    proboscides *pl*
procedural
procedure
proceed
  proceeded
  proceeding
process
procession
processional
processor
prochoice
proclaim
  proclaimed
  proclaiming
proclamation
proclivity
  proclivities *pl*
procrastinate
  procrastinated
  procrastinating
procrastination
procrastinator
procreate
  procreated
  procreating
procreative
procreator
proctor

proctorial
procurable
procuration
procurator
procure
  procured
  procuring
prod
  prodded
  prodding
  prods
prodigal
prodigality
prodigally
prodigious
prodigiously
prodigiousness
prodigy
  prodigies *pl*
produce
  produced
  producing
producer
product
production
productive
productively
productiveness
productivity
profanation
profane

profaned
profaning
profanely
profanity
  profanities *pl*
profess
profession
professional
professionalism
professionally
professor
professorial
proffer
  proffered
  proffering
proficiency
proficient
proficiently
profile
  profiled
  profiling
profit
  profited
  profiting
profitability
profitable
profitably
profiteer
  profiteered
  profiteering
profitless

profligacy
profligate
profligately
pro forma
profound
profounder
profoundly
profundity
profuse
profusely
profusion
progenitor (ancestor)
progenitrix
progeniture
progeny
prognosis
  prognoses *pl*
prognostic
prognosticate
  prognosticated
  prognosticating
prognostication
program
  programmed
  programming
  programs
programmer
progress
progression
progressive
progressively

prohibit
  prohibited
  prohibiting
prohibition
prohibitionist
prohibitive
prohibitively
project
projectile
projection
projector
prolapsed
proletarian
proletariat
prolife
proliferate
  proliferated
  proliferating
proliferation
prolific
prolifically
prolification
prolix
prolixity
prologue
prolong
prolongation
promenade
  promenaded
  promenading
promenader

prominence
prominent
prominently
promiscuity
promiscuous
promiscuously
promise
  promised
  promising
promissory
promontory
  promontories *pl*
promote
  promoted
  promoting
promoter
promotion
prompt
prompter
promptitude
promptly
promptness
promulgate
  promulgated
  promulgating
promulgation
promulgator
prone
prong
pronged
pronoun

pronounce
  pronounced
  pronouncing
pronounceable
pronouncement
pronunciation
proof
  proofs *pl*
proofreader
proofreading
prop
  propped
  propping
  props
propaganda
propagandist
propagate
  propagated
  propagating
propagation
propagator
propel
  propelled
  propelling
  propels
propellant (rocket
  fuel)
propellent (driving)
propeller
propensity
  propensities *pl*

proper
properly
propertied
property
  properties *pl*
prophecy (prediction)
  prophecies *pl*
prophesy (to predict)
  prophesied
  prophesies
  prophesying
prophet
prophetic
prophetically
prophylactic
prophylaxis
propinquity
  propinquities *pl*
propitiate
  propitiated
  propitiating
propitiator
propitiatory
propitious
propitiously
proponent
proportion
proportional
proportionally
proportionate
proposal

propose
  proposed
  proposing
proposer
proposition
propound
proprietary (legally
  owned)
proprietor (owner)
proprietress
propriety (decency)
  proprieties *pl*
propulsion
propulsive
pro rata
prorogation
prorogue
  prorogued
  proroguing
prosaic
prosaically
proscenium
proscribe (to outlaw)
  proscribed
  proscribing
proscription
proscriptive
prose
prosecute
  prosecuted
  prosecuting

prosecution
prosecutor
proselyte
proselytism
proselytize
  proselytized
  proselytizing
proselytizer
prosily
prosiness
prosody
prospect
prospective
prospector
prospectus
  prospectuses *pl*
prosper
  prospered
  prospering
prosperity
prosperous
prostate (gland)
prostitute
  prostituted
  prostituting
prostitution
prostrate
  prostrated
  prostrating
prostration
prosy

protagonist
protean (variable)
protect
protection
protective
protector
protectorate
protégé
protein (food
  chemical)
pro tempore, pro tem
protest
Protestant
Protestantism
protestation
protester, protestor
protocol
proton
protoplasm
prototype
protozoon
  protozoa *pl*
protract
protractor
protrude
  protruded
  protruding
protrusion
protuberance
protuberant
proud

prouder
proudly
provable
prove
  proved
  proving
proven (in law)
provenance
provender
proverb
proverbial
proverbially
provide
  provided
  providing
providence
provident
providential
providentially
provider
province
provincial
provincialism
provision
provisional
provisionally
proviso
  provisos pl
provisory
provocation
provocative

provocatively
provoke
  provoked
  provoking
provost
prow
prowess
prowl
prowler
proximate (nearest)
proximity
proxy
  proxies pl
prude
prudence
prudent
prudential
prudentially
prudery
prudish
prune
  pruned
  pruning
prurience
prurient
prussic
pry
  pried
  pries
  prying
psalm

psalmist
psalter (book of
  psalms)
pseudonym
pseudonymity
pseudonymous
psittacosis
psyche
psychedelic
psychiatric
psychiatrist
psychiatry
psychic
psychoanalysis
psychoanalyst
psychoanalytic
psychoanalytical
psychoanalyze
  psychoanalyzed
  psychoanalyzing
psychological
psychologist
psychology
psychometric
psychopath
psychopathic
psychosis
  psychoses pl
psychosomatic
ptarmigan
pterodactyl

ptomaine
pub
puberty
pubescence
pubescent
pubic
pubis
public
publican
publication
publicist
publicity
publicize
  publicized
  publicizing
publish
publisher
puce
puck
pucker
  puckered
  puckering
puckish
pudding
puddle
puerile
puerilely
puerility
puerperal
puff
puffin (sea-bird)

puffiness
puffy
  puffier
  puffiest
pug
pugilism
pugilist
pugnacious
pugnaciously
pugnacity
pukka
puling (whining)
pull
pullet
pulley
  pulleys pl
pullover
pullulate
  pullulated
  pullulating
pulmonary
pulp
pulpit
pulsar
pulsate
  pulsated
  pulsating
pulsation
pulse
  pulsed
  pulsing

pulseless
pulverization
pulverize
  pulverized
  pulverizing
puma
  pumas pl
pumice
pummel
  pummels
  pummeled
  pummeling
pump
pumpernickel
pumpkin
pun
  punned
  punning
  puns
punch
punctilious
punctiliously
punctiliousness
punctual
punctuality
punctually
punctuate
  punctuated
  punctuating
punctuation
puncture

punctured
puncturing
pundit
pungency
pungent
pungently
punish
punishable
punishment
punitive
punster
punt
punter
puny
  punier
  puniest
pup
pupa
  pupae *pl*
pupate
  pupated
  pupating
pupation
pupil
puppet
puppeteer
puppetry
puppy
  puppies *pl*
purblind
purchasable

purchase
  purchased
  purchasing
purchaser
purdah
pure
purée, puree(food)
  puréed, pureed
  puréeing, pureeing
  purées, purees
purely
purer
purgation
purgative
purgatorial
purgatory
purge
  purged
  purging
purification
purifier
purify
  purified
  purifies
  purifying
purism
purist
Puritan
puritanic
puritanical
puritanism

purity
purl (in knitting)
purloin
purple
purport
purpose
purposeful
purposeless
purposely
purr
purse
  pursed
  pursing
purser
pursuance
pursuant
pursue
  pursued
  pursuing
pursuit
purulence
purulent
purvey
  purveyed
  purveying
  purveys
purveyance
purveyor
purview
pus (from wound)
push

pusher
pushover
pusillanimity
pusillanimous
puss (cat)
pussy
  pussies *pl*
pustule
put (to place)
  puts
  putting
putative
putrefaction
putrefy
  putrefied
  putrefies
  putrefying
putrescence
putrescent
putrid
putt (in golf)
puttee (leggings)
putter
putty (for glazing)
puzzle
  puzzled
  puzzling
puzzlement
puzzler
pyelitis
pygmy

  pygmies *pl*
pyjamas
pylon
pyramid
pyramidal
pyre
pyrites
pyrotechnics
pyrrhic
python

quack
quackery
quadrangle
quadrangular
quadrant
quadraphonic
quadratic
quadrature
quadrilateral
quadrille
quadruped
quadruple
  quadrupled
  quadrupling
quadruplet

quadruplicate
  quadruplicated
  quadruplicating
quadruplication
quaff
quagmire
quail
  quailed
  quailing
quaint
quainter
quaintly
quaintness
quake
  quaked

quaking
Quaker
qualification
qualify
  qualified
  qualifies
  qualifying
qualitative
qualitatively
quality
  qualities *pl*
qualm
quandary
  quandaries *pl*
quantifiable
quantification
quantify
  quantified
  quantifies
  quantifying
quantitative
quantitatively
quantity
  quantities *pl*
quantum
  quanta *pl*
quarantine
quarrel
  quarrels
  quarreled
  quarreling

quarrelsome
quarry
 quarries *pl*
quart
quarter
 quartered
 quartering
quarterly
quartermaster
quartet
quarto
 quartos *pl*
quartz
quartzite
quasar
quash
quaternary
quatrain
quaver
 quavered
 quavering
quay (landing place)
 quays *pl*
queasiness
queasy
queen (sovereign)
queenly
queer
queerly
quell
quench

querulous
querulously
querulousness
query
 queries *pl*
 queried
 queries
 querying
quest
question
 questioned
 questioning
questionable
questionably
questioner
questionnaire
qui vive
quibble
 quibbled
 quibbling
quibbler
quick
quicken
 quickened
 quickening
quicker
quickly
quickness
quicksand
quicksilver
quid pro quo

quiescence
quiescent
quiet
quieter
quietly
quietude
quietus
quill
quilt
quince
quinine
quinquennial
quinquennium
 quinquenniums,
  quinquennia *pl*
quinsy
quintessence
quintet
quintuple
quintuplet
quip
 quipped
 quipping
 quips
quire (of paper)
quirk
quisling
quit
 quits
 quitted
 quitting

quite
quittance
quitter
quiver
  quivered
  quivering
quixotic
quixotically
quixotism
quiz
  quizzes *pl*
  quizzes
  quizzed
  quizzing
quizzically
quoit
quorum
  quorums *pl*
quota
  quotas *pl*
quotable
quotation
quote
  quoted
  quoting
quotidian
quotient

rabbi
  rabbis *pl*
rabbinical
rabbit
rabble
rabid
rabidly
rabies
race (to compete)
  raced
  racing
racecourse
racehorse
raceme
racetrack
racer
racial
racialism

racialist
racially
racily
racism
racist
rack
racket (disturbance;
  swindle)
racket, racquet
  (*eg* tennis)
racketeer
raconteur
racoon, raccoon
racquet, racket
  (*eg* tennis)
racy
radar
radial

radially
radiance
radiant
radiantly
radiate
  radiated
  radiating
radiation
radiator
radical
radicalism
radically
radio
  radios *pl*
  radioed
  radioing
  radios
radioactive
radioactivity
radiogram
radiographer
radiography
radioisotope
radiologist
radiology
radish
radium
radius
  radii, radiuses *pl*
radon
raffia

raffish

raffle
 raffled
 raffling

raft

rafter

ragamuffin

rage
 raged
 raging

ragged

raglan

ragout

rags

ragtime

raid
 raided
 raiding

raider

rail
 railed
 railing

raillery (teasing)

railroad

raiment

rain (water)
 rained
 raining

rainbow

raincheck

raincoat

rainfall

rainless

rainy

raise (to increase,
   bring up)
 raised
 raising

raisin (dried grape)

raison d'être

rajah, raja

rake
 raked
 raking

rakish

rally
 rallies pl
 rallied
 rallies
 rallying

ram
 rammed
 ramming
 rams

ramble
 rambled
 rambling

rambler

ramekin, ramequin

ramification

ramify
 ramified

ramifies

ramifying

ramp

rampage
 rampaged
 rampaging

rampancy

rampant

rampart

ramrod

ramshackle

ran (from run)

ranch

rancher

rancid

rancor

rancorous

random

randomly

rang (from ring)

range
 ranged
 ranging

rangy
 rangier
 rangiest

rank

ranker

rankle
 rankled
 rankling

ransack
ransom
  ransomed
  ransoming
rant
rap (to knock; music)
  rapped
  rapping
  raps
rapacious
rapacity
rape
  raped
  raping
rapid
rapidity
rapidly
rapier
rapine
rapist
rapport
rapprochement
rapscallion
rapt (engrossed)
rapture
rapturous
rapturously
rare
rarebit (Welsh)
rarefaction
rarefy

rarefied
rarefies
rarefying
rarely
rarer
rarity
  rarities *pl*
rascal
rascality
rash
rasher
rashly
rasp
raspberry
  raspberries *pl*
rat
  rats
  ratted
  ratting
ratchet
rate
  rated
  rating
rateable, ratable
ratepayer
rather
ratification
ratify
  ratified
  ratifies
  ratifying

ratio
  ratios *pl*
ratiocinate
  ratiocinated
  ratiocinating
ratiocination
ration
  rationed
  rationing
rational (reasonable)
rationale (basic
  reason)
rationalism
rationality
rationalization
rationalize
  rationalized
  rationalizing
rationally
rats
rattan
rattle
  rattled
  rattling
rattlesnake
raucous
raucously
raucousness
ravage
  ravaged
  ravaging

ravager

rave

  raved

  raving

ravel

  ravels

  raveled

  raveling

raven

ravening

ravenous

ravenously

raver

ravine (gorge)

ravioli

ravish

raw (uncooked)

rawboned

rawer

rawness

ray (beam)

  rays *pl*

rayon

raze (to destroy)

  razed

  razing

razor

razzle-dazzle

reach

react

reactance

reaction

reactionary

  reactionaries *pl*

reactivate

  reactivated

  reactivating

reactive

reactor

read (*eg* a book)

  reading

readable

readdress

reader

readily

readiness

readjust

readjustment

readmission

readmit

  readmits

  readmitted

  readmitting

readmittance

ready

  readied

  readies

  readying

readymade

reagent

real (true)

realism

realist

realistic

realistically

reality

  realities *pl*

realizable

realization

realize

  realized

  realizing

really

realm

ream (of paper)

reap

  reaped

  reaping

reaper

reappear

  reappeared

  reappearing

reappearance

rear

  reared

  rearing

rearguard

rearm

  rearmed

  rearming

rearmament

rearrange

  rearranged

rearranging
rearrangement
reason
reasoned
reasoning
reasonable
reasonableness
reasonably
reassemble
reassembled
reassembling
reassess
reassessment
reassurance
reassure
reassured
reassuring
reassuringly
rebate
rebel
rebelled
rebelling
rebels
rebellion
rebellious
rebirth
rebound
rebuff
rebuild
rebuilding
rebuilds

rebuilt
rebuke
rebuked
rebuking
rebut
rebuts
rebutted
rebutting
rebuttal
recalcitrance
recalcitrant
recall
recant
recantation
recap
recapped
recapping
recaps
recapitulate
recapitulated
recapitulating
recapitulation
recapture
recaptured
recapturing
recede
receded
receding
receipt
receivable
receive

received
receiving
receiver
receivership
recent
recently
receptacle
reception
receptionist
receptive
recess
recessed
recession
recessional
recessive
recharge
recharged
recharging
rechargeable
recherché
recidivism
recidivist
recipe
recipient
reciprocal
reciprocally
reciprocate
reciprocated
reciprocating
reciprocation
reciprocity

recital
recitation
recitative
recite
  recited
  reciting
reciter
reckless
recklessly
recklessness
reckon
  reckoned
  reckoning
reckoner
reclaim
  reclaimed
  reclaiming
reclamation
recline
  reclined
  reclining
recluse
reclusion
reclusive
recognition
recognizable
recognizance
recognize
  recognized
  recognizing
recoil

  recoiled
  recoiling
recollect
recollection
recommend
recommendation
recommit
  recommits
  recommitted
  recommitting
recommitment
recommittal
  recommitted
recompense
  recompensed
  recompensing
reconcilable
reconcile
  reconciled
  reconciling
reconcilement
reconciliation
recondite
recondition
  reconditioned
  reconditioning
reconnaissance
reconnoiter
  reconnoitered
  reconnoitering
reconquer

reconquered
reconquering
reconsider
  reconsidered
  reconsidering
  reconsideration
reconstruct
reconstruction
record
recorder
record player
recount (to count
  again)
recount (to tell)
recoup
  recouped
  recouping
recourse
recover
  recovered
  recovering
recovery
  recoveries pl
recreant
recreate (create
  again)
  recreated
  recreating
recreation
recreational
recreative

recriminate
  recriminated
  recriminating
recrimination
recriminatory
recrudescence
recrudescent
recruit
  recruited
  recruiting
rectal
rectangle
rectangular
rectifiable
rectification
rectifier
rectify
  rectified
  rectifies
  rectifying
rectilineal
rectilinear
rectitude
rector
rectorial
rectory
  rectories *pl*
rectum
  rectums *pl*
recumbent
recuperate

recuperated
recuperating
recuperation
recuperative
recur
  recurred
  recurring
  recurs
recurrence
recurrent
recusancy
recusant
recycle
  recycled
  recycling
red (color)
redbreast
redden
  reddened
  reddening
redder
redeem
  redeemed
  redeeming
redeemable
redeemer
redemption
redeploy
  redeployed
  redeploying
  redeploys

redeployment
redevelop
  redeveloped
  redeveloping
redevelopment
redid (*from* redo)
rediffusion
redirect
redirection
redistribute
  redistributed
  redistributing
redistribution
redo
  redid
  redoes
  redoing
  redone
redolence
redolent
redouble
  redoubled
  redoubling
redoubt
redoubtable
redound
redress
reduce
  reduced
  reducing
reducible

reductio ad absurdum
reduction
redundancy
  redundancies *pl*
redundant
reduplicate
  reduplicated
  reduplicating
reduplication
re-echo
  re-echoed
  re-echoes
  re-echoing
reed (water plant)
reef
reek (smell)
reel (dance; *eg* of
  cotton; to stagger)
reelect
reelection
reenter
  reentered
  reentering
reentrant
reentry
  reentries *pl*
reestablish
reestablishment
reexamination
reexamine
  reexamined

reexamining
reexport
reexportation
refectory
  refectories *pl*
refer
  referred
  referring
  refers
referable
referee
  refereed
  refereeing
reference
referendum
  referenda,
    referendums *pl*
refill
refillable
refine
  refined
  refining
refinement
refinery
  refineries *pl*
refit
  refits
  refitted
  refitting
reflate
  reflated

reflating
reflation
reflationary
reflect
reflection
reflective
reflector
reflex
  reflexes *pl*
reflexive (grammar)
refloat
  refloated
  refloating
reform
reformation
reformatory
  reformatories *pl*
reformed
reformer
refract
refraction
refractive
refractoriness
refractory
refrain
  refrained
  refraining
refresh
refresher
refreshment
refrigerant

refrigerate
  refrigerated
  refrigerating
refrigeration
refrigerator
refuel
  refuels
  refueled
  refueling
refuge
refugee
refulgence
refulgent
refund
refurbish
refurbishment
refusal
refuse
  refused
  refusing
refutable
refutation
refute
  refuted
  refuting
regain
  regained
  regaining
regal (royal)
regale (to entertain)
  regaled

  regaling
regalia
regally
regard
regardless
regatta
  regattas *pl*
regency
  regencies *pl*
regenerate
  regenerated
  regenerating
regeneration
regenerative
regenerator
regent
regicidal
regicide
regime (method of
  government)
regimen (strict
  routine)
regiment (of soldiers)
regimental
regimentation
region
regional
regionally
register (record)
  registered
  registering

registrar (*eg* of
  college)
registration
registry (where
  records are kept)
  registries *pl*
registry office
regress
regression
regressive
regret
  regrets
  regretted
  regretting
regretful
regretfully
regrettable
regrettably
regular
regularity
regularization
regularize
  regularized
  regularizing
regularly
regulate
  regulated
  regulating
regulation
regulator
regurgitate

regurgitated
regurgitating
regurgitation
rehabilitate
  rehabilitated
  rehabilitating
rehabilitation
rehearsal
rehearse
  rehearsed
  rehearsing
reign (to rule)
  reigned
  reigning
reimburse
  reimbursed
  reimbursing
reimbursement
rein (of horse)
reincarnation
reincarnate
  reincarnated
  reincarnating
reindeer
reinforce
  reinforced
  reinforcing
reinforceable
reinforcement
reinstate
  reinstated

  reinstating
reinstatement
reiterate
  reiterated
  reiterating
reiteration
reject
rejection
rejoice
  rejoiced
  rejoicing
rejoinder
rejuvenate
  rejuvenated
  rejuvenating
rejuvenation
relapse
  relapsed
  relapsing
relate
  related
  relating
relation
relationship
relative
relatively
relativity
relax
  relaxed
  relaxes
  relaxing

relaxation
relaxed
relay
  relayed
  relaying
  relays
release
  released
  releasing
relegate
  relegated
  relegating
relegation
relent
relentless
relentlessly
relevance
relevant
reliability
reliable
reliably
reliance
reliant
relic
relief
relieve
  relieved
  relieving
religion
religious
religiously

relinquish
reliquary
  reliquaries *pl*
relish
reluctance
reluctant
reluctantly
rely
  relied
  relies
  relying
remain
  remained
  remaining
remainder
  remaindered
  remaindering
remand
remark
remarkable
remarkably
remediable
remedial
remedy
  remedies *pl*
  remedied
  remedies
  remedying
remember
  remembered
  remembering

remembrance
remind
reminder
reminisce
  reminisced
  reminiscing
reminiscence
reminiscent
remiss
remissible
remission
remissness
remit
  remits
  remitted
  remitting
remittal
remittance
remnant
remonstrance
remonstrant
remonstrate
  remonstrated
  remonstrating
remonstration
remonstrator
remorse
remorseful
remorseless
remorselessly
remote

remotely
remotest
remount
removable
removal
remove
  removed
  removing
remover
remunerate
  remunerated
  remunerating
remuneration
remunerative
Renaissance
rend
render
  rendered
  rendering
rendezvous
rendition
renegade (turncoat)
renegation
renege
  reneged
  reneging
renew
  renewed
  renewing
renewable
renewal

rennet

renounce
  renounced
  renouncing
renouncement

renovate
  renovated
  renovating
renovation
renovator

renown
renowned

rent
rental
rentier

renunciate
  renunciated
  renunciating
renunciation

reopen
  reopened
  reopening
reorganization
reorganize
  reorganized
  reorganizing

repaid (*from* repay)

repair
  repaired
  repairing
repairer

reparable
reparation

repartee
  repartees *pl*

repast

repatriate
  repatriated
  repatriating
repatriation

repay
  repaid
  repaying
  repays

repayable
repayment

repeal
  repealed
  repealing

repeat
  repeated
  repeating
repeatedly
repeater

repel
  repelled
  repelling
  repels
repellent

repent
repentance
repentant

repercussion

repertoire (list of plays)

repertory (theater)
  repertories *pl*

repetition
repetitious
repetitive

rephrase
  rephrased
  rephrasing

repine
  repined
  repining

replace
  replaced
  replacing
replaceable
replacement

replay
  replays *pl*
  replayed
  replaying
  replays

replenish
replenishment

replete
repletion

replica
  replicas *pl*

reply

replies *pl*
replied
replies
replying
report
reportable
reportedly
reporter
repose
reposed
reposing
repository
repositories *pl*
repossess
repossession
reprehend
reprehensible
reprehension
represent
representation
representative
repress
repression
repressive
reprieve
reprieved
reprieving
reprimand
reprint
reprisal
reproach

reproached
reproachful
reproachfully
reprobate
reprobated
reprobating
reprobation
reproduce
reproduced
reproducing
reproducible
reproduction
reproductive
reproof (blame)
reproofs *pl*
reproval
reprove (to scold)
reproved
reproving
reprovingly
reptile
reptilian
republic
republican
republicanism
republication
republish
repudiate
repudiated
repudiating
repudiation

repugnance
repugnant
repulse
repulsed
repulsing
repulsion
repulsive
reputable
reputation
repute
reputedly
request
requiem
requiescat
require
required
requiring
requisite
requisition
requital
requite
requited
requiting
reroute
rerouted
reroutes
rerouting
rerun
reran
rerunning
reruns

rescind
rescission
rescript
rescue
  rescued
  rescuing
rescuer
research
researcher
researching
resemblance
resemble
  resembled
  resembling
resent
resentful
resentment
reservation
reserve
  reserved
  reserving
reservedly
reservist
reservoir
reset
  resets
  resetting
resettle
  resettled
  resettling
resettlement

reside
  resided
  residing
residence
residency
  residencies *pl*
residential
residual
residuary
residue
residuum
  residua *pl*
resign
  resigned
  resigning
resignation
resilience
resilient
resiliently
resin
resinous
resist
resistance
resistant
resister (person)
resistive
resistor (electrical)
resole
  resoled
  resoling
resolute

resolutely
resolution
resolve
  resolved
  resolving
resonance
resonant
resonate
  resonated
  resonating
resonator
resort
resound
resource
resourceful
respect
respectability
respectable
respectful
respectfully
respective
respectively
respiration
respirator
respiratory
respire
  respired
  respiring
respite
resplendence
resplendent

resplendently
respond
respondent
response
responsibility
  responsibilities *pl*
responsible
responsibly
responsive
rest (sleep)
restaurant
restaurateur
restful
restfully
restfulness
restitution
restive
restively
restiveness
restless
restlessly
restlessness
restoration
restorative
restore
  restored
  restoring
restorer
restrain
  restrained
  restraining

restraint
restrict
restriction
restrictive
restructure
  restructured
  restructuring
result
resultant
resume (review)
resume (take up)
  resumed
  resuming
resumption
resurgence
resurgent
resurrect
resurrection
resuscitate
  resuscitated
  resuscitating
resuscitation
retail
  retailed
  retailing
retailer
retain
  retained
  retaining
retainer
retaliate

retaliated
retaliating
retaliation
retaliatory
retard
retardation
retch (to vomit)
retention
retentive
rethink
  rethinking
  rethinks
  rethought
reticence
reticent
reticule
retina
  retinas *pl*
retinue
retire
  retired
  retiring
retirement
retort
retouch
retrace
  retraced
  retracing
retract
retractable
retractile

retraction
retractor
retread
  retreading
  retreads
  retrod
retreat
  retreated
  retreating
retrench
retrenchment
retribution
retributive
retrievable
retrieval
retrieve
  retrieved
  retrieving
retriever
retroactive
retrograde
retrogression
retrogressive
retro-rocket
retrospect
retrospection
retrospective
retrospectively
retrovirus
return
returnable

reunion
reunite
  reunited
  reuniting
reusable
reuse
  reused
  reusing
rev
  revs
  revved
  revving
revaluation
revalue
  revalued
  revaluing
revamp
  revamped
  revamping
reveal (to disclose)
  revealed
  revealing
reveille
revel (to make merry)
  revels
  reveled
  reveling
revelation
reveler
revelry
  revelries pl

revenge
  revenged
  revenging
revengeful
revenue
reverberate
  reverberated
  reverberating
reverberation
reverberator
revere (respect)
  revered
  revering
reverence
reverend
reverent
reverential
reverie
revers (turned back cloth)
reversal
reverse (back; move backwards)
  reversed
  reversing
reversible
reversion
revert
revetment
review (to examine critically)

reviewed
reviewing
reviewer
revile
  reviled
  reviling
revise
  revised
  revising
revision
revitalize
  revitalized
  revitalizing
revival
revive
  revived
  reviving
revocable
revocation
revoke
  revoked
  revoking
revolt
revolution
revolutionary
  revolutionaries *pl*
revolutionize
  revolutionized
  revolutionizing
revolve
  revolved

revolving
revolver
revue (entertainment)
revulsion
reward
rewrite
  rewrites
  rewriting
  rewritten
  rewrote
rhapsodize
  rhapsodized
  rhapsodizing
rhapsody
  rhapsodies *pl*
rheostat
rhesus
rhetoric
rhetorical
rhetorically
rheumatic
rheumatism
rheumatoid
rheumy
rhinoceros
  rhinoceroses *pl*
rhizome
rhododendron
  rhododendrons *pl*
rhomboid
rhombus

rhombuses *pl*
rhubarb
rhyme (verse)
  rhymed
  rhyming
rhythm
rhythmic
rhythmical
rhythmically
rib
  ribbed
  ribbing
  ribs
ribald
ribaldry
ribbon
rice
rich
riches
richly
richness
rick (of hay)
rickets
rickety
rickshaw, ricksha
ricochet
  ricocheted,
  ricocheting
rid
  ridding
  rids

ridable
riddance
ridden
riddle
  riddled
  riddling
ride
  ridden
  rides
  riding
  rode
rider
ridge
ridging
ridicule
  ridiculed
  ridiculing
ridiculous
ridiculously
rife
riff
riff-raff
rifle
  rifled
  rifling
rift
rig
  rigged
  rigging
  rigs
right (correct)

right angle
right-angled
righteous
righteousness
rightful
rightfully
rightly
rigid
rigidity
rigidly
rigmarole
rigor
rigor mortis (stiffness
  after death)
rigorous
rigorously
rile
  riled
  riling
rim
rime (frost)
rimmed
rind
ring (eg a bell)
  rang
  ringing
  rings
  rung
ring (to surround)
  ringed
  ringing

rings
ringer
ringleader
ringlet (of hair)
rink
rinse
  rinsed
  rinsing
riot
  rioted
  rioting
rioter
riotous
riotously
riotousness
rip
  ripped
  ripping
  rips
ripe
ripely
ripen
  ripened
  ripening
  ripens
ripeness
riper
riposte
ripple
  rippled
  rippling

rise
  rose
  rises
  rising
  risen
riser
risible
risk
riskily
riskiness
risky
  riskier
  riskiest
risotto
  risottos *pl*
risqué
rissole
rite (ceremony)
ritual
ritualism
ritualist
ritualistic
ritually
rival
  rivals
  rivaled
  rivaling
rivalry
  rivalries *pl*
river
rivet

riveted
riveting
riveter
Riviera
rivulet
roach
  roaches *pl*
road
roadblock
road hog
road map
roadway
  roadways *pl*
roadworthiness
roadworthy
roam
  roamed
  roaming
roan
roar (loud noise)
  roared
  roaring
roast
rob (to steal)
  robbed
  robbing
  robs
robber
robbery
  robberies *pl*
robe (dress)

robed
robing
robin
robot
robotics
robust
robustly
robustness
rock
rock and roll
rockery
  rockeries *pl*
rocket
  rocketed
  rocketing
rocketry
rocking horse
rocky
  rockier
  rockiest
rococo
rod
rode (*from* ride)
rodent
rodeo
  rodeos *pl*
roe (deer; of fish)
rogation
rogue
roguery
roguish

roisterer
role (actor's part)
roll
rollcall
roller
roller skate
  roller skated
  roller skating
rollick
roly-poly
  roly-polies *pl*
romance
  romanced
  romancing
romancer
romantic
romantically
romanticism
romanticize
  romanticized
  romanticizing
romp
romper
rondo
  rondos *pl*
roo (kangaroo)
rood (crucifix)
roof
  roofs *pl*
rook
rookery

  rookeries *pl*
rookie
room
roomful
roominess
roommate
room service
roomy
  roomier
  roomiest
roost
rooster (hen)
root (*eg* of a plant)
  rooted
  rooting
rootless
rope
  roped
  roping
rosary
  rosaries *pl*
rose (*from* rise; flower)
rosé (pink)
roseate
rose leaf
  rose leaves *pl*
rosemary
rosette
rosily
rosin
  rosined

  rosining
roster (list)
rostrum
  rostra, rostrums *pl*
rosy
rot
  rots
  rotted
  rotting
rota
  rotas *pl*
Rotarian
rotary
rotatable
rotate
  rotated
  rotating
rotation
rote (procedure)
rotisserie
rotor (of electric
  motor)
rotten
rottenness
rotter
rotund
rotunda
  rotundas *pl*
rotundity
roué
rouge

rough (coarse)
roughage
roughen
  roughened
  roughening
rougher
rough-hewn
roughly
roughness
roughshod
roulette
round
roundabout
roundelay
  roundelays *pl*
roundness
rouse
  roused
  rousing
rout (to defeat)
  routed
  routing
route (road taken)
  routed
  routing
routine (procedure)
rove
  roved
  roving
rover
row (boat)

rowdy
  rowdies *pl*
rowdily
rowdiness
rower
rowlock
royal
royalist
royally
royalty
  royalties *pl*
rub
  rubbed
  rubbing
  rubs
rubber
rubbish
rubbishy
rubble
rubicund
ruble (Russian
  money)
ruby
  rubies *pl*
rubric
ruche
ruck (crease)
  rucked
rucksack
ruction
rudder

ruddiness
ruddy
  ruddier
  ruddiest
rude (rough)
rudely
rudeness
rudiment
rudimentary
rue (herb; to regret)
  rued
  ruing
rueful
ruefully
ruff (collar)
ruffian
ruffle
  ruffled
  ruffling
rug
rugby
rugged
ruggedness
rugger
ruin (destroy)
  ruined
  ruining
ruination
ruinous
ruinously
rule

ruled

ruling

ruler

rum

rumble

  rumbled

  rumbling

ruminant

ruminate

  ruminated

  ruminating

rummage

  rummaged

  rummaging

rummy

rumor

rumored

rump

rumple

  rumpled

  rumpling

rumpus

  rumpuses *pl*

run

  ran

  running

  runs

runabout

runaway

  runaways *pl*

rune (letter)

rung (*from* ring;
  ladder)

runic

runner

runner-up

  runners-up *pl*

runny

  runnier

  runniest

runway

  runways *pl*

rupee (Indian money)

rupture

  ruptured

  rupturing

rural

rurally

ruse

rush

rush hour

rusk

russet

rust

rustic

rusticate

  rusticated

  rusticating

rustication

rusticity

rustiness

rustle

rustled

rustling

rustler

rustless

rustproof

  rustproofed

  rustproofing

  rustproofs

rusty

  rustier

  rustiest

rut

  ruts

  rutted

  rutting

ruthless

ruthlessly

ruthlessness

rye (grain)

Sabbatarian
sabbath
sabbatical
saber
sable
sabotage
  sabotaged
  sabotaging
saboteur
sac (pouch)
saccharin
sacerdotal
sachet (small bag)
sack (hessian)
sacked
sacrament
sacramental
sacred

sacredly
sacredness
sacrifice
  sacrificed
  sacrificing
sacrificial
sacrilege
sacrilegious
sacrosanct
sad
  sadder
  saddest
sadden
  saddened
  saddening
saddle
  saddled
  saddling

saddler
saddlery
  saddleries pl
sadism
sadist
sadistic
sadly
sadness
safari
  safaris pl
safe
safeguard
safely
safer
safety
saffron
sag
  sagged
  sagging
  sags
saga
  sagas pl
sagacious
sagaciously
sagacity
sage
sagely
sago
  sagos pl
sahib
said (from say)

sail (of ship)
sailer (ship)
sailor (man)
saint
sainthood
saintliness
saintly
sake
salaam
  salaamed
  salaaming
salacious
salacity
salad
salamander
salami (sausage)
  salamis *pl*
salariat
salary (wage)
  salaries *pl*
sale (at shop)
saleability
saleable
salesman
  salesmen *pl*
saleswoman
  saleswomen *pl*
salicin
salicylic
salient
saline

salinity
saliva
salivary
salivate
  salivated
  salivating
salivation
sallow
sallowness
sally
  sallies *pl*
  sallied
  sallies
  sallying
salmon
salmonella
  (bacterium)
salon (drawing room)
saloon (of pub)
salsify
  salsifies *pl*
salt
saltiness
saltpeter
salty
  saltier
  saltiest
salubrious
salubrity
salutary
salutation

salute
  saluted
  saluting
salvage (save)
  salvaged
  salvaging
salvation
salve
  salved
  salving
salver
salvo
  salvoes, salvos *pl*
Samaritan
same
samovar
sample
  sampled
  sampling
sampler
sanatorium
  sanatoriums,
    sanatoria *pl*
sanctification
sanctify
  sanctified
  sanctifies
  sanctifying
sanctimonious
sanctimoniously
sanctimoniousness

sanction
  sanctioned
  sanctioning
sanctity
sanctuary
  sanctuaries *pl*
sanctum
  sanctums, sancta *pl*
sand
sandal
sandalwood
sandbag
  sandbagged
  sandbagging
  sandbags
sandpaper
  sandpapered
  sandpapering
sandwich
  sandwiches *pl*
sandy
  sandier
  sandiest
sane (not mad)
sanely
sang (*from* sing)
sang-froid
sanguinary
sanguine
sanitarium
  sanitariums,

  sanitaria *pl*
sanitary
sanitation
sanity
sank (*from* sink)
Santa Claus
sap
  sapped
  sapping
  saps
sapience
sapient
sapling
sapper
sapphire
saprophyte
saprophytic
saraband
sarcasm
sarcastic
sarcastically
sarcoma
  sarcomas *pl*
sarcophagus
  sarcophagi *pl*
sardine
sardonic
sardonically
sari
  saris *pl*
sartorial

sash
sat (*from* sit)
Satan (devil)
satanic
satchel
sate
  sated
  sating
sateen (cotton)
satellite
satiable
satiate
  satiated
  satiating
satiation
satiety
satin (silk)
satinette
satire (sarcasm)
satirical
satirically
satirist
satirize
  satirized
  satirizing
satisfaction
satisfactorily
satisfactory
satisfiable
satisfy
  satisfied

satisfies
satisfying
satsuma
  satsumas *pl*
saturate
  saturated
  saturating
saturation
Saturday
  Saturdays *pl*
saturnine
satyr (a god)
sauce (food)
saucepan
saucer
saucily
sauciness
saucy
  saucier
  sauciest
sauerkraut
sauna (steam bath)
  saunas *pl*
saunter
  sauntered
  sauntering
sausage
sauté (fried)
  sautéed
  sautéing
savage

savaged
  savaging
savagely
savagery
savant
save
  saved
  saving
saver (keeper)
savior
savoir faire
savor (taste)
  savored
  savoring
savoriness
savory
  savories *pl*
saw (to cut; tool)
  sawed
  sawing
  sawn
  saws
saxifrage
saxophone
saxophonist
say
  said
  saying
  says
scab
scabbard

scabies
scaffold
scald (burn)
scale
  scaled
  scaling
scallop, scollop
scallywag
scalp
scalpel
scaly
scamp
scamper
  scampered
  scampering
scampi (prawns)
scan
  scanned
  scanning
  scans
scandal
scandalize
  scandalized
  scandalizing
scandalmonger
scandalous
scandalously
scanner
scansion
scant
scantily

scantiness
scanty
  scantier
  scantiest
scapegoat
scapula
  scapulas *pl*
scar
  scarred
  scarring
  scars
scarce
scarcely
scarcity
  scarcities *pl*
scare
  scared
  scaring
scarecrow
scarf
  scarfs, scarves *pl*
scarification
scarify
  scarified
  scarifies
  scarifying
scarlatina
scarlet
scarp
scat
  scats

scatted
scatting
scathe
  scathed
  scathing
scatheless
scatter
  scattered
  scattering
scatterbrain
scavenge
  scavenged
  scavenging
scavenger
scenario
  scenarios *pl*
scene (view)
scenery
scenic
scent (perfume)
scented
scepsis
scepter
schedule
  scheduled
  scheduling
schematic
schematically
scheme
  schemed
  scheming

schemer
scherzo
  scherzos *pl*
schism
schismatic
schist
schizoid
schizophrenia
schizophrenic
schnapps
scholar
scholarly
scholarship
scholastic
school
  schooled
  schooling
schoolboy
  schoolboys *pl*
schoolgirl
schoolmaster
schoolmistress
schoolteacher
schooner
sciatica
science
scientific
scientifically
scientist
scimitar
scintillate

scintillated
scintillating
scintillation
scion
scission (cutting)
scissors
sclerosis
scoff
scoffer
scold (to chide)
scollop, scallop
sconce
scone
scoop
scoot
scooter
scope
scorbutic
scorch
scorcher
score
  scored
  scoring
scoreboard
scorer
scorn
scornful
scornfully
scorpion
Scot
Scotch (whiskey)

scotch (to prevent;
  to wedge)
scot-free
Scotland
Scotsman
  Scotsmen *pl*
Scotswoman
  Scotswomen *pl*
Scottish
scoundrel
scour (scratch)
  scoured
  scouring
scourer
scourge
  scourged
  scourging
scout
  scouted
  scouting
scowl
scrabble
  scrabbled
  scrabbling
scrag
scraggy
scramble
  scrambled
  scrambling
scrap
  scrapped

scrapping
scraps
scrape
  scraped
  scraping
scraper
scrapie (disease)
scrappy
  scrappier
  scrappiest
scratch
scratched
scrawl
scrawny
  scrawnier
  scrawniest
scream
  screamed
  screaming
screech
screech owl
screed
screen
  screened
  screening
screenplay
  screenplays *pl*
screw
  screwed
  screwing
screwdriver

screwy
scribble
  scribbled
  scribbling
scribbler
scribe
scrimmage
  scrimmaged
  scrimmaging
scrimp
scrip (certificate)
script
scriptural
scripture
scriptwriter
scrofula
scrofulous
scroll
scrotum
  scrotums, scrota *pl*
scrounge
  scrounged
  scrounging
scrounger
scrub
  scrubbed
  scrubbing
  scrubs
scrubby
scruff
scruffily

scruffiness
scruffy
  scruffier
  scruffiest
scrum
scrummage
  scrummaged
  scrummaging
scrumptious
scrunch
scruple
scrupulous
scrupulously
scrupulousness
scrutineer
scrutinize
  scrutinized
  scrutinizing
scrutiny
scuba
scud
  scudded
  scudding
  scuds
scuff
scuffed
scuffle
  scuffled
  scuffling
scull (rowing)
sculler

scullery
  sculleries *pl*
scullion
sculpt
sculptor
sculptress
  sculptresses *pl*
sculpture
scum
scummy
scurf
scurrilous
scurrilously
scurry
  scurried
  scurries
  scurrying
scurvily
scurvy
scuttle
  scuttled
  scuttling
scythe
  scythed
  scything
sea (ocean)
seaboard
seaborne
seafarer
seafaring
seafood

seagull

seal

  sealed

  sealing

sea level

sealing wax

sea lion

sealskin

seam (in sewing)

seaman (sailor)

  seamen *pl*

seamanship

seamless

seamstress

seamy

seance

seaplane

sear (to scorch)

  seared

  searing

search

searcher

searchlight

seascape

sea serpent

seashore

seasick

seaside

season

  seasoned

  seasoning

seasonable

seasonably

seasonal

seasonally

seat

  seated

  seating

seat belt

seaweed

seaworthiness

seaworthy

sebaceous

sec (of wine; dry)

secant, sec. (maths.)

secateurs

secede

  seceded

  seceding

secession

seclude

  secluded

  secluding

seclusion

second

secondarily

secondary

  secondaries *pl*

secondary school

seconder

second guess

secondhand

secondment

second-rate

secrecy

secret

secretarial

secretariat

secretary

  secretaries *pl*

secrete

  secreted

  secreting

secretion

secretive

secretively

secretiveness

secretly

sect

sectarian

section

sectional

sector

secular

secure

  secured

  securing

securely

security

  securities *pl*

sedate

  sedated

  sedating

sedately
sedation
sedative
sedentary
sedge
sediment
sedimentary
sedimentation
sedition
seditious
seditiously
seduce
  seduced
  seducing
seducer
seduction
seductive
seductively
sedulity
sedulous
see (to view)
  saw
  seeing
  seen
  sees
seed (of a plant)
  seeded
  seeding
seediness
seedling
seedy

seedier
seediest
seek
  seeking
  seeks
  sought
seeker
seem (to appear)
  seemed
  seeming
seemingly
seemliness
seemly
see-saw
  see-sawed
  see-sawing
seen (*from* see)
seep
  seeped
  seeping
seepage
seer (prophet)
seethe
  seethed
  seething
segment
segmentation
segregate
  segregated
  segregating
segregation

segregative
seine (fishing net)
seismic
seismograph
seismologist
seismology
seize
  seized
  seizing
seizure
seldom
select
selection
selective
selectively
selectivity
selector
selenium
self
  selves *pl*
self-addressed
self-assured
self-catering
self-centered
self-conscious
self-consciously
self-consciousness
self-defense
self-employed
self-esteem
self-evident

self-explanatory
self-image
self-important
self-interest
selfish
selfishly
selfishness
selfless
self-made
self-portrait
self-possessed
self-regulating
self-righteous
self-righteousness
self-rising (flour)
selfsame
self-satisfied
self-service
self-starter
self-styled
self-sufficient
self-taught
sell (of goods)
seller (of goods)
sell-out
seltzer
selvedge, selvage
   (edge)
semantic
semaphore
semblance

semen (sperm)
semester
semiautomatic
semibreve
semicircle
semicircular
semicolon
semiconductor
semiconscious
semidetached
semifinal
seminal
seminar
seminary
   seminaries *pl*
semi-precious
semiquaver
semi-skilled
semitone
semitropical
semolina
senate
senator
senatorial
send
   sending
   sends
   sent
sender
senile
senility

senior
seniority
senna
   sennas *pl*
sensation
sensational
sensationalism
sensationally
sense
   sensed
   sensing
senseless
senselessly
senselessness
sensibility
sensible
sensibly
sensitive
sensitively
sensitivity
sensitize
   sensitized
   sensitizing
sensor (detecting
   device)
sensory
sensual
sensualist
sensuality
sensually
sensuous

sensuously
sensuousness
sent (*from* send)
sentence
  sentenced
  sentencing
sententious
sententiously
sententiousness
sentience
sentient
sentiment
sentimental
sentimentalist
sentimentality
sentimentalize
  sentimentalized
  sentimentalizing
sentimentally
sentinel
sentry
  sentries *pl*
separable
separate
  separated
  separating
separation
separatism
separator
sepia
sepoy

sepoys *pl*
sepsis
September
septic (infected)
septicemia
septuagenarian
septum
  septa *pl*
sepulcher
sepulchral
sequel
sequence
  sequenced
  sequencing
sequential
sequester
  sequestered
  sequestering
sequestrate
  sequestrated
  sequestrating
sequestration
sequestrator
sequin
sequined
seraglio
  seraglios *pl*
seraph
  seraphs, seraphim *pl*
seraphic
serenade

serenaded
serenading
serenader
serendipitous
serendipity
serene
serenely
serenity
serf (land slave)
serfdom
serge (cloth)
sergeant
sergeant major
serial (story in
  installments)
serialization
serialize
  serialized
  serializing
serially
series
serif
serious
seriously
seriousness
sermon
sermonize
  sermonized
  sermonizing
serpent
serpentine

serrated

serration

serum

  sera, serums *pl*

servant

serve

  served

  serving

server

service

  serviced

  servicing

serviceability

serviceable

servile

servility

servitude

sesame

session (period)

set

  sets

  setting

setback

settee

  settees *pl*

setter

settle

  settled

  settling

settlement

seven

seventeen

seventeenth

seventh

seventieth

seventy

  seventies *pl*

sever (to cut off)

  severed

  severing

several

severally

severance

severe (strict)

severely

severity

sew (to stitch)

  sewed

  sewing

  sewn

  sews

sewage

sewer (drain)

sewing machine

sex

  sexes *pl*

sexagenarian

sexed

sexiness

sexist

sextant

sextet

sexton

sextuple

sexual

sexuality

sexually

sexy

  sexier

  sexiest

shabbier

shabbily

shabbiness

shabby

  shabbier

  shabbiest

shack

shackle

  shackled

  shackling

shade

  shaded

  shading

shadily

shadow

shadowy

shady

  shadier

  shadiest

shaft

shaggy

  shaggier

  shaggiest

shagreen
Shah
shake
  shaken
  shakes
  shaking
  shook
shaker
shake-up
shakily
shakiness
shaky
shale
shall (will)
shallot
shallow
shallower
shallowness
shalt
sham
  shammed
  shamming
  shams
shamble
  shambled
  shambling
shame
  shamed
  shaming
shamefaced
shameful

shamefully
shameless
shamelessly
shampoo
  shampooed
  shampooing
  shampoos
shamrock
shandy
shanghai
  shanghaied
  shanghaiing
shan't (shall not)
shank
shantung
shanty
  shanties *pl*
shape
  shaped
  shaping
shapeless
shapeliness
shapely
shard, sherd
share
  shared
  sharing
shareholder
sharer
shark
sharp

sharpen
  sharpened
  sharpening
sharpener
sharper
sharply
sharpshooter
sharp-witted
shatter
  shattered
  shattering
shatterproof
shave
  shaved
  shaving
shaven
shaver
shawl
she
sheaf
  sheaves *pl*
shear (to cut)
  sheared
  shearing
  shears
  shorn
shearer
shears
sheath
sheathe
  sheathed

sheathing
sheath knife
shed
  shedding
  sheds
she'd (she would;
  she had)
sheen
sheep
sheepish
sheepishly
sheepskin
sheer (absolute; steep)
sheet
sheikh, sheik (ruler)
she'll (she will)
shelf
  shelves *pl*
shell
shellac
  shellacked
  shellacking
  shellacs
shellfish
shelter
  sheltered
  sheltering
shelterer
shelve
  shelved
  shelving

shenanigan
shepherd
  shepherded
  shepherding
shepherdess
sherbet
sherd, shard
sheriff
  sheriffs *pl*
sherry
  sherries *pl*
she's (she has; she is)
shied (*from* shy)
shield
shies (*from* shy)
shift
  shiftily
  shiftiness
  shifty
    shiftier
    shiftiest
shilling
shimmer
  shimmered
  shimmering
shin
shindy
  shindies *pl*
shine (to give out
  light)
  shines

shining
shone
shine (to polish)
  shined
  shines
  shining
shingle
  shingled
  shingling
shingles
shiny
  shinier
  shiniest
ship
  shipped
  shipping
  ships
shipmate
shipment
shipper
shipshape
shipwrecked
shipwright
shirk
shirker
shirr
shirring
shirt
shiver
  shivered
  shivering

shivers
shivery
shoal
  shoaled
  shoaling
shock
shock absorber
shocker
shocking
shod
shoddier
shoddily
shoddiness
shoddy
  shoddier
  shoddiest
shoe (footwear)
  shoes *pl*
  shod
  shoed
  shoeing
  shoes
shoelace
shone (*from* shine)
shoo (scare)
  shooed
  shooing
  shoos
shook (*from* shake)
shoot (*eg* with a gun)
  shooting

shoots
shot
shop
  shopped
  shopping
  shops
shopkeeper
shoplifting
shopped
shopper
shore (beach)
  shored
  shoring
shorn
short
shortage
shortbread
shortcake
short-circuit
  short-circuited
  short-circuiting
shortcoming
shorten
  shortened
  shortening
shorter
shorthand
short-lived
shortly
shortness
shortsighted

shortsightedness
short-tempered
shot
shotgun
should
shoulder
  shouldered
  shouldering
shoulder blade
shouldn't (should
  not)
shout
  shouted
  shouting
shove
  shoved
  shoving
shovel
  shovels
  shoveled
  shoveling
show
  showed
  showing
  shown
  shows
showdown
shower
showery
showily
showman

showmen *pl*
showmanship
showpiece
showy
shrank
shrapnel
shred
  shredded
  shredding
  shreds
shredder
shrew
shrewd
shrewdly
shrewdness
shrewish
shriek
  shrieked
  shrieking
shrift
shrike
shrill
shriller
shrillness
shrilly
shrimp
shrine
shrink
shrinkage
shrivel
  shrivels

shriveled
shriveling
shroud
shrub
shrubbery
  shrubberies *pl*
shrug
  shrugged
  shrugging
  shrugs
shrunk
shrunken
shuffle
  shuffled
  shuffling
shun
  shunned
  shunning
  shuns
shunt
shut
  shuts
  shutting
shutdown
shutters
shuttle
  shuttled
  shuttling
shuttlecock
shy
  shies *pl*

shy (timid)
  shied
  shies
  shying
  shyer
  shyest
shyly
shyness
sibilant
sibling
sic (thus)
sick
sick bay
sicken
  sickened
  sickening
sickle (for reaping)
sickly
sickness
side
  sided
  siding
sideboard
sideburns
sidelight
sideline
  sidelined
  sidelining
sidelong
sidesplitting
sidestep

sidestepped
sidestepping
sidesteps
sidetrack
sidewalk
sideways
siding
sidle
  sidled
  sidling
siege
sienna
  siennas *pl*
siesta
  siestas *pl*
sieve
  sieved
  sieving
sift
sigh
  sighed
  sighing
sight (vision)
sightless
sightlessness
sightliness
sightly
sightseeing
sightseer
sign (mark)
  signed

signing
signal
  signals
  signaled
  signaling
signaler
signally
signalman
  signalmen *pl*
signals
signatory
  signatories *pl*
signature
signer
signet (ring)
significance
significant
significantly
signify
  signified
  signifies
  signifying
signor
signora
  signoras *pl*
signorina
  signorinas *pl*
signpost
signwriter
signwriting
Sikh

silage
silence
  silenced
  silencing
silencer
silent
silently
silhouette
  silhouetted
  silhouetting
silica (*eg* in sand)
silicate
silicon (chem.
  element)
silicone (compound of
  silicon)
silicosis
silk
silken
silkworm
silky
  silkier
  silkiest
sill
sillabub, syllabub
  (sweet cream)
silliness
silly
  sillier
  silliest
silo

silos *pl*
silt
silver
  silvered
  silvering
silversmith
silver-tongued
silvery
simian
similar
similarity
  similarities *pl*
similarly
simile
  similes *pl*
similitude
simmer
  simmered
  simmering
simony
simper
  simpered
  simpering
simple
simpleminded
simpler
simpleton
simplex
simplicity
simplification
simplify

simplified
simplifies
simplifying
simplistic
simply
simulacrum
  simulacra *pl*
simulate
  simulated
  simulating
simulation
simulator
simultaneity
simultaneous
simultaneously
sin
  sinned
  sinning
  sins
since
sincere
sincerely
sincerity
sine (maths.)
sinecure
sine die
sine qua non
sinew
sine wave
sinewy
sinful

sinfully
sinfulness
sing
  sang
  singing
  sings
  sung
singe (to scorch)
  singed
  singeing
  singes
singer
single
  singled
  singling
single-minded
singlet
singleton
singly
singsong
singular
singularity
singularly
sinister
sinisterly
sink
  sank
  sinking
  sinks
  sunk
sinker

sinless
sinner
sinologist
sinology
sinuous (with curves)
sinuously
sinus
  sinuses *pl*
sinusitis
sinusoidal
sinusoidally
sip
  sipped
  sipping
  sips
siphon
  siphoned
  siphoning
sir
sire
  sired
  siring
siren
sirloin
sirocco
  siroccos *pl*
sisal
sister
sisterhood
sister-in-law
  sisters-in-law *pl*

sisterly
sit
  sits
  sat
  sitting
site (location)
sit-in
  sit-ins *pl*
sitter
situate
  situated
  situating
situation
sitz bath
six
  sixes *pl*
sixteen
sixteenth
sixth
sixthly
sixtieth
sixty
  sixties *pl*
sizable
sizably
size
  sized
  sizing
sizzle
  sizzled
  sizzling

skate
  skated
  skating
skateboard
skater
skedaddle
  skedaddled
  skedaddling
skein
skeletal
skeleton
skeptic
skeptical
skeptically
skepticism
sketch
sketcher
sketchily
sketchiness
sketchy
  sketchier
  sketchiest
skew
  skewed
  skewing
skewer
ski
  skied
  skiing
  skis
skid

skidded
skidding
skids
skied
skier
skiff
skill
skilled
skillet
skillful
skim
skimmed
skimming
skims
skimp
skimpily
skimpiness
skimpy
skimpier
skimpiest
skin
skinned
skinning
skins
skin-deep
skin diver
skin diving
skinflint
skinny
skinnier
skinniest

skintight
skip
skipped
skipping
skips
skipper
skirl
skirmish
skirt
skit
skittish
skittishly
skittishness
skua
skuas *pl*
skulduggery
skulk
skull (of head)
skullcap
skunk
sky
skies *pl*
skydiving
sky-high
skylark
skylight
skyscraper
slab
slack
slacken
slackened

slackening
slacker
slackness
slag
slagged
slagging
slags
slain (*from* slay)
slake
slaked
slaking
slalom
slam
slammed
slamming
slams
slander
slandered
slandering
slanderer
slanderous
slang
slangy
slant
slap
slapped
slapping
slaps
slapdash
slapstick
slash

slat
slate
  slated
  slating
slattern
slatternly
slaughter
  slaughtered
  slaughtering
slaughterhouse
slave
  slaved
  slaving
slaver
  slavered
  slavering
slavery
slavish
slavishly
slavishness
slay (kill)
  slain
  slayed
  slaying
  slays
  slew
sleaze
sleazy
  sleazier
  sleaziest
sled

sledge
sledgehammer
sleek
sleekness
sleep
  sleeps
  slept
  sleeping
sleeper
sleepily
sleepiness
sleepless
sleeplessness
sleepover
sleepwalk
  sleepwalked
  sleepwalking
sleepwalker
sleepy
  sleepier
  sleepiest
sleet
  sleeted
  sleeting
sleeve
sleeveless
sleigh (sledge)
sleight (skill)
slender
slenderness
slept (from sleep)

sleuth
slew (from slay)
slew (to swing
    around)
  slewed
  slewing
slice
  sliced
  slicing
slick
slicker
slide
  slid
  slides
  sliding
slide rule
slight (small)
  slighted
  slighting
  slighter
  slightest
slightly
slim
  slimmed
  slimming
  slims
slime (dirt)
slimmer
slimness
slimy
  slimier

slimiest

sling
  slinging
  slings
  slung

slink
  slinking
  slinks
  slunk

slip
  slipped
  slipping
  slips

slipknot
slipper
slipperiness
slippery
slipshod
slipstream
slit
  slits
  slitting
slither
  slithered
  slithering
sliver (to break up)
  slivered
  slivering
slobber
  slobbered
  slobbering

sloe (fruit)
sloe-eyed
sloe gin
slog
  slogged
  slogging
  slogs
slogan
slogger
sloop (ship)
slop
  slopped
  slopping
  slops
slope
  sloped
  sloping
sloppily
sloppiness
sloppy
  sloppier
  sloppiest
slosh
slot
  slots
  slotted
  slotting
sloth
slothful
slouch
slough (skin)

sloughed
sloughing
sloven
slovenliness
slovenly
slow (not fast)
  slowed
  slowing
  slower
  slowest
slowly
sludge
slug
  slugged
  slugging
  slugs
sluggard
sluggish
sluggishly
sluggishness
sluice
  sluiced
  sluicing
slum
  slummed
  slumming
  slums
slumber
  slumbered
  slumbering
slumberous, slumbrous

slump

slung (*from* sling)

slunk (*from* slink)

slur

  slurred

  slurring

  slurs

slurry

slush

slut

sluttish

sly

  slyer

  slyest

slyly

slyness

smack

small

smallness

smart

smarten

  smartened

  smartening

smartly

smartness

smash

smattering

smear

  smeared

  smearing

smell

smelled

smells

smelly

  smellier

  smelliest

smelt

smidgen, smidgin

smile

  smiled

  smiling

smirch

  smirched

smirk

smite

  smites

  smiting

  smitten

  smote

smith

smithereens

smithy

  smithies *pl*

smock

smocking

smog

smokable

smoke

  smoked

  smoking

smokeless

smoker

smoking

smoky

  smokier

  smokiest

smolder

  smoldered

  smoldering

smooth

smoother

smoothly

smoothness

smorgasbord

smote (*from* smite)

smother

  smothered

  smothering

smudge

  smudged

  smudging

smug

  smugger

smuggle

  smuggled

  smuggling

smuggler

smugly

smugness

smut

smuttiness

smutty

  smuttier

smuttiest

snack

snaffle
  snaffled
  snaffling

snag
  snagged
  snagging
  snags

snail

snake
  snaked
  snaking

snap
  snapped
  snapping
  snaps

snapdragon

snapper

snappily

snappish

snappy
  snappier
  snappiest

snaps

snapshot

snare
  snared
  snaring

snarl

snatch

sneak
  sneaked
  sneaking
  sneakers

sneer
  sneered
  sneering

sneeze
  sneezed
  sneezing

snicker
  snickered
  snickering

snide

sniff

sniffle
  sniffled
  sniffling

snifter

snigger
  sniggered
  sniggering

snip (to cut)
  snipped
  snipping
  snips

snipe (bird; to shoot)
  sniped
  sniping

snippet

snivel

snivels
sniveled
sniveling
sniveler

snob
snobbery
  snobberies *pl*
snobbish
snobbishly
snobbishness

snooker
snookered
snookering

snoop
snooped
snooping
snooper

snooze
snoozed
snoozing

snore
snored
snoring
snorer

snorkel
snorkels
snorkeled
snorkeling

snort

snot

snotty

snout

snow
  snowed
  snowing
snowball
snowballing
snowdrop
snowfall
snowflake
snowmobile
snowplow
snowshoe
  snowshoes *pl*
snub
  snubbed
  snubbing
  snubs
snub-nosed
snuff
snuffers
snuffle
  snuffled
  snuffling
snug
snuggle
  snuggled
  snuggling
snugly
soak
  soaked
  soaking

soap
  soaped
  soaping
soapsuds
soapy
soar (to fly high)
  soared
  soaring
sob
  sobbed
  sobbing
  sobs
sober
  sobered
  sobering
sobriety
sobriquet
soccer
sociability
sociable
sociably
social
social security
Socialism
Socialist
socialite
socialization
socialize
  socialized
  socializing
  socially

society
  societies *pl*
socioeconomic
sociological
sociologist
sociology
sock
socket
sod (turf)
soda
  sodas *pl*
soda water
sodden
sodium
sodomy
sofa
  sofas *pl*
soft
softball
soften
  softened
  softening
softer
softly
softness
software
soggy
  soggier
  soggiest
soil
  soiled

soiling

soirée

sojourn

solace

solacing

solar

solar system

solarium

  solariums, solaria *pl*

sold (*from* sell)

solder

  soldered

  soldering

soldering iron

soldier

  soldiered

  soldiering

sole (alone; fish; of

  shoe)

solecism

solely

solemn

solemnity

  solemnities *pl*

solemnization

solemnize

  solemnized

  solemnizing

solemnly

solenoid

solicit

solicited

soliciting

solicitation

solicitor

solicitous

solicitously

solicitude

solid

solidarity

solidification

solidify

  solidified

  solidifies

  solidifying

solidity

solidly

solid-state

soliloquize

  soliloquized

  soliloquizing

soliloquy

  soliloquies *pl*

soling

solitaire (single gem)

solitarily

solitariness

solitary

solitude

solo

  solos, soli *pl*

  soloed

soloes

soloing

soloist

solstice

solstitial

solubility

soluble

solution

solvable

solve

  solved

  solving

solvency

solvent

somatic

somber

somberly

somberness

sombrero

  sombreros *pl*

some (a few)

somebody

somehow

someone

somersault

somewhat

somewhere

somnambulism

somnambulist

somnolence

somnolent

son
sonar
sonata
  sonatas *pl*
sonatina
  sonatinas *pl*
son-in-law
  sons-in-law *pl*
song
songster
sonic
sonnet
sonny
sonority
sonorous
sonorously
soon
  sooner
  soonest
soot
soothe
  soothed
  soothing
soothsayer
sop
  sopped
  sopping
  sops
sophism
sophist
sophisticated

sophistry
sophomore
soporific
soprano
  sopranos *pl*
sorcerer
sorceress
sorcery
sordid
sordidly
sordidness
sore (painful)
sorely
soreness
sorority
sorrel
sorrow
sorrowful
sorrowfully
sorrowfulness
sorry
  sorrier
  sorriest
sort (kind; to arrange
  in groups)
sorter
sortie
  sorties *pl*
sot
sottish
sotto voce (in a

whisper)
soubrette
soufflé
sought (*from* seek)
soul (spirit; music)
soulful
soulfully
soulless
sound
sounder
soundless
soundlessly
soundly
soundness
soundproof
  soundproofed
  soundproofing
  soundproofs
soup
soupçon
sour
source (origin)
  sourced
  sourcing
sourly
sourness
souse
  soused
  sousing
south
southerly

southern
southerner
southward
souvenir
sou'wester
sovereign
sovereignty
soviet
sow (female pig;
    seeds)
  sowed
  sowing
  sown
  sows
soya
soybean
spa
  spas *pl*
space
  spaced
  spacing
spacecraft
spaceship
spacesuit
spacious
spaciousness
spade
spaghetti
span
  spanned
  spanning

spans
spangle
  spangled
  spangling
spaniel
spank
spar
  sparred
  sparring
  spars
spare
  spared
  sparing
sparingly
spark
sparkle
  sparkled
  sparkling
sparkler
sparrow
sparse
sparsely
spasm
spasmodic
spasmodically
spastic
spat (*from* spit)
spate
spatial
spatter
  spattered

spattering
spatula
  spatulas *pl*
spavin
spavined
spawn
spay
  spayed
  spaying
  spays
speak
  speaking
  speaks
  spoke
  spoken
speaker
spear
  speared
  spearing
spearhead
special
specialist
speciality
  specialities *pl*
specialization
specialize
  specialized
  specializing
specially
specialty
  specialties *pl*

specie (coins)
species
  species *pl*
specific
specifically
specification
specify
  specified
  specifies
  specifying
specimen
specious (plausible)
speck (fleck)
speckled
spectacle
spectacles
spectacular
spectacularly
spectator
specter
spectral
spectroscope
spectroscopic
spectrum
  spectra *pl*
speculate
  speculated
  speculating
speculation
speculative
speculatively

speculator
speech
speechify
  speechified
  speechifies
  speechifying
speechless
speechlessly
speed
  sped
  speeded
  speeding
  speeds
speedily
speedometer
speedy
  speedier
  speediest
spell
  spelled
  spelling
  spells
  spelt
spellbinding
spellbound
speller
spelt
spelter
spend
  spending
  spends

spent
spender
spendthrift
sperm
spermaceti
sperm whale
spew
  spewed
  spewing
sphagnum
  sphagna *pl*
sphere
spherical
spherically
spheroid
sphincter
sphinx
  sphinxes *pl*
sphygmomanometer
spice
spicily
spiciness
spick and span
spicy
  spicier
  spiciest
spider
spidery
spied (*from* spy)
spigot
spike

spiked
spiking
spiky
  spikier
  spikiest
spill
  spilled
  spilling
  spills
  spilt
spillage
spin
  spinning
  spins
  spun
spinach
spinal
spinal column
spindle
spindly
spine
spineless
spinet
spinnaker
spinner
spinneret
spinning wheel
spin-off
spinster
spinsterhood
spiral

spirals
  spiraled
  spiraling
spirally
spire
spirit
  spirited
  spiriting
spiritedly
spiritless
spiritual
spiritualism
spiritualist
spiritualistic
spiritually
spirituous
spirt, spurt
spit
  spits
  spitted
  spitting
spite
spiteful
spitefully
spitefulness
spitfire
spitter
spittle
spittoon
splash
splashdown

splatter
  splattered
  splattering
splay
  splayed
  splaying
  splays
spleen
splendid
splendidly
splendor
splice
  spliced
  splicing
splint
splinter
  splintered
  splintering
split
  splits
  splitting
splurge
  splurged
  splurging
splutter
  spluttered
  spluttering
spoil
  spoiled
  spoiling
  spoils

spoilt

spoke (*from* speak;
  thin rod)

spoken (*from* speak)

spokeshave

spokesman

  spokesmen *pl*

spokeswoman

  spokeswomen *pl*

spoliation

spoliator

sponge

  sponged

  sponging

sponger

spongy

sponsor

  sponsored

  sponsoring

spontaneity

spontaneous

spontaneously

spoof

  spoofed

  spoofing

spool

  spooled

  spooling

spoon

  spooned

  spooning

spoonerism

spoon-feed

  spoon-fed

  spoon-feeding

  spoon-feeds

spoonful

  spoonfuls *pl*

spoor (track)

sporadic

sporadically

spore (for
  reproduction)

sporran

sport

sportive

sportively

sportsman

  sportsmen *pl*

sportsmanship

spot

  spots

  spotted

  spotting

spot-check

spotless

spotlessness

spotlight

  spotlighted

  spotlighting

  spotlights

spotlit

spotty

  spottier

  spottiest

spouse

spout

sprain

  sprained

  spraining

sprang (*from* spring)

sprat

sprawl

spray

  sprays *pl*

  sprayed

  spraying

  sprays

sprayer

spread

  spreading

  spreads

spreadeagle

  spreadeagled

  spreadeagling

spree

sprig

sprightliness

sprightly

  sprightlier

  sprightliest

spring

  sprang

springing
springs
sprung
pringboard
pring-cleaning
pringtime
prinkle
sprinkled
sprinkling
prinkler
print
printer
prite
pritzer
procket
prout
sprouted
sprouting
pruce
spruced
sprucing
prucely
pruceness
prue
prung (*from* spring)
pry
pryer
pryly
pryness
pud
pume

spun (*from* spin)
spunk
spur
  spurred
  spurring
  spurs
spurious
spurn
spurt, spirt
sputnik
sputter
  sputtered
  sputtering
sputum
  sputa *pl*
spy
  spies *pl*
  spied
  spies
  spying
squabble
  squabbled
  squabbling
squad
squadron
squadron leader
squalid
squalidly
squall
squally
squalor

squander
  squandered
  squandering
square
  squared
  squaring
squarely
squash
squat
  squats
  squatted
  squatting
  squatter
squaw
squawk
squawker
squeak
  squeaked
  squeaking
squeal
  squealed
  squealing
squeamish
squeamishness
squeegee
squeeze
  squeezed
  squeezing
squelch
squib
squid

squiggle
  squiggled
  squiggling
squill
squint
squire
squirearchy
  squirearchies *pl*
squirm
squirrel
squirt
stab
  stabbed
  stabbing
  stabs
stability
stabilization
stabilize
  stabilized
  stabilizing
stabilizer
stable
  stabled
  stabling
staccato
  staccatos *pl*
stack
stadium
  stadiums, stadia *pl*
staff
  staffed

staffing
staffs
stag
stage
  staged
  staging
stagecraft
stagey, stagy
stagger
  staggered
  staggering
staggers (sheep
  disease)
stagnant
stagnate
  stagnated
  stagnating
stagnation
staid (steady)
staidly
staidness
stain
  stained
  staining
stainless
stair (step)
staircase
stake (post; to bet)
  staked
  staking
stakeholder

stakeholding
stalactite
stalagmite
stale
stalemate
staleness
stalk (to hunt)
stalker
stall
stallion
stalwart
stamen
stamina
stammer
  stammered
  stammering
stammerer
stamp
stamp album
stamp collecting
stamp collector
stampede
  stampeded
  stampeding
stance
stanchion
stand
standard
standardization
standardize
  standardized

standardizing
standby
  standbys *pl*
stank
stanza
  stanzas *pl*
staple
  stapled
  stapling
stapler
star
  starred
  starring
  stars
starboard
starch
stardom
stare (to gaze)
  stared
  staring
stark
starless
starlet
starry
start
starter
startle
  startled
  startling
starvation
starve

starved
starving
starveling
state
  stated
  stating
stateless
stateliness
stately
statement
statesman
  statesmen *pl*
statesmanship
static
station
  stationed
  stationing
stationary (not
  moving)
stationer
stationery (paper)
stationmaster
statistical
statistically
statistician
statistics
statuary
statue
  statues *pl*
statuesque
statuette

stature
status
  statuses *pl*
status quo
statute (law)
statutory
staunch (loyal; to stop
  bleeding)
staunchly
staunchness
stave
  staved
  staving
stave off
stay
  stayed
  staying
  stays
steadfast
steadfastly
steadfastness
steadier
steadily
steadiness
steady
  steadied
  steadies
  steadying
steak (meat)
steal (to rob)
  stealing

steals
stole
stolen
stealth
stealthily
stealthiness
stealthy
 stealthier
 stealthiest
steam
 steamed
 steaming
steam engine
steamer
steamroller
 steamrollered
 steamrollering
steed
steel (metal; to
 prepare oneself)
 steeled
 steeling
steely
steep
 steeped
 steeping
steeper
steeple
steeplechase
steeplejack
steeply

steepness
steer
 steered
 steering
steerable
steerage
steersman
 steersmen *pl*
stele, stela (Greek
 gravestone)
stellar
stem
 stemmed
 stemming
 stems
stench
stencil
 stencils
 stenciled
 stenciling
stenographer
stenographic
stenography
stenotype
stentorian
step
 stepped
 stepping
 steps
stepbrother
stepfather

stepladder
stepmother
steppe (plain)
stepsister
stereo
stereophonic
stereoscope
stereoscopic
stereotype
 stereotyped
 stereotyping
sterile
sterility
sterilization
sterilize
 sterilized
 sterilizing
sterilizer
sterling
stern
sterner
sternly
sternness
sternum
 sternums *pl*
steroid
stertorous
stet
stethoscope
stevedore
stew

stewed
stewing
steward
stewardess
stick
sticker
stickily
stickiness
stickleback
stickler
sticky
  stickier
  stickiest
sticky
stiff
stiffen
  stiffened
  stiffening
stiffener
stiffly
stiff-necked
stifle
  stifled
  stifling
stigma
  stigmas, stigmata *pl*
stigmatize
  stigmatized
  stigmatizing
stile (over a hedge)
stiletto

stilettos *pl*
still
stillbirth
stillborn
stillness
stilt
stilted
stimulate
  stimulated
  stimulating
stimulation
stimulative
stimulus
  stimuli *pl*
sting
  stings
  stinging
  stung
stinger
stingily
stinginess
stingless
stingy
  stingier
  stingiest
stink
  stank
  stinking
  stinks
  stunk
stinker

stint
stipend
stipendiary
  stipendiaries *pl*
stipple
  stippled
  stippling
stipulate
  stipulated
  stipulating
stipulation
stir
  stirred
  stirring
  stirs
stirrup
stitch
stitched
stoat
stock
stock exchange
stockade
stockbroker
stocked
stockholder
stockiness
stockinette, stockinet
stocking
stockpile
  stockpiled
  stockpiling

stock-still
stocktaking
stocky
  stockier
  stockiest
stockyard
stodge
stodgily
stodgy
  stodgier
  stodgiest
stoic
stoical
stoically
stoicism
stoke
  stoked
  stoking
stoker
stole (*from* steal; robe)
stolen (*from* steal)
stolid
stolidity
stolidly
stomach
stomachache
stone
  stoned
  stoning
stone-deaf
stonemason

stonewalling
stonily
stony
  stonier
  stoniest
stood (*from* stand)
stooge
stoop
  stooped
  stooping
stop
  stopped
  stopping
  stops
stopcock
stopgap
stopover
stoppage
stopper
stopwatch
storage
store
  stored
  storing
storekeeper
stork (bird)
storm
stormbound
stormily
stormy
  stormier

stormiest
story (tale; of a
    building)
  stories *pl*
storyteller
stoup (flagon)
stout
stoutly
stoutness
stove
stow
  stowed
  stowing
stowage
stowaway
  stowaways *pl*
straddle
  straddled
  straddling
strafe
  strafed
  strafing
straggle
  straggled
  straggling
straggler
straight (direct)
straighten
  straightened
  straightening
straighter

straightforward

strain
  strained
  straining

strainer

strait (narrow)

straiten
  straitened
  straitening

straitjacket

straitlaced

straits (difficulties)

strand

stranded

strange

strangely

stranger

strangle
  strangled
  strangling

stranglehold

strangulate
  strangulated
  strangulating

strangulation

strap
  strapped
  strapping
  straps

straphanger

stratagem (trickery)

strategic

strategically

strategist

strategy (war tactics)
  strategies *pl*

stratification

stratify
  stratified
  stratifies
  stratifying

stratosphere

stratospheric

stratum (layer)
  strata *pl*

stratus (cloud)
  strati *pl*

straw

strawberry
  strawberries *pl*

stray
  strayed
  straying
  strays

streak
  streaked
  streaking

streaky

stream
  streamed
  streaming

streamline

streamlined

streamlining

street

streetcar

streetwise

strength

strengthen
  strengthened
  strengthening

strenuous

strenuously

strenuousness

streptococcal

streptococcus
  streptococci *pl*

streptomycin

stress

stretch

stretcher

strew
  strewed
  strewing
  strewn
  strews

striate
  striated
  striating

striation

stricken

strict

stricter (more

disciplined)
strictly
strictness
stricture (scolding)
stride
  strides
  striding
  strode
stridency
strident
stridently
strife
strike (to hit)
  strikes
  striking
  struck
strike (affected)
  strikes
  striking
  stricken
strikebound
strikebreaker
strikebreaking
striker
string
  strings
  stringing
  strung
stringed
stringency
stringent

stringently
stringy
strip
  stripped
  stripping
  strips
stripe
  striped
  striping
stripling
stripper
striptease
strive
  striven
  strives
  striving
  strove
stroboscope
stroboscopic
strode (*from* stride)
stroke
  stroked
  stroking
stroll
stroller
strong
stronger
stronghold
strongly
strontium
strop

stropped
stropping
strops
strove (*from* strive)
struck (*from* strike)
structural
structurally
structure
  structured
  structuring
strudel
struggle
  struggled
  struggling
strum
  strummed
  strumming
  strums
strummer
strung (*from* string)
strut
  struts
  strutted
  strutting
strychnine
stub
  stubbed
  stubbing
  stubs
stubble
stubborn

stubbornly
stubbornness
stucco
  stuccoed
  stuccoes
  stuccoing
stuck (*from* stick)
stud
  studded
  studding
  studs
student
studied
studio
  studios *pl*
studious
studiously
study
  studies *pl*
  studied
  studies
  studying
stuff
stuffed
stuffier
stuffiness
stuffy
  stuffier
  stuffiest
stultification
stultify

stultified
stultifies
stultifying
stumble
  stumbled
  stumbling
stumbling block
stump
  stumped
stun
  stunned
  stunning
  stuns
stung (*from* sting)
stunk (*from* stink)
stunt
  stunted
stupefaction
stupefy
  stupefied
  stupefies
  stupefying
stupendous
stupendously
stupid
  stupider
  stupidity
stupor
sturdily
sturdiness
sturdy

sturdier
sturdiest
sturgeon
stutter
  stuttered
  stuttering
stutterer
sty
  sties *pl*
style (method,
  elegance)
stylish
stylishly
stylishness
stylist
stylize
  stylized
  stylizing
stylus (gramophone
  needle)
  styluses, styli *pl*
stymie
  stymied
  stymieing
  stymies
styptic
styrene
suave
suavely
suavity
subaltern

subcommittee
subconscious
subconsciously
subconsciousness
subcontract
subcontractor
subdivide
  subdivided
  subdividing
subdivisible
subdivision
subdual
subdue
  subdued
  subduing
subeditor
subject
subjection
subjective
subjectively
subjectivity
sub judice
subjugate
  subjugated
  subjugating
subjugation
subjunctive
sublet
  sublets
  subletting
sublimate

  sublimated
  sublimating
sublimation
sublime
sublimely
subliminal
sublimity
submarine
submerge
  submerged
  submerging
submergence
submersible
submersion
submission
submissively
submissiveness
submit
  submits
  submitted
  submitting
subnormal
subnormality
subnormally
subordinate
  subordinated
  subordinating
subordination
suborn (to bribe)
subornation
suborner

subplot
subpoena
  subpoenaed
  subpoenaing
  subpoenas
sub rosa
subscribe
  subscribed
  subscribing
subscriber
subscription
subsequent
subsequently
subservience
subservient
subside
  subsided
  subsiding
subsidence
subsidiary
  subsidiaries *pl*
subsidies *pl*
subsidize
  subsidized
  subsidizing
subsidy
  subsidies *pl*
subsist
subsistence
subsoil
subsonic

substance
substandard
substantial
substantially
substantiate
  substantiated
  substantiating
substantiation
substantive
substation
substitute
  substituted
  substituting
substitution
substratum
  substrata *pl*
substructure
subtenancy
  subtenancies *pl*
subtenant
subtend
subterfuge
subterranean
subtitle
  subtitled
  subtitling
subtle
subtlety (ingenuity)
  subtleties *pl*
subtly
subtract

subtraction
subtropical
suburb
suburban
suburbanite
suburbia
subvention
subversion
subversive
subvert
subverter
subway
  subways *pl*
succeed
  succeeded
  succeeding
success
successful
successfully
succession
successive
successively
successor
succinct
succor
  succored
  succoring
succulence
succulent
succumb
  succumbed

  succumbing
such
suck
sucker
suckle
  suckled
  suckling
sucrose
suction
sudden
suddenly
suddenness
suds
sue
  sued
  sues
  suing
suede (kind of
  leather)
suet
suffer
  suffered
  suffering
sufferance
sufferer
suffice
  sufficed
  sufficing
sufficiency
sufficient
sufficiently

suffix
  suffixes *pl*
suffocate
  suffocated
  suffocating
suffocation
suffragan
suffrage
suffragette
suffuse
  suffused
  suffusing
suffusion
sugar
  sugared
  sugaring
sugary
suggest
suggestion
suggestive
suggestively
suicidal
suicide
suit (clothes; to be
    convenient)
  suited
  suiting
suitability
suitable
suitably
suitcase

suite (furniture;
    rooms)
suitor
sulfate
sulfide
sulfur
sulfuric acid
sulk
sulkily
sulkiness
sulky
sullen
sullenly
sullenness
sully
  sullied
  sullies
  sullying
sultan
sultana
  sultanas *pl*
sultanate
sultrier
sultrily
sultriness
sultry
sum (total)
  summed
  summing
  sums
summarily

summariness
summarize
  summarized
  summarizing
summary (short)
  summaries *pl*
summation
summer
summertime
summery (warm)
summit
summitry
summon
  summoned
  summoning
summons
  summonses *pl*
sump
sumptuary
sumptuous
sumptuously
sumptuousness
sums
sun (star)
  sunned
  sunning
  suns
sunbathe
  sunbathed
  sunbathing
sunbeam

sunburn
sunburned
sunburnt
sundae (ice-cream)
  sundaes *pl*
Sunday
sundial
sundry
  sundries *pl*
sunflower
sung (*from* sing)
sunglasses
sunk (*from* sink)
sunken
sunless
sunlight
sunnier
sunny
sunrise
sunspot
sunstroke
suntan
  suntanned
  suntanning
  suntans
sup
  supped
  supping
  sups
superabundance
superabundant

superannuate
  superannuated
  superannuating
superannuation
superb
  superbly
supercargo
  supercargoes *pl*
supercharge
  supercharged
  supercharging
supercilious
  superciliously
  superciliousness
superconductivity
superconductor
superficial
superficiality
superficially
superfluity
superfluous
  superfluously
superglue
superheterodyne
superhuman
superimpose
  superimposed
  superimposing
superimposition
superintend
superintendence

superintendent
superior
superiority
superlative
superlatively
superman
  supermen *pl*
supermarket
supernatural
supernaturalism
supernaturally
supernumerary
  supernumeraries *pl*
superpose
  superposed
  superposing
superposition
supersaturate
  supersaturated
  supersaturating
supersaturation
supersede
  superseded
  superseding
supersedure
supersonic
superstition
superstitious
superstructure
supervene
  supervened

supervening
supervention
supervise
  supervised
  supervising
supervision
supervisory
supine
supped
supper
supperless
supplant
supplanter
supple
supplely
supplement
supplementary
supplementation
suppleness
suppliant
supplicate
  supplicated
  supplicating
supplication
supplier
supply
  supplies *pl*
  supplied
  supplies
  supplying
support

supporter
suppose
  supposed
  supposing
supposedly
supposition
suppository
  suppositories *pl*
suppress
suppressible
suppression
suppressor
suppurate
  suppurated
  suppurating
suppuration
supremacy
supreme
supremely
surcharge
  surcharged
  surcharging
sure (certain)
surely
surety
  sureties *pl*
surf (sea)
  surfed
  surfing
surface
  surfaced

surfacing
surfboard
surfeit
  surfeited
  surfeiting
surfer
surfing
surge (to rush)
  surged
  surging
surgeon
surgery
  surgeries *pl*
surgical
surgically
surlily
surliness
surly
  surlier
  surliest
surmise
  surmised
  surmising
surmount
surname
surpass
surplice (clergyman's)
surplus (excess)
  surpluses *pl*
surprise
  surprised

surprising
surrealism
surrealist
surrender
  surrendered
  surrendering
surreptitious
surreptitiously
surrogate
surround
surtax
  surtaxes *pl*
surveillance
survey
  surveyed
  surveying
  surveys
surveyor
survival
survive
  survived
  surviving
survivor
susceptibility
susceptible
suspect
suspend
suspender
suspense
suspension
suspicion

suspicious
suspiciously
sustain
  sustained
  sustaining
sustenance
suture
  sutured
  suturing
svelte
swab
  swabbed
  swabbing
  swabs
swaddle
  swaddled
  swaddling
swag
swagger
  swaggered
  swaggering
  swaggerer
swain
swallow
  swallowed
  swallowing
swam (*from* swim)
swamp
swampy
swanky
swank

swap
  swapped
  swapping
  swaps
sward (of grass)
swarm
swarthily
swarthiness
swarthy
  swarthier
  swarthiest
swash
swashbuckler
swastika
  swastikas *pl*
swat (a fly)
  swats
  swatted
  swatting
swath, swathe (strip)
swathe (to bandage)
  swathed
  swathing
swatter
sway
  swayed
  swaying
  sways
swear
  swearing
  swears

swore
  sworn
sweat
  sweated
  sweating
sweater
sweaty
  sweatier
  sweatiest
swede (kind of turnip)
Swede (person from
  Sweden)
Swedish
sweep
  sweeping
  sweeps
  swept
sweeper
sweepstake
sweet (sugary)
sweet pea
sweetbread
sweeten
  sweetened
  sweetening
sweeter
sweetheart
sweetly
sweetmeat
swell
  swelled

swelling
swells
swollen
swelter
  sweltered
  sweltering
swept (*from* sweep)
swerve
  swerved
  swerving
swift
swifter
swiftly
swiftness
swig
  swigged
  swigging
  swigs
swill
swim
  swam
  swimming
  swims
  swum
swimmer
swimmingly
swindle
  swindled
  swindling
swindler
swine

swing
  swinging
  swings
  swung
swinish
swipe
  swiped
  swiping
swirl
  swirled
  swirling
switch
switchback
switchboard
swivel
  swivels
  swiveled
  swiveling
swizzle
swollen (*from* swell)
swoon
  swooned
  swooning
swoop
  swooped
  swooping
swop, swap
  swopped, swapped
  swopping, swapping
  swops, swaps
sword

swore (*from* swear)

sworn (*from* swear)

swum (*from* swim)

swung (*from* swing)

sybarite

sybaritic

sycamore

sycophant

syllabic

syllable (part of a
  word)

syllabub, sillabub

syllabus
  syllabuses, syllabi *pl*

syllogism

sylph

symbiosis

symbol (sign)

symbolic

symbolical

symbolically

symbolism

symbolize
  symbolized
  symbolizing

symmetrical

symmetrically

symmetry
  symmetries *pl*

sympathetic

sympathetically

sympathize
  sympathized
  sympathizing

sympathizer

sympathy
  sympathies *pl*

symphonic

symphony
  symphonies *pl*

symposium
  symposia *pl*

symptom

symptomatic

synagogue

synchromesh

synchronism

synchronization

synchronize
  synchronized
  synchronizing

synchronous

synchronously

syncopate
  syncopated
  syncopating

syncopation

syncope

syndicalism

syndicate

syndication

syndrome

synod

synonym

synonymous

synopsis
  synopses *pl*

syntactic

syntax

synthesis
  syntheses *pl*

synthesize
  synthesized
  synthesizing

synthetic

synthetically

syphilis

syphilitic

syringe
  syringed
  syringing

syrup

syrupy

system

systematic

systematically

systematize
  systematized
  systematizing

systole

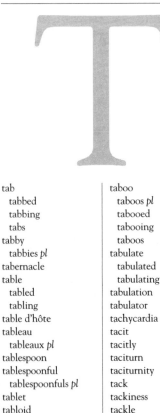

tab
  tabbed
  tabbing
  tabs
tabby
  tabbies *pl*
tabernacle
table
  tabled
  tabling
table d'hôte
tableau
  tableaux *pl*
tablespoon
tablespoonful
  tablespoonfuls *pl*
tablet
tabloid

taboo
  taboos *pl*
  tabooed
  tabooing
  taboos
tabulate
  tabulated
  tabulating
tabulation
tabulator
tachycardia
tacit
tacitly
taciturn
taciturnity
tack
tackiness
tackle

tackled
tackling
tackler
tacky (sticky)
taco
  tacos *pl*
tact
tactful
tactfully
tactic
tactical
tactician
tactile
tactless
tactlessly
tadpole
taffeta
tag
  tagged
  tagging
  tags
tagliatelle
tail (of animal)
  tailed
  tailing
tailless
tailor
  tailored
  tailoring
tailor-made
taint

tainted
take
  taken
  takes
  taking
  took
takeoff
taker
talc
talcum
tale (story)
talent
talented
talisman
  talismans *pl*
talk
talkative
talkativeness
talker
tall
tallness
tallow
tally
  tallies *pl*
  tallied
  tallies
  tallying
talon
tambourine
tame
  tamed

  taming
tameable
tameness
tamer
tam-o'-shanter
tamp
tamper
  tampered
  tampering
tampon
tan
  tanned
  tanning
  tans
tandem
tang
tangent
tangential
tangentially
tangerine
tangibility
tangible
tangibly
tangle
  tangled
  tangling
tango
  tangos *pl*
  tangoed
  tangoing
  tangos

tank
tankage
tankard
tanker
tankful
  tankfuls *pl*
tanner
tannery
  tanneries *pl*
tannic
tannin
tantalize
  tantalized
  tantalizing
tantalizingly
tantalum
tantalus
  tantaluses *pl*
tantamount
tantrum
  tantrums *pl*
tap
  tapped
  tapping
  taps
tape
  taped
  taping
tape recorder
taper
  tapered

tapering

tapestry

  tapestries *pl*

tapeworm

tapioca

tappet

taproot

taproom

tar

  tarred

  tarring

  tars

tarantella (dance)

  tarantellas *pl*

tarantula (spider)

  tarantulas *pl*

tardily

tardiness

tardy

tare (weight)

target

tariff

  tariffs *pl*

tarmac

tarn

tarnish

tarnished

tarot

tarpaulin

tarragon

tarry

tarried

tarries

tarrying

tart

tartan

tartar

tartaric acid

tartness

tartrate

task

task force

taskmaster

tassel

tasseled

taste

  tasted

  tasting

tasteful

tastefully

tastefulness

tasteless

taster

tasty

  tastier

  tastiest

tatter

tatterdemalion

tattered

tattle

  tattled

  tattling

tattoo

  tattoos *pl*

  tattooed

  tattooing

  tattoos

tattooist

tatty

  tattier

  tattiest

taught (*from* teach)

taunt

taupe

taut (tight)

tauten

  tautened

  tautening

tautly

tautness

tautological

tautology

  tautologies *pl*

tavern

tawdrily

tawdry

tawny

tax

  taxes *pl*

  taxed

  taxes

  taxing

taxable

taxation

taxi

  taxis *pl*

  taxied

  taxiing

  taxis

taxicab

taxidermist

taxidermy

taximeter

taxonomy

  taxonomies *pl*

taxpayer

tea (drink)

tea bag

teach

  taught

  teaches

  teaching

teacher

teacup

teak

tea leaf

  tea leaves *pl*

tea party

  tea parties *pl*

teapot

team (*eg* of players)

teammate

teamster

teamwork

tear (to rip; crying)

  tearing

  tears

  tore

  torn

tearful

tearfully

tearfulness

tearless

tease

  teased

  teasing

teaser

teaspoon

teaspoonful

  teaspoonfuls *pl*

teat

technical

technicality

  technicalities *pl*

technically

technician

technique

technocracy

  technocracies *pl*

technological

technologically

technology

  technologies *pl*

teddy bear

Te Deum

tedious

tediously

tediousness

tedium

tee (in golf)

  teed

  teeing

teem (to be

  abundant)

  teemed

  teeming

teenage

teenager

teens (age)

teeth (*from* tooth)

teethe

  teethed

  teething

teetotal

teetotaler

teetotalism

telecommunications

telegram

telegraph

telegraphic

telemeter

telepathic

telepathy

telephone

  telephoned

  telephoning

telephonic
telephonist
telephony
telephoto
teleprinter
teleprompter
telescope
  telescoped
  telescoping
telescopic
telescopy
teletext
teletype
televise
  televised
  televising
television
teleworker
teleworking
telex
  telexes *pl*
  telexed
  telexes
  telexing
tell
  telling
  tells
  told
telltale
temerity
temper

tempered
  tempering
tempera
temperament
temperamental
temperamentally
temperance
temperate
temperature
tempest
tempestuous
template
temple
tempo
  tempi, tempos *pl*
temporal
temporally
temporarily
temporary
temporize
  temporized
  temporizing
temporizer
tempt
temptation
tempter
temptress
ten
tenability
tenable
tenacious

tenaciously
tenacity
tenancy
  tenancies *pl*
tenant
tenantry
tendency
  tendencies *pl*
tendentious
tender
  tendered
  tendering
tenderer
tenderhearted
tenderize
  tenderized
  tenderizing
tenderly
tendon
tendril
tenement
tenet
tenfold
tennis
tennis court
tennis racket
tenon
tenor
tense
  tensed
  tensing

tensely
tenseness
tensile
tension
tent
tentacle
tentative
tentatively
tenterhooks
tenth
tenthly
tenuity
tenuous
tenuously
tenure
tepid
tepidly
tercentenary
tercentennial
term
termagant
terminable
terminal
terminally
terminate
  terminated
  terminating
termination
terminological
terminology
  terminologies *pl*

terminus
  termini,
    terminuses *pl*
termite
tern (bird)
terra firma
terrace
  terraced
  terracing
terracotta
terrain
terrapin
terrestrial
terrible
terribly
terrier
terrific
terrifically
terrify
  terrified
  terrifies
  terrifying
territorial
territorially
territory
  territories *pl*
terror
terrorism
terrorist
terrorization
terrorize

terrorized
terrorizing
terse
tersely
terseness
tertian
tertiary
test
testament
testamentary
testate
testator
testatrix
  testatrices *pl*
testicle
testicular
testify
  testified
  testifies
  testifying
testily
testimonial
testimony
  testimonies *pl*
testiness
test tube
testy
tetanus
tetany
tetchily
tetchiness

tetchy
tête-à-tête
tether
  tethered
  tethering
tetragon
tetragonal
tetrahedral
tetrahedron
tetralogy
  tetralogies *pl*
tetrarch
tetrarchy
  tetrarchies *pl*
tetrode
Teuton
Teutonic
text
textile
textual
textually
texture
than
thank
thankful
thankfully
thankfulness
thankless
thanksgiving
that
thatch

thatcher
thaw
  thawed
  thawing
theater
theatrical
theatrically
thee
theft
their (of them)
theirs
theism
theist
them
thematic
theme
themed
themselves
then
thence
thenceforth
thenceforward
theocracy
  theocracies *pl*
theodolite
theologian
theological
theologist
theology
theosophical
theorem

theoretic
theoretical
theoretically
theoretician
theorize
  theorized
  theorizing
theory
  theories *pl*
theosophist
theosophy
therapeutic
therapist
therapy
  therapies *pl*
there (at that place)
thereabouts
thereafter
thereby
therefore
thereupon
therm
thermal
thermally
thermionic
thermite
thermocouple
thermodynamic
thermometer
thermos
thermostat

thesaurus
 thesauri *pl*
these
thesis
 theses *pl*
they
they'd (they would;
 they had)
they'll (they will)
they're (they are)
they've (they have)
thick
thicken
 thickened
 thickening
thickener
thicker
thicket
thickheaded
thickly
thickness
thickset
thick-skinned
thief
 thieves *pl*
thieve
 thieved
 thieving
thigh
thimble
thin

thinned
thinning
thins
thine
thing
think
 thinking
 thinks
thought
thinker
thinner
thin-skinned
third
thirdly
thirst
thirstily
thirsty
 thirstier
 thirstiest
thirteen
thirteenth
thirtieth
thirty
 thirties *pl*
this
thistle
thither
thong
thoracic
thorax
 thoraxes *pl*

thorn
thornless
thorny
 thornier
 thorniest
thorough (absolute)
thoroughbred
thoroughfare
thoroughgoing
thoroughly
thoroughness
those
thou (you)
though (in spite of)
thought (*from* think)
thoughtful
thoughtfully
thoughtfulness
thoughtless
thoughtlessness
thousand
thousandth
thrash
thread
 threaded
 threading
threadbare
threat
threaten
 threatened
 threatening

three
three-cornered
three-dimensional
threefold
three-quarters
threescore
thresh
thresher
threshold
threw (*from* throw)
thrice
thrift
thriftily
thriftless
thrifty
  thriftier
  thriftiest
thrill
thrilled
thriller
thrilling
thrive
  thrived
  thriving
throat
throb
  throbbed
  throbbing
  throbs
throe (suffering)
  throes *pl*

thrombosis
  thromboses *pl*
throne (chair)
throng
throttle
  throttled
  throttling
throttler
through (from end to
  end)
throughout
throve
throw (to fling)
  threw
  throwing
  thrown
  throws
thrush
thrust
thud
  thudded
  thudding
  thuds
thug
thumb
  thumbed
  thumbing
thump
  thumped
  thumping
thunder

thundered
  thundering
thunderbolt
thunderer
thunderstorm
thunderstruck
Thursday
  Thursdays *pl*
thus
thwart
thwarted
thy
thyme (herb)
thyroid
thyself
tiara
  tiaras *pl*
tibia
  tibias *pl*
tic (twitch)
tick (insect; sound of
  clock)
ticked
ticker
ticker tape
ticket
  ticketed
  ticketing
tickle
  tickled
  tickling

ticklish
tidal
titbit
tiddlywinks
tide (ocean)
tideless
tidily
tidiness
tidings
tidy
  tidied
  tidies
  tidying
  tidier
  tidiest
tie (to bind)
  tied
  ties
  tying
tie-dye
  tie-dyed
  tie-dying
tier (row of seats)
tierce (set of three)
tiered
tiff
tiger
tight
tighten
  tightened
  tightening

tighter
tightlaced
tight-lipped
tightly
tightrope
tights
tigress
tile
  tiled
  tiling
till
tillable
tillage
tiller
tilt
tilth
timber
timbered
timbre (quality of
  sound)
time (clock)
  timed
  timing
time-honored
timekeeper
timeless
timely
timepiece
timer
time warp
timid

timidity
timidly
timorous
timorously
timorousness
timpani
timpanist
tin
  tinned
  tinning
  tins
tincture
tinder
tinfoil
tinge
  tinged
  tingeing
tingle
  tingled
  tingling
tinker
  tinkered
  tinkering
tinkle
  tinkled
  tinkling
tinnitus
tinny
  tinnier
  tinniest
tinplate

tinsel

tinseled

tint

tinted

tintinnabulation

tiny

  tinier

  tiniest

tip

  tipped

  tipping

  tips

tip-off

tipped-off

tipper

tippet

tipple

  tippled

  tippling

tippler

tipsily

tipsiness

tipstaff

  tipstaffs, tipstaves *pl*

tipster

tipsy

tiptoe

  tiptoed

  tiptoeing

  tiptoes

tiptop

tirade

tire (to get tired;
    wheel)

  tired

  tiring

tiredness

tireless

tirelessly

tiresome

tiresomely

tissue

tit

tit for tat

titan

titanic

titbit

tithe

  tithed

  tithing

titillate

  titillated

  titillating

titillation

titivate (to smarten)

  titivated

  titivating

titivation

title

  titled

titmouse

  titmice *pl*

titrate

  titrated

  titrating

titration

titter

  tittered

  tittering

tittle-tattle

  tittle-tattled

  tittle-tattling

titular

to (towards)

to-and-fro

toad

toadstool

toady

toadying

toast

toaster

tobacco

tobacconist

toboggan

  tobogganed

  tobogganing

tobogganer

tobogganist

toccata

  toccatas *pl*

tocsin (alarm bell)

today

toddle

toddled
toddling
toddler
toddy (drink)
  toddies *pl*
to-do
toe (foot)
  toed
  toeing
  toes
toehold
toffee
tog
together
toggle
togs (clothes)
toil
  toiled
  toiling
toiler
toilet
toiletry
  toiletries *pl*
token
told (*from* tell)
tolerable
tolerably
tolerance
tolerant
tolerantly
tolerate

tolerated
tolerating
toleration
toll
toll call (telephone)
tomahawk
tomato
  tomatoes *pl*
tomato sauce
tomb
tombola
  tombolas *pl*
tomboy
  tomboys *pl*
tombstone
tomcat
tome (volume)
tomfoolery
tomorrow
tomtit
ton (imperial weight)
tonal
tonality
tone (sound)
toneless
tongs (pincers)
tongue (in mouth)
  tongued
  tongues
  tonguing
tongue-tied

tonic
tonight
tonnage
tonne (metric ton)
tonsil
tonsillectomy
tonsillitis
tonsorial
tonsure
too (also)
took (*from* take)
tool
  tooled
  tooling
tooth
toothache
toothless
toothsome
tootle
  tootled
  tootling
top
  topped
  topping
  tops
toper (drinker)
top-heavy
topiary
topic
topical
topically

topknot
topless
topmost
top-notch
topographer
topographic
topography
topper
topple
  toppled
  toppling
topsy-turvy
toque (small hat)
torch
tore (*from* tear)
toreador
torment
tormentor
torn (*from* tear)
tornado
  tornadoes *pl*
torpedo
  torpedoes *pl*
  torpedoed
  torpedoes
  torpedoing
torpid
torpidity
torpidly
torpidness
torpor

torque (twisting)
torrent
torrential
torrid
torsion
torso
  torsos *pl*
tort (law)
tortilla
  tortillas *pl*
tortoise
tortoiseshell
tortuosity
tortuous
tortuously
tortuousness
torture
  tortured
  torturing
torturer
tosh
toss
tossed
toss-up
tot
  tots
  totted
  totting
total
  totals
  totaled

  totaling
totalisator
totalitarian
totality
totalizator
totally
tote
totem
totter
  tottered
  tottering
touch
touché
touched
touchy
  touchier
  touchiest
tough
toughen
  toughened
  toughening
tougher
toughly
toughness
toupee
tour (trip)
  toured
  touring
tour de force
tourism
tourist

tournament

tournedos

tourniquet

tousle

  tousled

  tousling

tout

  touted

  touting

touter

tow (pull)

  towed

  towing

towage

toward

towards

towel

  towels

  toweled

  toweling

tower

  towered

  towering

town hall

town

townie

township

townspeople

towpath

toxemia

toxic

toxicologist

toxicology

toxin (poison)

toy

  toys *pl*

  toyed

  toying

  toys

trace

  traced

  tracing

traceable

tracer

tracery

trachea (windpipe)

  tracheas *pl*

trachoma

track

tract

tractable

traction

traction engine

tractor

trade

  traded

  trading

trademark

trader

tradesman

  tradesmen *pl*

tradition

traditional

traditionally

traduce

  traduced

  traducing

traducer

traffic

trafficker

trafficking

tragedian

tragedienne (fem)

tragedy

  tragedies *pl*

tragic

tragically

tragicomedy

tragicomic

trail

  trailed

  trailing

trailblazer

trailer

train

  trained

  training

trainee

trainer

traipse

  traipsed

  traipsing

trait

traitor
traitorous
trajectory
  trajectories *pl*
tram
trammel
  trammels
  trammeled
  trammeling
tramp
trample
  trampled
  trampling
trampoline
trance
tranquil
tranquilization
tranquilize
  tranquilized
  tranquilizing
tranquilizer
tranquilly
transact
transaction
transatlantic
transceiver
transcend
transcendent
transcendental
transcontinental
transcribe

  transcribed
  transcribing
transcript
transcription
transept
transsexual
transfer
  transferred
  transferring
  transfers
transferable
transference
transfiguration
transfigure
  transfigured
  transfiguring
transfix
  transfixed
  transfixes
  transfixing
transform
transformation
transformer
transfuse
  transfused
  transfusing
transfusion
transgress
transgression
transgressor
transience

transient
transistor
transistorization
transistorize
  transistorized
  transistorizing
transit
transition
transitional
transitive
transitorily
translatable
translate
  translated
  translating
translation
translator
transliterate
  transliterated
  transliterating
transliteration
translucence
translucent
transmigrate
  transmigrated
  transmigrating
transmigration
transmission
transmit
  transmits
  transmitted

transmitting
transmitter
transmutation
transmute
  transmuted
  transmuting
transoceanic
transom
transpacific
transparence
transparency
transparent
transparently
transpiration
transpire
  transpired
  transpiring
transplant
transplantation
transport
transportable
transportation
transporter
transpose
  transposed
  transposing
transposition
transship
  transshipped
  transshipping
  transships

transshipment
transubstantiate
transubstantiation
transverse
transversely
transvestism
transvestite
trap
  trapped
  trapping
  traps
trapeze
trapezium
trapper
trash
trauma
  traumas *pl*
traumatic
travail (painful effort)
travel
  travels
  traveled
  traveling
traveler
travelogue
traverse
  traversed
  traversing
travesty
  travesties *pl*
trawl

trawled
trawling
trawls
trawler
tray
  trays *pl*
treacherous
treacherously
treachery
  treacheries *pl*
tread
  treading
  treads
  trod
  trodden
treadle
treason
treasonable
treasonably
treasure
  treasured
  treasuring
treasurer
treasury
  treasuries *pl*
treat
  treated
  treating
treatable
treatise
treatment

treaty
  treaties *pl*
treble
trebly
tree
trefoil
trek
  trekked
  trekking
  treks
trekker
trellis
tremble
  trembled
  trembling
tremendous
tremendously
tremolo
  tremolos *pl*
tremor
tremulous
tremulously
tremulousness
trench
trenchancy
trenchant
trenchantly
trencher
trend
trendy
  trendier

  trendiest
trepan
  trepanned
  trepanning
  trepans
trepidation
trespass
trespassed
trespasser
trestle
trial
trials
triangle
triangular
triangulate
  triangulated
  triangulating
triangulation
tribal
tribalism
tribe
tribulation
tribunal
tribune
tributary
  tributaries *pl*
tribute
trice
trick
trickery
trickily

trickle
  trickled
  trickling
trickster
tricky
  trickier
  trickiest
tricycle
trident
tried (*from* try)
triennial
trier
tries (*from* try)
trifle
  trifled
  trifling
trifler
trigger
  triggered
  triggering
trigonometric
trigonometrical
trigonometry
trill
trilogy
  trilogies *pl*
trim
  trimmed
  trimming
  trims
trimmer

trinity
  trinities *pl*
trinket
trio
  trios *pl*
triode
trip
  tripped
  tripping
  trips
tripartite
tripe
triphthong
triple
  tripled
  tripling
triplet
triplicate
triplication
triply
tripod
tripodal
tripos
tripper
triptych (picture)
triptyque (travel
  document)
trite
tritely
triumph
triumphal

triumphant
triumphantly
triumvirate
trivia
trivial
triviality
  trivialities *pl*
trivialize
  trivialized
  trivializing
trivially
trod (*from* tread)
trodden (*from* tread)
troll
trolley
  trolleys *pl*
trollop
trombone
troop (soldiers)
  trooped
  trooping
trooper
trophy
  trophies *pl*
tropic
tropical
tropism
troposphere
tropospheric
trot
  trots

trotted
trotting
trotter
troubadour
trouble
  troubled
  troubling
troublesome
trough
trounce
  trounced
  trouncing
troupe (of actors)
trouper
trousers
trousseau
  trousseaus,
    trousseaux *pl*
trout
trowel
truancy
truant
truce
truck
truckle
truckling
truculence
truculent
truculently
trudge
  trudged

trudging
true
true-blue
truer
truffle
truism
truly
trump
trumped-up
trumpery
trumpet
  trumpeted
  trumpeting
trumpeter
truncate
  truncated
  truncating
truncation
truncheon
trundle
  trundled
  trundling
trunk
trunnion
truss
trussed
trust
trustee
trusteeship
trustful
trustfully

trustworthiness
trustworthy
truth
truthful
truthfully
truthfulness
try
  tries *pl*
  tried
  tries
  trying
tryout
tryst
tsetse fly
  tsetse flies *pl*
T-shirt
tub
tuba (music)
  tubas *pl*
tubbiness
tubby
  tubbier
  tubbiest
tube
tuber (swelling)
tubercle
tubercular
tuberculosis
tuberculous
tubing
tubular

tuck
Tuesday
  Tuesdays *pl*
tuft
tufted
tug
  tugged
  tugging
  tugs
tuition
tulip
tumble
  tumbled
  tumbling
tumbler
tumescence
tumescent
tumor
tumult
tumultuous
tun (barrel)
tuna
  tuna, tunas *pl*
tundra
tune
  tuned
  tuning
tune up
tuneful
tunefully
tunefulness

tuner

tungsten

tunic

tunnel

  tunnels

  tunneled

  tunneling

tunneler

tunneling

tunny

  tunny, tunnies *pl*

turban

turbaned

turbid

turbidity

turbine

turbogenerator

turbojet

turboprop

turbot

turbulence

turbulent

tureen

turf

  turfs, turves *pl*

turgid

turkey

  turkeys *pl*

turmeric

turmoil

turn (to rotate)

turncoat

turner

turnip

turnstile

turntable

turpentine

turpitude

turps

turquoise

turret

turreted

turtle

tusk

tussah

tussle

  tussled

  tussling

tutelage

tutelary

tutor

  tutored

  tutoring

tutorial

tutti-frutti

tutu

  tutus *pl*

tuxedo

  tuxedoes, tuxedos *pl*

twaddle

twain

tweak

tweaked

tweaking

tweed

tweezers

twelfth

twelve

twentieth

twenty

  twenties *pl*

twice

twiddle

  twiddled

  twiddling

twig

twilight

twilit

twill (fabric)

twin

  twins *pl*

  twinned

  twinning

  twins

twine (thread)

twinge

twinkle

  twinkled

  twinkling

twirl

twist

twister

twit

twitch
twitter
  twittered
  twittering
two (number)
twofold
tycoon
tying (*from* tie)
tympanum (eardrum)
  tympanums,
    tympana *pl*
type
  typed
  typing
typecast
  typecasting
typescript
typewriter
typewriting
typewritten
typhoid
typhoon
typhus
typical
typically
typify
  typified
  typifies
  typifying
typist
typographic

typography
tyrannical
tyrannically
tyrannize
  tyrannized
  tyrannizing
tyrannous
tyranny
  tyrannies *pl*
tyrant
tyro
  tyros *pl*
tzar, tsar, czar
tzigane

ubiquitous
ubiquity
udder
ugliness
ugly
  uglier
  ugliest
ukase
ukulele
ulcer
ulcerated
ulceration
ulcerous
ulterior
ultimate
ultimately
ultimatum
  ultimatums,

ultimata *pl*
ultraconservative
ultramarine
ultramicroscopic
ultramodern
ultrasonic
ultraviolet
umber
umbilical
umbilicus
  umbilici,
    umbilicuses *pl*
umbrage
umbrella
  umbrellas *pl*
umpire
  umpired
  umpiring

umpteen
umpteenth
unable
unabridged
unacceptable
unaccompanied
unaccountable
unaccountably
unaccustomed
unacquainted
unaffected
unafraid
unalterable
unanimity
unanimous
unanimously
unanswerable
unanswered
unapproachable
unarmed
unashamed
unasked
unassisted
unassuming
unattached
unattainable
unattended
unauthorized
unavailable
unavailing
unavoidable

unaware
unawares
unbalanced
unbearable
unbearably
unbeatable
unbeaten
unbecoming
unbeknown
unbelievable
unbelievably
unbeliever
unbend
unbent
unbiased
unbidden
unblemished
unblushing
unborn
unbounded
unbowed
unbroken
unburdened
unburied
unbuttoned
uncannily
uncanniness
uncanny
unceremonious
uncertain
uncertainty

uncertainties *pl*
unchangeable
unchanged
uncharitable
uncharted
unchristian
uncivilized
unclaimed
uncle
unclean
uncomfortable
uncomfortably
uncommitted
uncommon
uncommonly
uncommunicative
uncompleted
uncompromising
unconcern
unconditional
unconditionally
unconfirmed
uncongenial
unconnected
unconquerable
unconscious
unconsciously
unconsciousness
unconstitutional
unconstitutionally
uncontrollable

uncontrollably
uncontrolled
unconventional
unconventionally
uncooperative
uncoordinated
uncorroborated
uncouple
uncoupled
uncoupling
uncouth
uncouthly
uncouthness
uncover
uncovered
uncovering
uncritical
uncritically
unction
unctuous
unctuously
unctuousness
uncultivated
undated
undaunted
undecided
undefended
undeniable
undeniably
under
underarm

underclothes
underclothing
undercover
undercurrent
undercut
  undercuts
  undercutting
underdeveloped
underdog
underdone
underexposed
undergo
  undergoes
  undergoing
  undergone
  underwent
undergraduate
underground
undergrowth
underhand
underlay
underlie
  underlain
  underlay
  underlies
  underlying
underline
  underlined
  underlining
underling
undermanned

undermanning
undermine
  undermined
  undermining
underneath
undernourished
undernourishment
underpass
underprivileged
underrate
  underrated
  underrating
undersigned
understand
  understanding
  understands
  understood
understandable
understatement
understrapper
understudied
understudy
  understudies *pl*
  understudied
  understudies
  understudying
undertake
  undertaken
  undertakes
  undertaking
  undertook

undertaker
underwater
underwear
underweight
underwent
underworld
underwrite
  underwrites
  underwriting
  underwritten
  underwrote
underwriter
undeserved
undesirable
undesirably
undetermined
undeterred
undigested
undignified
undisciplined
undo
  undid
  undoes
  undoing
  undone
undoubted
undoubtedly
undress
undressed
undue
undulate

undulated
undulating
undulation
undulatory
unduly
undying
unearned
unearth
unearthly
uneasily
uneasy
uneatable
uneconomic
uneconomical
uneconomically
uneducated
unemployable
unemployed
unemployment
unenterprising
unequal
unequaled
unequally
unerring
uneven
unevenly
unevenness
uneventful
unexceptionable
unexceptional
unexpected

unfailing
unfair
unfairly
unfairness
unfaithful
unfaithfully
unfaithfulness
unfashionable
unfasten
unfastened
unfastening
unfavorable
unfavorably
unfeeling
unfeelingly
unfeigned
unfit
unfits
unfitted
unfitting
unfitness
unfold
unforeseen
unforgettable
unforgettably
unfortunate
unfortunately
unfounded
unfriendliness
unfriendly
unfurl

unfurled
unfurnished
ungainly
ungodly
ungovernable
ungrammatical
ungrammatically
ungrateful
ungratefully
unguarded
unguent
unhappily
unhappiness
unhappy
unhappier
unhappiest
unharmed
unhealthy
unhealthier
unhealthiest
unheard-of
unhinge
unhinged
unhoped for
unicellular
unicorn
unidentifiable
unidentified
unification
unified
uniform

uniformity
uniformly
unify
  unified
  unifies
  unifying
unilateral
unilaterally
unimpeachable
unimpeachably
uninhabited
uninhibited
uninspiring
unintelligibility
unintelligible
unintelligibly
union
unionism
unionist
unionization
unionize
  unionized
  unionizing
unique
uniquely
uniqueness
unison
unit
unitary
unite
  united

  uniting
unity
universal
universality
universally
universe
university
  universities *pl*
unjust
unjustifiable
unjustifiably
unjustified
unkempt
unkind
unkindly
unkindness
unknowing
unknown
unlawful
unlawfully
unleaded
unleavened
unless
unlettered
unlicensed
unlike
unlikelihood
unlikely
unlimited
unload
  unloaded

  unloading
unlock
unlocked
unluckily
unlucky
  unluckier
  unluckiest
unmanageable
unmarried
unmask
unmentionable
unmistakable
unmistakably
unmitigated
unmoved
unnamed
unnatural
unnaturally
unnecessarily
unnecessary
unnerved
unnerving
unnumbered
unobservant
unobtrusive
unobtrusively
unobtrusiveness
unoccupied
unofficial
unofficially
unopened

unpack
unpacked
unpaid
unparalleled
unparliamentary
unpleasant
unpleasantly
unpleasantness
unprecedented
unprejudiced
unprepared
unprincipled
unprintable
unprofessional
unprofessionally
unqualified
unquestionable
unquestionably
unravel
  unravels
  unraveled
  unraveling
unreadable
unreadiness
unready
unreal
unrealistic
unrealistically
unreasonable
unreasonably
unrecognizable

unrecognized
unreliable
unreliably
unreserved
unreservedly
unresponsive
unrest
unrestrained
unrighteous
unripe
unrivaled
unruffled
unruly
  unrulier
  unruliest
unsafe
unsaid
unsatisfactorily
unsatisfactoriness
unsatisfactory
unsatisfied
unsavoriness
unsavory
unscathed
unscientific
unscientifically
unscrupulous
unscrupulously
unscrupulousness
unseasonable
unseasonably

unseeing
unseemliness
unseemly
  unseemlier
  unseemliest
unseen
unserviceable
unsettle
  unsettled
  unsettling
unsightliness
unsightly
  unsightlier
  unsightliness
unskilled
unskillful
unskillfully
unsociable
unsociably
unsophisticated
unspeakable
unspeakably
unspoiled
unstable
unstably
unsteadily
unsteadiness
unsteady
unsubstantiated
unsuccessful
unsuccessfully

unsuitable
unsuitably
unsupported
unsuspected
untactful
untactfully
untenable
unthinkable
untidiness
untidy
  untidier
  untidiest
untie
  untied
  unties
  untying
until
untimely
unto
untold
untouchable
untoward
untraceable
untrue
untruth
untruthful
untruthfully
unusual
unusually
unveil
  unveiled

unveiling
unwanted
unwarily
unwarranted
unwary
  unwarier
  unwariest
unwell
unwholesome
unwieldiness
unwieldy
  unwieldier
  unwieldiest
unwind
unwinding
unwise
unwisely
unwitting
unwittingly
unwonted (unusual)
unworkable
unworldliness
unworldly
unworthily
unworthiness
unworthy
  unworthier
  unworthiest
unwound
unwrap
  unwrapped

unwrapping
unwraps
unwritten
up-to-date
upbraid
  upbraided
  upbraiding
upbringing
update
  updated
  updating
upheaval
uphold
  upheld
  upholding
  upholds
uphill
upholster
  upholstered
  upholstering
  upholsterer
  upholstery
upkeep
upon
upper
uppercut
uppermost
uppish
uppishness
upright
uprightness

uprising
uproar
uproarious
upset
  upsets
  upsetting
upshot
upside
upside-down
upstairs
upstart
uptight
upward
upwards
uranium
urban (town)
urbane (polite)
urbanely
urbanity
urchin
urea
uremia
urethra
  urethrae *pl*
urge
  urged
  urging
urgency
urgent
urgently
urinal

urinary
urinate
  urinated
  urinating
urine
urn (pot)
urologist
urology
usable
usage
use
  used
  using
useful
usefully
usefulness
useless
uselessly
uselessness
user
usher
  ushered
  ushering
usherette
ushers
usual
usually
usurer
usurious
usurp
usurpation

usurper
usury
utensil
uterine
uterus
  uteri *pl*
utilitarian
utility
  utilities *pl*
utilizable
utilization
utilize
  utilized
  utilizing
utmost
utopia
utopian
utter
  uttered
  uttering
utterance
utterly
uttermost
uvula
  uvulae *pl*
uvular
uxorious

V

vacancy
  vacancies *pl*
vacant
vacate
  vacated
  vacating
vacation
vaccinate (to
  inoculate)
  vaccinated
  vaccinating
vaccination
vaccine
vacillate
  vacillated
  vacillating
vacillation
vacuity

vacuole
vacuous
vacuum
  vacuums, vacua *pl*
vade mecum
  vade mecums *pl*
vagabond
vagabondage
vagary
  vagaries *pl*
vagina
  vaginas *pl*
vagrancy
vagrant
vague
vaguely
vagueness
vaguer

vain (conceited;
  useless)
vainer
vainglorious
vainglory
vainly
valance (frill)
vale (valley)
valediction
valedictory
valence (chem.)
valency
  valencies *pl*
valentine
valerian
valet
  valeted
  valeting
valetudinarian
Valhalla
valiant
valiantly
valid
validate
  validated
  validating
validation
validity
valise
valley
  valleys *pl*

valor
valorous
valuable
valuation
value
  valued
  valuing
valueless
valuer
valve
valvular
vamp
vampire
van
vandal
vandalism
vandalize
  vandalized
  vandalizing
vane (weathercock)
vanguard
vanilla
vanish
vanity
  vanities *pl*
vanquish
vantage
vapid
vapor
vaporization
vaporize

vaporized
vaporizing
vaporizer
vaporous
variability
variable
variance
variant
variation
varicolored
varicose
varicose veins
varied
variegated
variegation
variety
  varieties *pl*
various
varlet
varnish
varsity
  varsities *pl*
vary
  varied
  varies
  varying
vascular
vase
vast
vaster
vastly

vastness
vat (tank)
Vatican
vaudeville
vault
vaunt
veal
vector
vectorial
veer
  veered
  veering
vegetable
vegetarian
vegetarianism
vegetate
  vegetated
  vegetating
vegetation
vegetative
vehemence
vehement
vehicle
vehicular
veil (cover)
  veiled
  veiling
vein (blood vessel;
  manner; thin strip)
veiny
  veinier

veiniest
vellum
velocity
  velocities *pl*
velour
velvet
velveteen
velvety
venal
venality
venally
vend
vended
vender
vendetta
  vendettas *pl*
vendor (seller)
veneer
  veneered
  veneering
venerable
venerate
  venerated
  venerating
veneration
venereal (disease)
vengeance
vengeful
venial (pardonable)
venison
venom

venomous
venous
vent
ventilate
  ventilated
  ventilating
ventilation
ventilator
ventral
ventrally
ventricle
ventricular
ventriloquism
ventriloquist
venture
  ventured
  venturing
venturer
venturesome
venue
veracious (honest)
veracity
veranda
  verandas *pl*
verb
verbal
verbalize
  verbalized
  verbalizing
verbally
verbatim

verbena
  verbenas *pl*
verbiage
verbose
verbosity
verdancy
verdant
verdict
verdigris
verdure
verdurous
verge
  verged
  verging
verger
verifiable
verification
verify
  verified
  verifies
  verifying
verily
verisimilitude
veritable
veritably
verity
  verities *pl*
vermicelli
vermilion
vermin
verminous

vermouth
vernacular
vernal
vernier
veronal
verruca
  verrucae *pl*
versatile
versatility
verse
versed
versification
versifier
versify
  versified
  versifies
  versifying
version
versus (against)
vertebra
  vertebrae *pl*
vertebral
vertebrate
vertex
  vertices, vertexes *pl*
vertical
vertically
vertiginous
vertigo
verve
very

vesper
vessel
vest
vestibule
vestige
vestigial
vestment
vestry
  vestries *pl*
vesture
vet
  vets
  vetted
  vetting
vetch
veteran
veterinarian
veterinary
veto
  vetoes *pl*
  vetoed
  vetoes
  vetoing
vex
  vexed
  vexing
vexation
vexatious
via
viability
viable

viaduct
vial (tube)
viand
vibrant
vibrate
  vibrated
  vibrating
vibration
vibrato
vibrator
vibratory
vicar
vicarage
vicarious
vice
vice versa
vice-chancellor
vice president
vice-presidential
viceregal
viceroy
  viceroys *pl*
viceroyalty
vichyssoise
vicinity
  vicinities *pl*
vicious (evil)
viciously
viciousness
vicissitude
victim

victimization
victimize
  victimized
  victimizing
victor
victorious
victory
  victories *pl*
victuals
victualer
video
  videos *pl*
videocassette
videodisc
video-signal
videotape
videotext
vie (to compete with)
  vied
  vies
  vying
view
viewer
viewpoint
vigil
vigilance
vigilant
vigilante
vigilantly
vignette
vigor

vigorous
vigorously
vigorousness
vile (bad)
vilely
vileness
viler
vilification
vilifier
vilify
  vilified
  vilifies
  vilifying
villa
  villas *pl*
village
villager
villain
villainous
villainously
villainy
villein (serf)
vim
vinaigrette
vindicate
  vindicated
  vindicating
vindication
vindicator
vindictive
vindictively

vindictiveness
vine
vinegar
vinegary
vinery
  vineries *pl*
vineyard
viniculture
vinous
vintage
vintner
vinyl
viol
viola
  violas *pl*
viola da gamba
  viola da gambas *pl*
violate
  violated
  violating
violation
violator
violence
violent
violently
violet
violin
violoncello
  violoncellos *pl*
viper
virago

viragoes, viragos *pl*
viral
virgin
virginal (harpsichord)
virginity
  virginities *pl*
virile
virility
virtu (love of art)
virtual
virtually
virtue (goodness)
virtuosity
virtuoso
  virtuosi, virtuosos *pl*
virtuous
virtuously
virulence
virulent
virulently
virus
  viruses *pl*
vis-à-vis
visa
  visas *pl*
visage
viscera
visceral
viscid
viscidity
viscosity

viscount
viscountess
viscous (thick)
visage
vise
  vised
  vising
visibility
visible
visibly
vision
visionary
  visionaries *pl*
visit
  visited
  visiting
visitation
visitor
visor
vista
  vistas *pl*
visual
visualization
visualize
  visualized
  visualizing
visually
vital
vitality
vitalization
vitalize

vitalized
vitalizing
vitally
vitals
vitamin
vitiate
  vitiated
  vitiating
vitiation
viticulture
vitreous
vitrification
vitrify
  vitrified
  vitrifies
  vitrifying
vitriol
vitriolic
vituperate
  vituperated
  vituperating
vituperation
vituperative
vivace
viva voce
vivacious
vivacity
vivid
vividly
vividness
vivify

vivified

vivifies

vivifying

viviparous

vivisect

vivisection

vivisector

vixen

vizier

vocabulary

  vocabularies *pl*

vocal

vocal cord

vocalist

vocalization

vocalize

  vocalized

  vocalizing

vocally

vocation

vocational

vocative

vociferate

  vociferated

  vociferating

vociferation

vociferous

vociferously

vociferousness

vodka

  vodkas *pl*

vogue

voice

  voiced

  voicing

voiceless

voiceprint

void

voidable

voile

volatile

volatility

volatilize

  volatilized

  volatilizing

vol-au-vent

volcanic

volcano

  volcanoes *pl*

volition

volley

  volleys *pl*

volleyball

volt

voltage

voltaic

volte-face

voltmeter

volubility

voluble

volubly

volume

volumetric

voluminous

voluntarily

voluntary

volunteer

  volunteered

  volunteering

volunteers

voluptuary

  voluptuaries *pl*

voluptuous

voluptuously

voluptuousness

vomit

  vomited

  vomiting

voodoo

voracious (greedy)

voraciously

voracity

vortex (whirlwind)

  vortexes, vortices *pl*

votary

  votaries *pl*

vote

  voted

  voting

voter

votive

vouch

voucher

vouchsafe
  vouchsafed
  vouchsafing
vow
  vowed
  vowing
vowel
voyage
  voyaged
  voyaging
voyager
voyeur
vulcanization
vulcanize
  vulcanized
  vulcanizing
vulgar
vulgarism
vulgarity
vulgarization
vulgarize
  vulgarized
  vulgarizing
vulnerability
vulnerable
vulpine
vulture
vulva
  vulvas *pl*
vying (*from* vie)

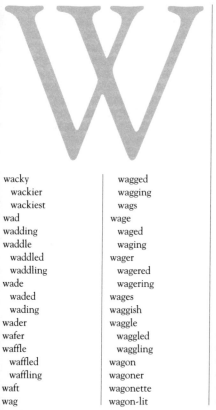

wacky
  wackier
  wackiest
wad
wadding
waddle
  waddled
  waddling
wade
  waded
  wading
wader
wafer
waffle
  waffled
  waffling
waft
wag

wagged
wagging
wags
wage
  waged
  waging
wager
  wagered
  wagering
wages
waggish
waggle
  waggled
  waggling
wagon
wagoner
wagonette
wagon-lit

wagtail
waif
  waifs *pl*
wail (to cry)
  wailed
  wailing
wainscot
wainscoting
waist (body)
wait (at table; bide
    time)
  waited
  waiting
waiter
waitress
waive (to forgo)
  waived
  waiving
waiver (in law)
wake
  waking
  woke
  woken
  wakes
  waked
wakeful
wakefulness
walk
walker
walking stick
walkover

wall
wallaby
  wallabies *pl*
wallah
wallet
wallflower
wallop
  walloped
  walloping
wallow
  wallowed
  wallowing
wallpaper
walnut
walrus
  walruses *pl*
waltz
  waltzes *pl*
wan (pale)
wand
wander (to walk)
  wandered
  wandering
wanderer
wanderlust
wane
  waned
  waning
wangle
  wangled
  wangling

wangler
want
wanting
wanton (free and
  easy)
wantonly
wantonness
war
  warred
  warring
  wars
warble
  warbled
  warbling
warbler
ward
warden
wardress
wardrobe
ware
  wares *pl*
warehouse
warfare
warier
warily
wariness
warm (heat)
warmer
warmhearted
warmly
warmonger

warmongering
warmth
warm-up
warn (signal)
warning
warp
warped
warrant
warranty
  warranties *pl*
warring
warren
warrior
wart (lump)
wary
  warier
  wariest
wash
washable
washer
wasn't (was not)
wasp
waspish
wassail
wastage
waste (to squander)
  wasted
  wasting
wasteful
wastefully
wastefulness

waster
wastrel
watch
watcher
watchful
watchfully
watchfulness
watchmaker
watchword
water
  watered
  watering
waterborne
watercolor
watercress
waterfall
waterlogged
watermark
waterproof
watershed
water-ski
  water-skied
  water-skiing
  water-skis
watertight
waterworks
watt (unit of power)
wattage
wattle
wattmeter
wave (ocean)

waved
  waving
waveform
wavelength
waver (to sway)
  wavered
  wavering
waverer
wavy
wax
  waxed
  waxes
  waxing
waxwork
way (method; route)
  ways pl
wayfare
wayfarer
wayfaring
waylaid
waylay
  waylaid
  waylaying
  waylays
wayside
wayward
waywardness
we (us)
weak (feeble)
weaken
  weakened

weakening
weaker
weak-kneed
weakling
weakly (feebly)
weak-minded
weakness
weal (scar; welfare)
weald (former forest)
wealth
wealthy
  wealthier
  wealthiest
wean
  weaned
  weaning
weapon
weaponry
wear (clothes)
  wearing
  wears
  wore
  worn
wear and tear
wearable
wearier
wearily
weariness
wearisome
weary
  wearier

weariest
weasel
weather (climate)
  weathered
  weathering
weather-beaten
weathercock
weave (cloth)
  weaves
  weaving
  wove
  woven
weaver
we'd (we had; we
  would)
we'll (we will)
we're (we are)
we've (we have)
web
  webbed
  webbing
web-footed
wed (to marry)
  wedded
  wedding
  weds
wedge
  wedged
  wedging
wedlock
Wednesday

  Wednesdays *pl*
wee (tiny)
week (seven day)
weekday
  weekdays *pl*
weekend
weekly (each week)
  weeklies *pl*
weep
  weeping
  weeps
  wept
weevil
weft
weigh
  weighed
  weighing
weight
  (measurement)
weightily
weightless
weightlessness
weighty
  weightier
  weightiest
weir (across a river)
weird
weirdly
weirdness
welcome
  welcomed

welcoming
weld
welder
welfare
welkin
well
we'll (we will)
well-being
wellborn
well-bred
well-known
well-meant
well-nigh
well-read
well-to-do
Welsh
welt
welter
welterweight
wen (swelling)
wench
went (*from* go)
wept (*from* weep)
were (*from* be)
we're (we are)
weren't (were not)
werewolf
  werewolves *pl*
west
westerly
western

westernization
westernize
  westernized
  westernizing
westward
wet (damp)
  wets
  wetted
  wetting
wet blanket
wether (sheep)
wetness
wetsuit
whack
whacked
whacko
whale (sea mammal)
whalebone
whaler
whaling
wharf
  wharfs, wharves *pl*
wharfage
wharfinger
what (question)
whatever
whatnot
whatsoever
wheat
wheaten
wheatmeal

wheedle
  wheedled
  wheedling
wheel
  wheeled
  wheeling
wheelbarrow
wheelchair
wheelwright
wheeze
  wheezed
  wheezing
wheezily
whelk
whelp
when (question)
whence
whenever
whensoever
where (place)
whereabouts
whereas
whereat
wherefore
whereupon
wherever
wherewithal
wherry
  wherries *pl*
whet (to sharpen)
  whets

whetted
whetting
whether (if)
whetstone
whey (from milk)
which (what)
whichever
whiff
while (time)
  whiled
  whiling
whilst
whim
whimper
  whimpered
  whimpering
whimsical
whimsy
  whimsies *pl*
whine (to cry)
  whined
  whining
whinny
  whinnied
  whinnies
  whinnying
whip
  whipped
  whipping
  whips
whipcord

whip hand
whippet (dog)
whir
whirl (spin)
whirligig
whirlpool
whirlwind
whirr
whisk
whisker
whiskered
whiskey
  whiskeys *pl*
whisper
  whispered
  whispering
whisperer
whist
whistle
  whistled
  whistling
whistler
whit (small amount)
white
whitebait
white-headed
whiten
  whitened
  whitening
whiter
whitewash

whither (where to)
whiting (fish)
whitlow
Whitsun
whittle
  whittled
  whittling
whizz
  whizzed
  whizzes
  whizzing
who
whoever
whole (entire)
wholehearted
wholesale
wholesaler
wholesome
wholesomely
wholesomeness
wholly (entirely)
whom
who's (who is or has)
whoop (to shout)
  whooped
  whooping
whoopee
whooping cough
whopper
whore
whoremonger

whoring
whorl (circle)
whortleberry
  whortleberries *pl*
whose
why
wick
wicked (bad)
wickedly
wickedness
wicker
wickerwork
wicket
wide
wide awake
widely
widen
  widened
  widening
wider
widespread
width
widow
widowed
widower
wield
wife
  wives *pl*
wifely
wig
wiggle

wiggled
wiggling
wigwam
wild
wildebeest
wilder
wilderness
wildfire
wild-goose chase
wildlife
wildly
wildness
wile (trick)
will
willful
willfully
willfulness
willing
willingly
willingness
will-o'-the-wisp
willow
willowy
willpower
willy-nilly
wilt (thou)
wilt (to droop)
wily
wimple
win
  winning

wins
won
wince
  winced
  wincing
winch
wind
  winding
  winds
  wound
winder
windfall
windlass
windless
windmill
window
windowpane
window-shopping
windowsill
windward
windy
  windier
  windiest
wine (drink)
wine cellar
wing
wingspan
wingspread
wink
winner
winnow

winnowed
winnowing
winsome
winsomely
winsomeness
winter
  wintered
  wintering
wintry
wipe
  wiped
  wiping
wire
wireless
wiriness
wiry
wisdom
wise
wiseacre
wisecrack
wisely
wiser
wish
wishful
wishfully
wishy-washy
wisp
wisteria
  wisterias *pl*
wistful
wistfully

wistfulness
wit (humor)
witch (magician)
  witches *pl*
witchcraft
witchery
  witcheries *pl*
with
withal
withdraw
  withdrawing
  withdrawn
  withdraws
  withdrew
withdrawal
wither (to shrivel)
  withered
  withering
withers (of a horse)
withhold
  withheld
  withholding
  withholds
within
without
withstand
  withstanding
  withstands
  withstood
witless
witness

witness-box
  witness-boxes *pl*
witticism
wittily
wittiness
witty
  wittier
  wittiest
wizard
wizardry
wizened
woad
wobble
  wobbled
  wobbling
woe
woebegone
woeful
woefully
woke (*from* wake)
woken (*from* wake)
wold (open hilly
  country)
wolf
  wolves *pl*
woman
  women *pl*
womanly
womankind
womb
womenfolk

won (*from* win)
wonder (to think)
  wondered
  wondering
wonderful
wonderfully
wondrous
wont (accustomed)
won't (will not)
wonted
woo
  wooed
  wooing
  woos
wood
wooden
woodenly
woodenness
woodland
wooer
woofer
wool
woolen
woolly
word
wordily
wordy
wore (*from* wear)
work
workable
workaholic

worker
workman
  workmen *pl*
workmanship
workshop
world
worldliness
worldly
worldwide
worm (creature)
worm-eaten
worn (*from* wear)
worn-out
worrier
worry
  worries *pl*
  worried
  worries
  worrying
worse
worsen
  worsened
  worsening
worship
  worships
  worshiped
  worshiping
worshiper
worshipful
worst
worsted

worth
worthier
worthily
worthless
worthwhile
worthy
  worthier
  worthiest
would
wouldn't (would not)
wound
wounded
wound-up
wove (*from* weave)
woven (*from* weave)
woven
wrack (seaweed)
wraith (ghost)
wrangle
  wrangled
  wrangling
wrangler
wrap (to cover)
  wrapped
  wrapping
  wraps
wraparound
wrapper
wrath (anger)
wrathful
wreak (to inflict)

wreath (of flowers)
  wreaths *pl*
wreathe (twist)
  wreathed
  wreathing
wreck
wreckage
wrecked
wrecker
wren
wrench
wrest (to snatch)
wrestle
  wrestled
  wrestling
wrestler
wretch
wretched
wretchedly
wretchedness
wriggle
  wriggled
  wriggling
wriggler
wring (to twist)
  wringing
  wrings
  wrung
wrinkle
  wrinkled
  wrinkling

wrinkly
wrist
wristband
wristlet
wristwatch
writ (legal document)
write (letter)
  writes
  writing
  written
  wrote
write-up
writer
writhe
  writhed
  writhing
wrong
  wronged
  wronging
wrongdoer
wrongdoing
wrongful
wrongfully
wrote (*from* write)
wrought (shaped)
wrung (*from* wring)
wry (twisted)
wryly
wryness

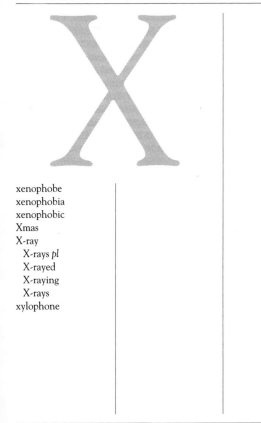

xenophobe
xenophobia
xenophobic
Xmas
X-ray
  X-rays *pl*
  X-rayed
  X-raying
  X-rays
xylophone

Y

yacht
yachtsman
  yachtsmen *pl*
Yankee
yap
  yapped
  yapping
  yaps
yard
yardage
yardstick
yarn
yashmak
yawl
yawn
  yawned
  yawning
yea

year
yearling
yearlong
yearly
year-round
yearn
yeast
yell
yellow
yelp
yen (longing)
yeoman
  yeomen *pl*
yeomanry
  yeomanries *pl*
yes
yesterday
  yesterdays *pl*

yesteryear
yet
yeti
yew (tree)
Yiddish
yield
yippee
yodel
  yodels
  yodeled
  yodeling
yodeler
yoga
yogi
yogurt
yoke (fitted on neck)
yokel (peasant)
yolk (of egg)
yonder
yore (long ago)
you (person)
you'd (you had)
you'll (you will)
young
  younger
  youngest
youngster
you're (you are)
your
yours
yourself

yourselves *pl*
youth
  youths *pl*
youthful
you've (you have)
yowl
yo-yo
  yo-yos *pl*
yule (Christmas)
Yuletide

zoos *pl*
zoological
zoologist
zoology
zoom
  zoomed
  zooming
zoom lens
zygote

zany
  zanies *pl*
zeal
zealot
zealous
zebra
  zebras *pl*
zen
zenith
zephyr
  zephyrs *pl*
zero
  zeros *pl*
zest
zestful
zigzag
  zigzagged
  zigzagging

zigzags
zinc
zinnia
  zinnias *pl*
Zion
Zionism
Zionist
zip
  zipped
  zipping
  zips
zipper
zither
zodiac
zombie
zonal
zone
zoo